The EVERYTHING® Landscaping Book

Dear Reader,

I've been growing plants of all types since my early days in 4-H, and won my first gardening prize when I was 12 years old. Ever since those good old days, I've enjoyed growing a wide range of plants and have always shared the harvests of knowledge veteran gardeners and gardening experts shared with me. In the process, I've written several dozen books about gardening, been a nationally syndicated garden columnist in hundreds of papers for over 25 years, and done radio and TV features as "Doctor Plant."

In this book I'll share with you many growing secrets I've learned from veteran gardeners, top plant breeders, horticultural authorities, and other helpful garden experts. Gardening is America's number one family hobby and continues to grow in popularity. I hope you'll dig in with family and friends; plan, plant, and enjoy your own attractive landscapes; and share what you learn from this book and your gardening experience with many others. My living and writing theme is down-to-earth, for everyone all across America—Let's grow better together!

Your gardening friend,

Allan A. Swenson

The EVERYTHING® Series

Editorial

Publishing Director	Gary M. Krebs
Managing Editor	Kate McBride
Copy Chief	Laura MacLaughlin
Acquisitions Editor	Eric Hall
Development Editor	Lesley Bolton
Production Editor	Khrysti Nazzaro

Production

Production Director	Susan Beale
Production Manager	Michelle Roy Kelly
Series Designers	Daria Perreault Colleen Cunningham
Cover Design	Paul Beatrice Frank Rivera
Layout and Graphics	Colleen Cunningham Rachael Eiben Michelle Roy Kelly Daria Perreault Erin Ring
Series Cover Artist	Barry Littmann
Interior Illustrator	Kathie Kelleher
Insert Photography	©PhotoDisc, Inc.

Page 4, center, *Little Girl Overlooking the "River of Muscari,"* courtesy of Netherlands Flower Bulb Information Center; page 6, top left, *New for Fall 2001: My Favorite Mum "Autumn Red,"* courtesy My Favorite Company; page 6, center, *1993 AAS Winner Pumpkin Baby Bear,* courtesy of All-American Selections; page 7, bottom right, courtesy of Allan A. Swenson

THE EVERYTHING® LANDSCAPING BOOK

From planning to planting, mulching to maintenance—simple steps to beautify your property

Allan A. Swenson

Adams Media Corporation
Avon, Massachusetts

To every gardener who helps another person grow better.

An Everything® Series Book.
Everything® is a registered trademark of Adams Media Corporation.

Published by Adams Media Corporation
57 Littlefield Street, Avon, MA 02322 U.S.A.
www.adamsmedia.com

ISBN: 1-58062-861-3
Printed in the United States of America.

J I H G F E D C B A

Library of Congress Cataloging-in-Publication Data
Swenson, Allan A.
The everything landscaping book / Allan A. Swenson.
p. cm. (An everything series book)
ISBN 1-58062-861-3
1. Landscape gardening. I. Title. II. Series: Everything series.
SB473 .S929 2003
712—dc21
2002152392

This publication is designed to provide accurate and authoritative information with regard to the subject matter covered. It is sold with the understanding that the publisher is not engaged in rendering legal, accounting, or other professional advice. If legal advice or other expert assistance is required, the services of a competent professional person should be sought.

—From a *Declaration of Principles* jointly adopted by a Committee of the American Bar Association and a Committee of Publishers and Associations

Many of the designations used by manufacturers and sellers to distinguish their products are claimed as trademarks. Where those designations appear in this book and Adams Media was aware of a trademark claim, the designations have been printed with initial capital letters.

Additional illustrations courtesy of Dover Publications.

This book is available at quantity discounts for bulk purchases.
For information, call 1-800-872-5627.

Contents

Acknowledgments

Profuse thanks to many gardening experts and hundreds of friends who shared their knowledge, ideas, tips, and advice with me so I may share their experience, wit, and wisdom with others every way I can.

Top Ten Things You Will Know
After Reading This Book

1. It's possible to increase your property value by up to 10 percent by landscaping your home.
2. Creating a design plan before you begin can help you get organized and set a budget.
3. If you identify the plants that are ideally suited to your climate, you'll have a better chance at keeping your vegetation alive.
4. "Framing" doors, walkways, and patios with attractive plants can make your home even more inviting.
5. Planting trees in strategic areas around your home can lower air conditioning costs and provide windbreaks.
6. Your landscape design should be organized—learn techniques for mixing various types of flowers, shrubs, and trees.
7. By watching the nutrient levels in your soil, you can improve your growing ground to ensure healthy plant life.
8. Attracting desirable wildlife to your yard can be as easy as planting certain shrubs and trees.
9. To add a unique flair to your yard, try adding a biblical garden with flowers of the scriptures.
10. Making water gardens or outdoor living rooms is not as complicated as it sounds—and they can be beautiful accents to your landscape.

Introduction

▶WELCOME TO A WONDERFUL NEW WORLD of landscaping and plantscaping. You'll discover exciting new growing horizons in this book that will enable you to enjoy a more colorful world of blooming beauty; fragrant outdoor living rooms; and other glorious displays of flowers, shrubs, trees, and attractive landscape designs.

Gardening is America's number one family hobby for good reason. Not only do you get lots of fresh air and sunshine and the opportunity to plant and see entire landscapes come alive, bloom, and bear abundantly, but it's also great exercise. You'll find new ideas in this book, harvested from some of the top plant breeders, horticulturists, and gardening authorities in America. They have graciously shared their knowledge, as most gardeners gladly will, to help others grow better on their own land.

This book offers secrets of the time-honored European gardens that you can transplant to your own land, as well as abundant ideas and growing advice for the popular Oriental gardens and container gardens. In addition, you'll get a feel for other new trends from water and pond gardening to planting more dramatic, year-round color and fragrance gardens.

Read on and you'll learn to grow more fruitfully. There's nothing like sun-ripened, plump, juicy blackberries, blueberries, raspberries, and strawberries picked fresh from your own plants. There are other treats in store. You'll discover many more varieties of delicious apples, pears, peaches, and plums that you just can't find in the supermarket. Even better, new dwarf-sized trees take little space but have banquets of full-sized fruit. There are abundant reasons to grow fruitfully and this book will show you how.

Hundreds of test and demonstration gardens and arboretums offer knowledge for the asking and pleasure for the viewing. You'll find many places to visit where you can see examples of exceptional landscaping and samples of the best plants to use for your home grounds. You'll also be able to take trips to great gardens across America and around the world via the super garden Web sites listed in this book and available on the Internet. Gardeners are a sharing bunch. They gladly answer questions, offer ideas, and often share some of their plants and friendship with all who share their love of the land and the plants you can all enjoy in your gardens.

It has been well said that great oaks from tiny acorns grow. You'll discover many secrets of master gardeners about selecting the best trees for landscape beauty, shade, and use as windbreaks and filters for noise as well as energy savers. In addition, there are many useful tips, ideas, and bits of wit and wisdom about colorful, multipurpose shrubs and perennials, and ways to make your property bloom from spring to fall.

There's much more. Even if you have poor soil, you'll learn ways to improve your growing ground to have more profuse flowering plants, better shrubs, and a healthier, more appealing landscape. How to use fertilizer well and wisely and make the most of mulch are other key points.

Plantscaping is the path that takes you beyond landscaping to expanding growing horizons of all types. With this book in hand, you, too, will be able to look years ahead and envision more beautiful landscapes, and then dig in to plant the panoramas that you want and deserve. It's your growing guide to a more beautiful, enjoyable outdoor living environment.

Chapter 1
Improving Home Value

Upgrading your landscaping with attractive, colorful shrubs, flowers, and trees can increase the value of your home 8 to 10 percent and more, according to a variety of reports. That's not all. Landscaping can also help you cut down on energy bills. This chapter shows you how.

Landscaping Boosts Property Value

You know that landscaping adds a touch of beauty and wonder to your home. But did you know that it also adds value? From a monetary perspective, landscaping is a good investment. If you aren't convinced, consider the following statistics:

- Landscaping can add between 7 and 15 percent to a home's value according to one Gallop Organization survey.
- Homes with "excellent" landscaping can expect a sale price about 6 to 7 percent higher than equivalent houses with only "good" landscaping. What's more, improving landscaping from "average" to "good" can result in a 4 to 5 percent increase according to a study by Clemson University.
- Landscaping beats other home improvement investments according to *Money* magazine. Their report stated that landscaping can bring a recovery value of 100 to 200 percent at selling time. Compare that to kitchen remodeling, which brought a 75 to 125 percent recovery rate; bathroom remodeling, a 20 to 120 percent recovery rate; and the addition of a swimming pool, a 20 to 50 percent recovery rate.
- In a report by the National Gardening Association, 95 percent of real estate appraisers concurred that attractive landscaping improves the sales appeal of real estate.
- In another study, 83 percent of realtors believe that mature trees have a "strong or moderate impact" on the salability of homes listed for under $150,000; on homes over $250,000, this perception increases to 98 percent.
- Mature landscapes can reduce air conditioning costs by up to 50 percent by shading windows and walls of a home from the sun, according to the American Public Power Association.

For people who have rental property, other facts are worth knowing. Several different independent surveys have indicated that a well-designed landscape invites customers in the door and produces higher occupancy rates, increased rentals, and lower vacancies. One conclusion is that tenants attracted to good landscaping also tend to want to maintain the attractive outdoor living areas. People who enjoy plants, it seems, also tend to be more desirable tenants in houses and apartments.

Key research points about gardening worth knowing: The main reasons people garden are to be outdoors (44 percent), to be around beautiful things (42 percent), to relax and escape the pressures of everyday life (39 percent), and to stay active and get exercise (35 percent).

Landscaping Saves Energy, Too

Energy costs have a way of climbing higher every year. While there isn't much that homeowners can do about that, landscaping can help you save energy. Proper selection and placement of plant material can lower heating and cooling costs by as much as 20 percent, while creating a healthy, more attractive environment.

During summer months, one large tree can absorb as much heat as several window air conditioners and can lower the temperature in its shade by 10°F.

Plan for Your Climate

In climates with frigid winters, your goal should be to block winter winds with trees and shrubs while trying to capture the heat of the winter sun. In warmer climates, your goal is to block the summer sun while channeling in summer breezes to cool your home.

In temperate climates, it pays to use both strategies. For example, a dense row of evergreens to the north and northwest works effectively. They block frigid winds that would otherwise hit your home. Deciduous trees and shrubs should be planted to the east and west. A semicircular row of deciduous trees and shrubs planted from southeast to southwest, with a break to the south, usually will work to funnel in summer breezes. Naturally, these points are dependent on prevailing winds in your area, which can be influenced by topography and other factors, including nearby woodlands or buildings.

Cooling Benefits

Cities can be 5 to 10° warmer than suburbs. This is called the urban heat island effect. It is caused by heat-absorbing surfaces such as roads, buildings, driveways, and homes. Research reveals that as much as 8 percent of current electricity demand for air conditioning is used to compensate for this heat island effect. By planting trees, shrubs, and hedges, you can achieve substantial heat reductions achieved from the shade provided by trees and their cooling effect as they give off moisture. Tall shrubs around home foundations also offer cooling benefits.

There are three ways in which trees and shrubs cool the air. First, they provide shade from solar radiation. You'll note the difference just standing under a tree. Second, they reduce air temperature through evaporation and transpiration. Third, trees absorb heat themselves, which further reduces the need for air conditioning.

FACT

Planting trees means improved water quality because it results in less runoff and erosion. This allows more recharging of the ground water supply. Wooded areas also help prevent runoff of sediment and chemicals into streams, according to the U.S. Forest Service.

Additional Benefits

There are other benefits as well. Trees and plants absorb pollutants and block noise levels. For example, a thick hedge planted along the front of a property can reduce street noise by 5 decibels. Trees also help dampen noise. Today town planners recommend tree belts along highways to reduce noise levels from road traffic.

A Worthwhile Focus

To make landscaping pay off, you must first focus on how your house looks from an overview. Drive past and see what others see. Be honest with yourself. Other main points to think about as you plan your future landscaping include a colorful and welcoming entryway, blooming flowers and shrubs, a cutting-flower garden, flavorful and useful herbs that have fragrance, some special specimen shrubs or trees with eye appeal, and fruit and vegetable gardens for tastier living.

Trees Are Permanent Assets

Trees are lasting landscape assets. They deserve to be the first thing planted on your property, with others added periodically. Many homeowners advise planting fast-growing multipurpose trees that provide blooms, fruits, berries, or vibrant foliage color.

Bright foliage trees for reds include scarlet oak, sassafras, red maples, and sweet gum. For yellows, think about purchasing yellowwood, birch, beech, poplar, aspen, and Norway maples. For oranges and browns, consider hickory, black oak, hornbeam, white oak, and horse chestnut trees. Equally important are different types of trees hosting differing shades of green foliage. You can select trees that are covered with yellow or reddish or even variegated leaves. Some even have blue or multicolored foliage. Look around every fall to appreciate what color combinations may be available as you envision your new landscape look for the future.

Pick trees with the brightest colors at local nurseries. The brilliance of a tree's foliage as a sapling will be retained throughout its life. Buy them for fall or next spring planting.

Choose Multipurpose Shrubs

Consider planting blooming shrubs in front of your home to enhance your property. Select those that have flowers in spring and colorful fruits, berries, or foliage in fall. Also consider flowering perennials such as azalea, rhododendron, mountain laurel, burning bush, and lilacs. (You'll find more selections in Chapter 4.)

Ask local nurseries to suggest plants that grow best in your area. Locally grown shrubs, trees, and perennials are acclimated to your climate and growing conditions. That can be important—some shrubs may please you but won't survive growing conditions in your area.

Perennial Flowers, Please

Dress up your entryway with perennial flowers. They bloom every year with minimal care. Crocuses, daffodils, hyacinths, tulips, irises, and lilies provide color from earliest spring through summer. You also get to select different varieties to extend the blooming season of daffodils, tulips, irises, and lilies. You'll discover many selections and worthwhile tips in Chapter 6.

Think Fragrance, Too

As you plan landscapes, inhale deeply and think sweet smells. Then, plan to add fragrance to outdoor living areas with sweet-smelling shrubs and flowers. Place plants upwind so prevailing breezes blow pleasing scents where you spend time outdoors.

Some of the best include lily of the valley, lilacs, sweet clematis, old-time roses, and viburnum. You can also grow fragrant annuals from seeds, including such smell-good flowers as carnations, pinks, mignonette, lavender, fragrant nicotiana, sweet pea, and violas. Check mail-order catalogs. Many feature their fragrant flowers of all types and can give you ideas for bulbs, plants, and seeds.

Enjoy Tuneful Landscapes

Birds are fun to watch and they will cheer you with their songs and antics. Select trees that attract songbirds and provide wildlife habitats. Aromatic sumac, bayberry, firethorn, holly, and American cranberry bush look great and offer abundant food for birds. Avoid bittersweet and barberry, which are invasive plants and can take over areas of your landscape. Your local garden centers and nurseries will be able to advise you on those that are best for your area.

Think About Dramatic Specimen Plants

Some plants offer dramatic appearances that provide focal points for landscapes. You can utilize them for specimen plantings or groupings. For instance, consider these trees: autumn olive, mountain ash, ornamental crabapple of all types, and dogwood. Hawthorn is also popular for its hardiness, blooms, and fall berries. You'll find more lists in the chapters specific to trees, shrubs, bulbs, and perennials. But for now, just form a general idea in the back of your mind of what you may want.

Think tastefully when you redo landscapes. Just a few bushes or rows of blueberries and raspberries or strawberry beds are attractive and tasty. Realtors report that berry patches are "berry" good sales aids for homebuyers.

New Looks in Landscaping

Real estate research can provide useful information relating to landscaping. With a strong national housing market, more than 21 million U.S. households spent a record $16.8 billion on professional landscape/lawn care/tree care services in 1998, according to a just-released Gallup survey. This represents a $2.2 billion increase on total spending over the previous year and a 32 percent increase in the average amount spent by each household on these professional services. The key point is that that amount is only what was spent for contractors. No doubt billions more have been spent by people like yourself who want to dig in and improve their home grounds and property themselves.

Reengineering Your Garden

Reengineering is a popular buzzword today. In essence, it means taking a look at where you are and reassessing what you can do to capitalize on what you have. That's corporate talk, but the same reengineering approach holds true for home gardens and home landscapes.

There are good reasons to sit back some day and take a good look at what you have. As landscapes mature, a variety of things changes. Trees get taller and cast deeper shade over a wider area. Their roots spread out farther to draw water and nutrients away from other plants. Shrubs and bushes outgrow their original compactness, meaning pruning may be needed to keep them in bounds, or at least to restore their desired shapes and avoid the appearance of a crowded landscape.

Regardless of whether you have purchased a home with plantings you don't care for or whether you are simply in need of a change, the time comes in almost every landscape plan when reengineering is the way to go. Be imaginative and visionary. Sometimes cutting back and pruning hard is one of the first steps you should take.

Take a Long, Hard Look

Take a walk around your land and take a hard, honest look at what you have. Changes in your plantscape happen subtly over years. Although some years produce lush growth, other years, trees and shrubs grow more slowly. Trimming, pruning, or perhaps replacing may be needed.

Before you dig to plant new trees and shrubs, especially near the street, call your local utilities. You may have seen news stories about people who dug into buried power lines or gas pipes that burst. Take a pledge: No digging until you find out from utility companies where underground lines or pipes may be. Try ✆ 888-Dig-Safe in your area. And be sure to give the utility companies 2 to 3 days notice before your shrubs arrive, otherwise they will dry out while you're waiting for authorization to dig.

Also consider the changes to your outdoor living area. For example, perhaps when you added a deck you changed outdoor traffic patterns. Pretend you are the new owner of the house. Look at the landscape with as much objectivity as you can. Does it have a pleasant look or is it somewhat disorganized? Be honest with yourself.

Sketch Out a Plan

Take a notebook and sketch out a base plan. Depending on the size of your gardens and how fancy you want to make them, you can plan it yourself or call on professional help for advice and/or contracting. You're well advised to review one area at a time. That process lets you focus on one piece of the Big Picture without becoming confused by too many details, which you can eventually accomplish in time, project by project.

FACT

Planting trees means improved water quality because it results in less runoff and erosion. This allows more recharging of the ground water supply. Wooded areas also help prevent runoff of sediment and chemicals into streams, according to the U.S. Forest Service.

Think about how you want one specific area to look. Make a quick sketch and some notes. Then, move on to the next area. If your garden doesn't have different "areas," think about creating them by varying garden bed sizes, shapes, and what plants they will contain. A total landscape doesn't have to happen all at once. Besides time constraints, budgets must be considered, too.

Early on you'll want to develop an overall plan that will achieve the total landscape look you want. However, by doing smaller specific designs and plans, you can work on one or two areas at a time. Then, just postpone work on other areas for later in the year or until the next season or two. You'll find more step-by-step landscape designing and planning tips and advice in the next chapter.

A Landscape Panorama

When you take a look at your land, you'll see many different views. As you browse through mail-order catalogs and visit garden centers and nurseries, you'll undoubtedly begin to envision the glories your landscape and gardens can have. Dreaming of vistas of blooming beauty, colorful shrubs, and dramatic trees is one of a gardener's greatest pleasures.

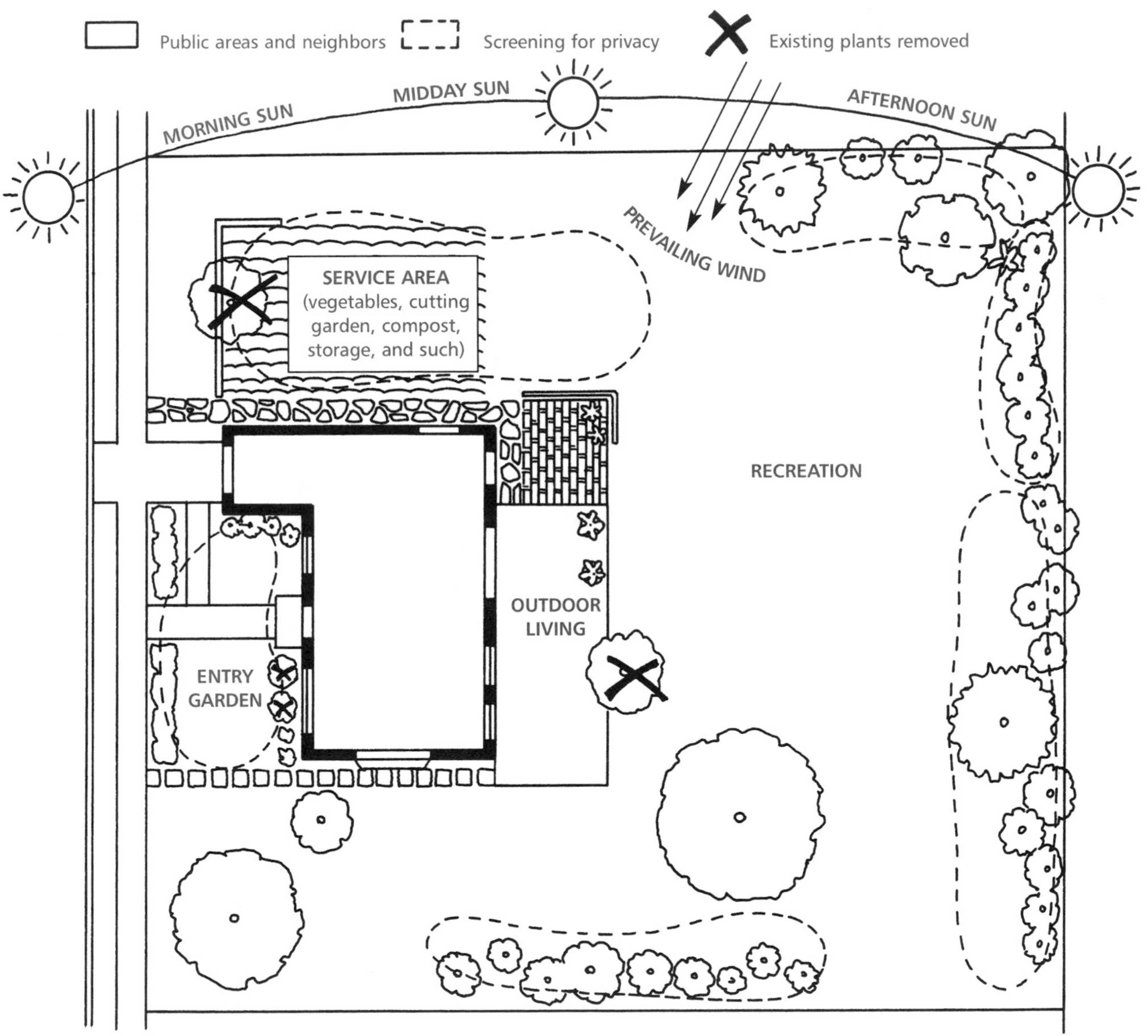

▲ Example of design or plan of home landscaping.

Time for Trees and Shrubs

Once you walk your land, you'll undoubtedly see opportunities to add trees to the landscape. Whether you decide to re-tree your property, add beds and borders, grow more fruitfully, or otherwise dress up your property graciously, this book can help. You'll find many details about trees, from which ones work best for city streets and urban environments to how to pick the best for your area. You'll also find tips about multipurpose trees, how to choose the best ones for fall foliage displays, and how to select those that attract singing birds for tuneful gardening.

FACT

Trees have a calming effect on people. In laboratory research conducted by Texas A&M University, it was found that visual exposure to settings with trees produced significant recovery from stress within 5 minutes, as indicated by changes in blood pressure and muscle tension.

Shrubs also offer many choices and opportunities to beautify home grounds. Many types are unfortunately often overlooked but offer such marvelous color, fragrance, and appealing shapes and textures that they deserve to be considered. In Chapter 4, you'll find details about many shrubs that fit into wet, dry, shady, or sunny spots, so you can match the right ones for your land areas.

Bulbs and Perennial Beauty

Bulbs are one of a gardener's sure-fire winners. They provide you with a way to add many dramatic displays of color and fragrance to your gardens. Bulbs of colorful flowers such as crocuses, daffodils, hyacinths, and tulips can be creatively used in beds, borders, or as massed displays. Some types also can be naturalized in lawns, on slopes, or among shrubs and trees for beauty and easy care.

Perennial bulbs provide advantages. Once planted, they emerge each year to bloom and add their beauty to your garden. Some are low growing and ideal as ground cover, while others deserve to be featured in their own site as dramatic specimen planting or accents. One of the

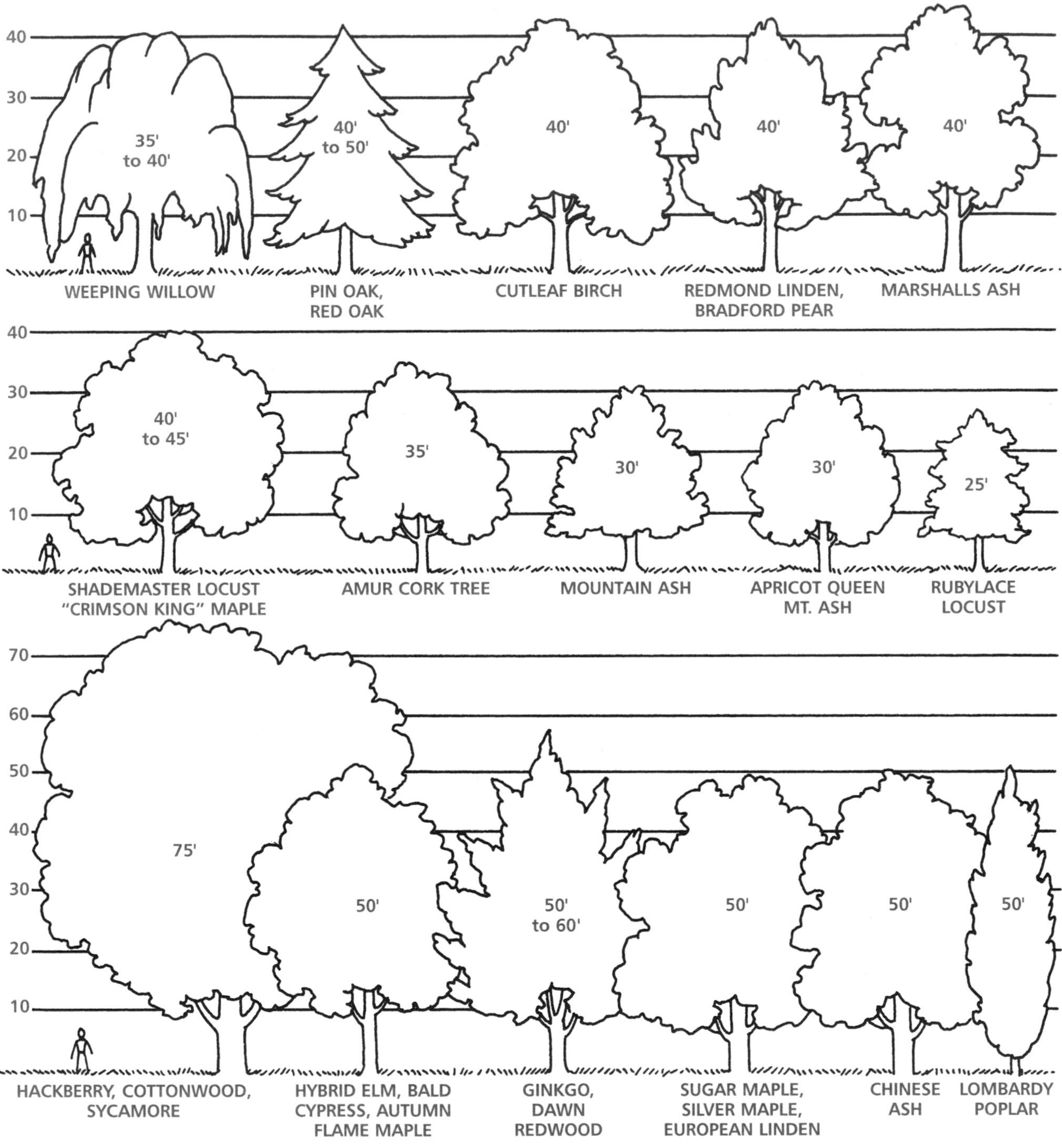

▲ Shapes and sizes of popular landscaping trees.

most striking uses for spring-flowering bulbs and perennials is to spotlight your front door with bright and colorful welcoming blooms.

Annuals Are Appealing

Annual flowers are an annual delight, as millions of gardeners know. Americans buy seeds and seedlings to plant a few billion flowers every year, giving their gardens a fountain of color. You'll find many new varieties in mail-order catalogs, which also provide information about the benefits of these exciting new hybrids. The All-America Selections and National Garden Bureau are two nonprofit organizations that provide a wealth of free information to home gardeners (visit *www.all-americaselections.org* and *www.ngb.org* for more information).

FACT

According to the National Wildlife Service, there are about 60 to 200 million spaces along our city streets where trees could be planted. This translates to the potential to absorb 33 million more tons of carbon dioxide every year and a savings of $4 billion in energy costs.

Tasty Additions

Fruitful gardening is another treat in store for you. You'll be amazed how easy it is to plant, tend, and enjoy a home miniorchard and bountiful berry patches. You'll find tips for selecting the best varieties, especially those that are disease resistant and require less care or pesticide use.

Apples, cherries, pears, peaches, and plums abound in many different, distinctive flavors that you'll never find in a supermarket. Blackberries; blueberries; and red, black, and purple raspberries also yield abundantly from small backyard plots. There are some varieties of fruit that are sweeter and more delicious than those that you find at the store. The explanation is that some of the tastiest fruit varieties don't ship well, so are not grown commercially. But they are ideal for home gardens.

One of the best new developments has been dwarf and semidwarf root stocks. Desired fruit varieties are grafted on these stocks to keep tree size small, but they still yield full-size, mouth-wateringly good, juicy fruits.

Roses Are Favorites

Roses of all types are available for use in many ways in home landscapes today. Climbing roses will grace the sides of homes and grow over arbors and along fences in a variety of bright colors. Hybrid tea and compact miniature roses have their places as well. Newer ground-cover roses are prolific, exceedingly colorful, and hardy. For rose lovers, new Hellebores bloom even during winter when the snow may be on the ground. You will find an entire chapter about roses, so you can pick and grow whichever you prefer as blooming additions to your landscape.

For those who like the soothing sound of water, you can add water gardens to your landscape. Water gardening is one of America's fastest-growing gardening projects. You'll learn how to do some basics in Chapter 15, if you wish to try your hand at this new growing horizon.

How to Know How

Gardening isn't all fun and games. Problems can come up. You'll find helpful hints about problem solving, including how to improve soil for better growing of all types of plants and how to deal with problem areas such as shady, wet, dry, or other difficult spots. To guide you even further there are Web sites filled with gardening know-how and advice and places where you can e-mail or call toll free to get your own questions answered by experts.

Thumb through this book now and check out the Web sites that you'll find listed in Appendix B. Take a walk around your land. Look carefully at what you have and envision what you would like to see. Then, with this book in hand, begin your landscaping plans. You'll be amazed at how well you will be able to transform your land and achieve a more colorful, dramatic, appealing outdoor living area. As you do, you'll earn a bonus. Better landscaping just naturally boosts your property values.

Chapter 2

Planning Your Landscape

While books, friends, family, and experts can offer you suggestions, tips, and advice, the fact is this is your project. You should create a landscape that suits your tastes and is beautiful in your eyes. This chapter will help you plan your strategy and overcome any fears that may be holding back the landscaping artist inside you.

So Many Decisions!

While the idea of landscaping is very appealing, once you actually look over your property to get started, you may become panic-stricken. How will you ever decide on what goes where with all the possibilities available to you? Don't worry; you aren't alone. Even some veteran gardeners find the prospect of designing a landscape terrifying.

What you need to keep in mind is that there are no "right" decisions in gardening. There is no ultimate garden design for any property. There are as many different landscape designs as there are gardeners. Some gardeners even like to redesign their gardens and replant them periodically. Try to think of landscaping as a delightful way to express yourself.

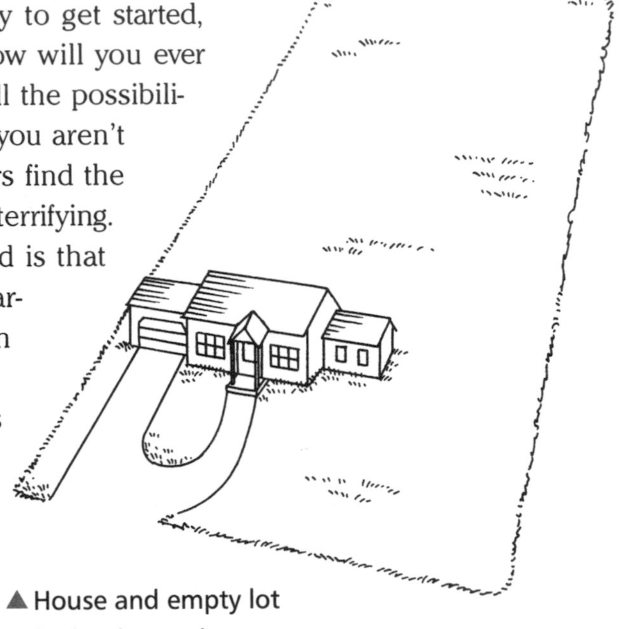

▲ House and empty lot to be landscaped.

Do a Site Analysis

Scrutinize your site. Take note of the way the sun affects your house and site at different times of day and different seasons. Note the direction of prevailing winds. Walk around your property several times and carefully observe the views. Consider the following questions:

- Do you have a pleasant view from the road to your front door?
- What do you hear at different places, such as areas that could use plantings to help screen out street noises?
- What do you see from your porch or deck? How can you improve that view?

Note good and bad views and also sources of noises so you can plan to solve those problems with effective, creative landscaping.

Consider access to your house:

- Walks–width, appearance, drainage, lighting, safety, condition
- Driveways–type of surface and condition plus turnaround space and snow storage
- Parking–on street or on property for family, guests, boat, bikes, camper

Focus on family activities:

- Outdoor entertaining areas for cookouts, seating, patio access, games
- Children's play area for swings, games, sports
- Pets' runs, fencing, housing

Think about storage and maintenance needs, too:

- Storage for gardening equipment, including mowers, tools, supplies
- Storage of fertilizers and pesticides
- Garbage cans, firewood, recycling bins
- Paints, gardening chemicals, and materials secured from children
- Your special hobby storage needs

Assess your family needs. Enjoy a relaxed meal with your family. Ask them what they would like to see in the way of flowers, shrubs, trees, special garden accents, or special privacy areas. Use this book to help you gather input to create the best landscape design you can devise.

Value of a Garden Designer

As you begin making plans yourself, the obvious question arises: Should you hire a professional landscaper or garden designer? If you have the means and desire to do so, it will probably be money well spent. Professional advice can give you a valuable new perspective on your yard and gardens. Most designers are willing to focus their attention on a particular area that is giving you difficulty. As you might expect, though, their advice can be costly.

However, with this book as your guide, most likely you will be able to do your own basic landscape plans. Just be sure to keep three goals in mind: Organize your garden areas for maximum use and pleasure; create a visual relationship between the house and your gardens; and keep landscape maintenance to a practical, doable level.

Don't Rush Design

Too often people get carried away with grand plans and waste money landscaping their businesses and homes without thoughtful planning. Some think that any sort of landscaping will improve their business's or home's appearance without using thoughtful planning. Several years later, poorly sited plants are struggling to survive because of a lack or excess of sun or shade, or plants that looked "just right" when first planted have overgrown their allotted space and are obscuring views, paths, or living areas.

FACT

Some think any landscaping improves the appearance of their place, while others just like to grow plants. Masses of plants or other materials in the landscape may take up a large portion of the space and leave little room for people. Landscaping should serve you and your family, so focus on what you want.

Landscape Lingo

Landscape designers have special terms describing aspects of design. It helps to know what they mean as you discuss your plans with nursery staff, veteran gardeners, and others.

Naturally, beauty still is in the eye of the beholder, so vary your landscape plans as you wish, so long as they please you and your family. But, try to observe the basic design elements that will guide you to more attractive results.

Flow

Flow is a key word. A garden is more pleasing if there is a logical flow or progression from one area to the next. Think about how you would like someone to see your gardens and move through them. Paths are one way to connect different parts of the garden to achieve a sense of cohesiveness. Focal points such as a piece of sculpture, a distinctive tree, or a mass of floral color can be used to draw people forward into a new area.

Scale

Scale is all about the proportions—sizes and shapes—of things that relate to each other. For instance, a small tree or shrub in front of a two-story house will be seriously out of scale. So would a 1-foot-wide bed of flowers amid a large lawn. Most scale problems are due to skimpiness, such as beds and paths that are too narrow, or plantings that are too small. It usually is better to be bolder with larger plants and masses of flowers for dramatic effect. On the other hand, avoid overplanting, which will eventually overgrow an area.

Rhythm

Consider creating rhythm by repeating plants and materials. Too much repetition can be monotonous, but as in music, variations on a theme are pleasing. Consider repeating certain distinctive plant materials such as the spearlike foliage of Siberian irises or the dramatic sweep of massed tulips or a grouping of peonies with varied color coordination.

Focusing on just one aspect of design and not considering others may limit your landscaping endeavor. All elements of design actually relate to each other. For instance, creating a rhythm with repeating splashes of color helps to guide the eye. That also is a part of the flow in your garden.

Symmetry and Balance

Symmetry and balance are important, too. Humans seem attracted to the symmetry of balanced features. Used judiciously, balance and symmetry can be an appealing design technique, especially in formal landscapes. However, carried to excess, it can be stiff.

The natural landscape, of course, is not governed by symmetry. Something subtler is at work, which artists and landscape designers refer to as balance. In truth, balance is an essential factor in garden design. Balance refers to "visual weight." For example, a birch clump is balanced by a large bed of hosta around the base, or a cluster of orange poppies is balanced by deep blue lupines or blue pansies. As you visit other gardens, you'll see examples of these design elements.

Sketch Your Site

The first step to designing a landscape is easy: Sketch your site. Grab a pencil, some graph paper, and a ruler. The site plan is going to be like a bird's-eye view of your yard. When you see your site on paper, it's easier to identify basic design elements such as traffic patterns, scale, and symmetry.

A drawing board and T-square will make the job easier, but they aren't essential. All you need are pieces of graph paper large enough to draw your yard on. Use a convenient scale, such as 1 to 4, in which 1 inch equals 4 feet or ¼ inch equals 1 foot. The larger your second number of the scale, the smaller everything will appear on paper. Graph paper is best because it already has lines on it and can represent whatever scale you wish. Sketch in all existing major features on your plan. Be sure to make note of the location of buried gas, water, and electric lines.

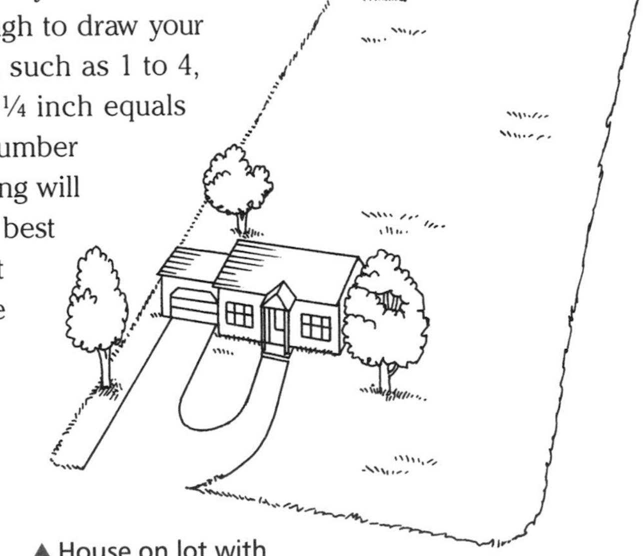

▲ House on lot with some trees added.

Analyze Each Area

It pays to have a guide or checklist for each specific area. This helps as you begin to actually draw your landscaping plans on paper. Veteran gardeners and landscape contractors emphasize the value of a simple checklist.

The Public Area

The area most seen by passersby and guests is referred to as the public area. It usually includes your front yard, drive, walks, and main entrance to your house. Focus on that important "face to the world," your front door. You will want the front door to be attractive and inviting. What about the front walk? Can you make it more appealing with a different surface? Outdoor lighting also helps direct people to your door after dark and is a safety feature as well.

Do a checklist of your plants for the public area. First, list what you have, and on graph paper, measure plants and sketch in their size. That will give you a basic plot plan to review. From there you can research and add other plants that will make the public area more attractive and fulfill your vision.

FACT

Studies show that about half of home sales are decided during the first minute at the house. An astounding 50 percent of home-purchasing decisions are made at the first impression, and that is often based on how the house looks as the buyers approach it, looking at the front door and nearby foundation plantings.

Foundation Plants

Foundation plants greet visitors, add dimension to the area, and complement the structural lines of your house. When planning foundation areas, consider the size, color, texture, and number of plants needed to direct visitors to the entrance in a pleasing way.

Choose plants that will grow well in your site conditions, sunny or shady as they are.

Refrain from installing new plants too close to your foundation.

Shrubs should never be planted closer than 3 to 4 feet from a foundation, and trees shouldn't be nearer than half their expected mature diameter. Choose good-quality, semimature plants instead of overplanting with many smaller shrubs. This helps to overcome the temptation to put plants too close to your home's foundation. Use a few plants of specimen size, which will be more impressive than a clutter of smaller ones. Remember that small plants will grow, and perhaps overgrow, which will require periodic pruning or removal of crowded ones.

▲ House, trees, gardens, and hedges as landscape is put into place with plants.

Outdoor Living

Once you have focused on your front door and the entryway approach, take time to consider and appraise the important parts of your outdoor living rooms. Don't overlook what most people overlook, the service areas. From garbage cans and equipment storage to compost piles and vegetable patches, think of how you can screen such areas from view. You can make them less obvious by using hedges, shrubs, and other plants to hide unsightly views, perhaps of your neighbor's backyard areas, too. Here's a simple checklist as you plan your outdoor entertaining, dining, and living areas. Think a few years ahead.

- Do you need or want a patio, deck, or terrace?
- Will you be cooking and eating outdoors very often?
- Can walls, hedges, shrubs, and trees help hide unsightly areas?
- Can landscaping hide storage areas?
- Will container gardens brighten your outdoor areas?
- Do you want a kitchen herb garden?
- Would you like a cutting garden for indoor flower bouquets?

The outdoor features you will choose depend on your family's needs and desires. They may include a patio for entertaining, a children's play area, or a sport and game area. Perhaps you like to brighten your house with cut flowers, in which case a cutting garden will probably make the cut. Maybe you want to enjoy tastier living with a vegetable garden, berries, miniature fruit trees, and an herb garden.

Once you have a list, set priorities of what you want first. Rearrange your list and renumber priorities. Keep in mind that trees and shrubs are likely to be permanent landscape features, so you may want to start with these and plan your flowers and gardens around them.

Creating a Base Plan

Once you have done your analysis, it is time to take pencil in hand and focus on making your world the more beautiful place and space you want and deserve to have. Place tracing paper over the original site sketch and sketch in possible ideas and solutions to your landscape needs. Make several variations, if you wish, as options.

FACT

Always indicate compass directions in relation to the house by drawing an arrow pointing north. It also helps to show the direction of the rising sun. In summer, the sun rises somewhat north of east and sets somewhat north of west. In winter, the sun rises and sets a little south of east and west respectively.

If you have a large property, you may want to make one sketch of the whole yard on a small scale first and later make separate plans of individual areas on a larger scale. This may seem like busywork, but pushing a pencil on paper is far easier than pushing a wheelbarrow filled with plants and then having to move them later because you made a planting mistake.

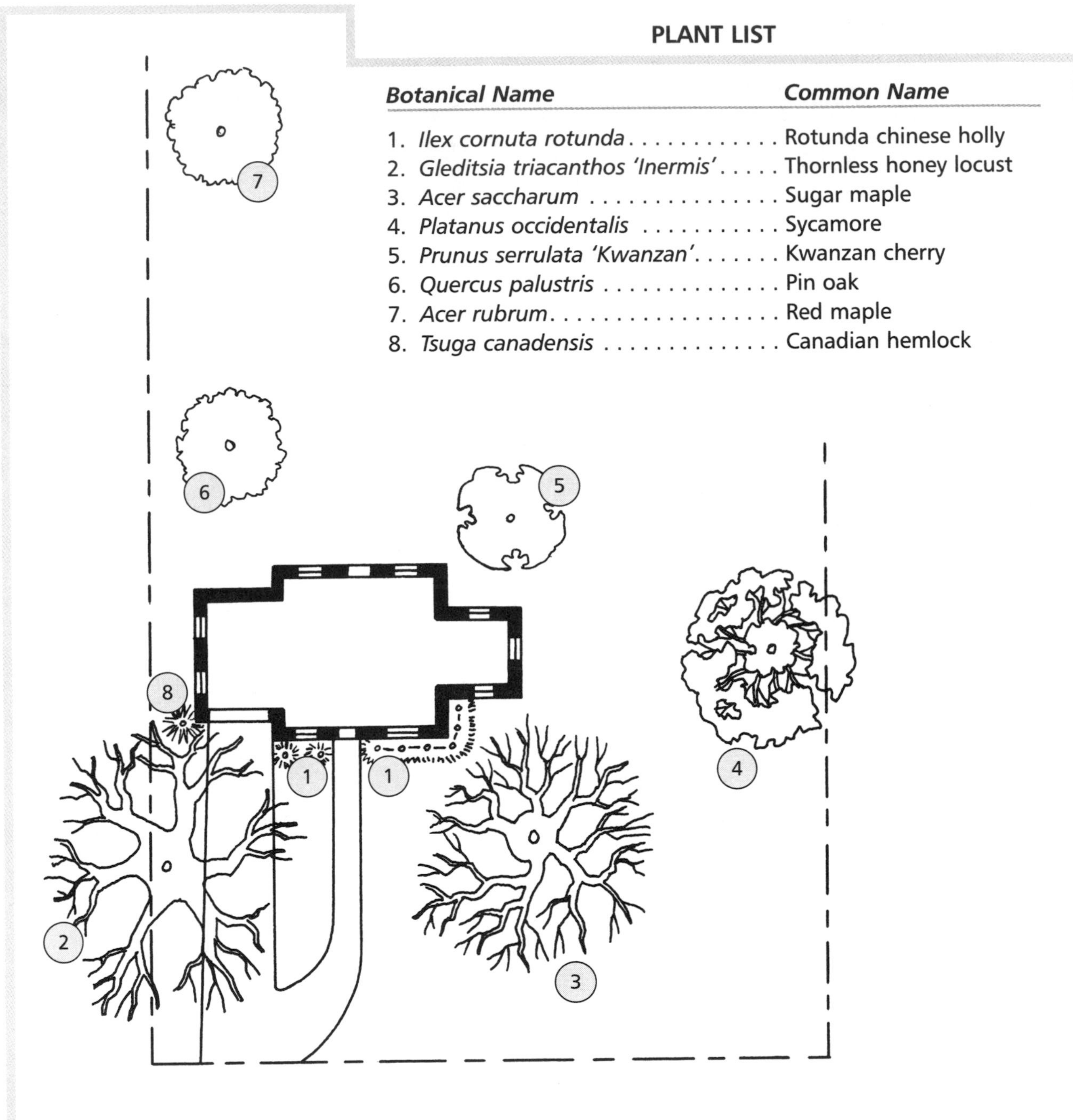

PLANT LIST
Botanical Name
Common Name
1. Ilex cornuta rotunda . . . . Rotunda chinese holly
2. Gleditsia triacanthos 'Inermis' . . . . . Thornless honey locust
3. Acer saccharum . . . . Sugar maple
4. Platanus occidentalis . . . . Sycamore
5. Prunus serrulata 'Kwanzan' . . . . Kwanzan cherry
6. Quercus palustris . . . . Pin oak
7. Acer rubrum . . . . Red maple
8. Tsuga canadensis . . . . Canadian hemlock
7
6
5
4
8
1
1
2
3

▲ Example of landscape with suggested trees in position.

Study Homes You Admire

It helps to study homes you admire. Focus on the most attractively landscaped homes and take a look at how trees are used to frame the house and how they provide background for it. Do they have special accent trees and shrubs? What does their entryway say? Is it welcoming? A sweep of lawn and plants with an attractive walkway usually is more appealing than a concrete path from street to front door that detracts from the natural living look.

Plan Your Site Thoughtfully

Place needs and activities where they can serve best and provide enough space for each need. For example, will your outdoor barbecue area be big enough for the size of the groups you usually entertain? Will your work or service area be convenient and reasonably attractive? Remember that lawnmowers, wheelbarrows, tools, insecticides, and fertilizers all need to be stored in a convenient, dry location. Service areas are most convenient on a wall or area of a garage or carport.

Terraces or decks and patios are an integral part of many homes

▲House with slope, including trees and plants.

today. Plan for where they will receive summer breezes and afternoon shade. If sun is a problem, plan to add trees or overhead shading structures.

Please feel free to copy and use the designs included with this chapter as landscape design elements. Just reduce them on a copy machine and paste up on your design representations of trees and other plants with your own code for identification.

Compare costs for outdoor living rooms with the cost of adding interior floor space to a home. Most likely you'll discover that outdoor living areas add entertaining and living space at a much lower cost. Attractive, long-lasting outdoor furniture and accessories such as water garden features, sculptures, and container plants can also be useful and enrich outdoor living areas.

Focus on Your Front Entrance

Friends, visitors, and passersby see you when they see your home's entranceway. Consider how your house looks from a distance and as you approach your front door. For improving overall appearance, plant attractive shrubs along the front. Flowering shrubs offer spring and summer beauty.

▲ Focus shrubs and plants around a doorway or an entrance to improve its appeal.

Use multipurpose trees that have blooms in spring and colorful fruits or berries in the fall to frame your house and showcase gardens. Local landscapers can suggest attractive plants to enhance the overview of your property. They also know which plants grow best in the area. As you develop your plans, write for free garden catalogs that give blooming dates so you can select the right plants to have blooms from different flowers all season long. The more you learn about plants, the better you'll be able to plan more beautiful and functional landscapes.

Enjoy Texture

The texture of plants is often overlooked, but it is a worthwhile design tool. Think of how the glossy leaves of holly, magnolia, and roses contrast with the suedelike foliage of lamb's ears, heliotrope, and coleus. You also have a variety of shapes of leaves from thick and shiny to multicolored, feathery, and airy. Flowers also provide textural interest. They can be rich and velvety like a rose or as thin and translucent as a poppy. Even tree and shrub bark contributes textural interest, especially during the winter months. You can and should use texture to good advantage.

Color Combinations

Color is a very personal feature for many people who have their favorites. You may have your favorite color or colors and are entitled to grow the colors you wish. Every color is represented in literally hundreds of different flowers. As you design your landscape, consider the following thoughts about color.

Combining floral colors in new and interesting ways offers a lifetime of growing possibilities. As a general rule, red, orange, and yellow are colors that jump out at you. Product packaging experts use them as hot, "buy" colors that excite customers. They are lively and stimulating. However, if you plant too many hot-colored flowers and don't balance them with cool-colored, less assertive plants, your garden may shout too loudly. In contrast, green, blue, and violet are cool colors. In the garden, these flowers create a more soothing, restful feeling and tend to recede into the distance. The palette of colors you wish to combine is up to you, but remember, in most great works of art, colors are subtly combined for artistic effect. You, too, can do that with your own gardens.

Consider Nonplant Elements

Other landscape factors also deserve attention beyond plants. Think about walls, fences, and paths. When designing your own garden use these aspects to create "rooms" in which plants are arranged in a context. For example, old-time English flower borders almost always had a background behind them, often a tall stone or brick wall or an evergreen hedge. Such a backdrop gives a focus on the intended plants. You can transplant that design idea to your garden.

FACT

Landscape designing, like rearranging furniture, is much easier on your back when you use graph paper to map out plans first. Would you rather move a tree on paper or transplant a living one?

Consider roofing for a portion of your garden especially in hot areas of the country or on the sun-baked sides of your house. For instance, you may wish to include arbors, bowers, and pergolas. Something like a series of overhead beams that support an arbor of grapes or flowering vines may create a quiet meditation or spiritual garden spot, or can be used as an entrance to another garden dimension.

Paths perform a purpose, leading us through a garden as they link one area to another. The paving material and the way you design a path can help define the style of the garden. For instance, a wide brick path suggests neatness and order.

Paths also create edges along which new plants or garden beds can be located. Many new types of path-making materials are available today from cast stones and bricks to gravel or slate. Basically, you should try to match the paving material to the feel of your garden—formal, informal, or free form.

Consider Landscape Accessories

Landscape accessories add character and dimension to a garden. Sculptures; chairs and benches; and bird feeders, baths, and houses can be part of your landscape planning. To determine whether or not to use an accessory consider these three basic points:

1. Does it have practical use?
2. Is it attractive by itself?
3. Does it fit into the overall landscape design?

Garden furniture offers a real opportunity to add utility, color, and beauty to the landscape. Birdbaths and bird feeders are often used in home landscapes. Sculptures also have their place, including statues and other replicas of nature. More accessories are becoming readily available in stores and from specialty mail-order firms. Cast iron is making a comeback. So is statuary. Elves, trolls, and pixies, as well as replicas of wild animals, are available, too. Think carefully to determine which will work for you and enhance the landscape, not detract from it.

Consulting Resources

Sometimes the best ideas for garden designs may be growing right next door, down the street, or where you work. Visiting other people's gardens may be the best source of landscaping inspiration. Knock on doors. Introduce yourself and compliment the homeowners on the gardens that captured your attention. Take along a camera or sketchpad and ask if you may take photos of garden plants and features that are especially appealing. Ask questions about their designs, their favorite plants that do best in your area, and whatever else you need to know. Most gardeners will be delighted to share their love of gardens. In fact, new friendships may sprout as well as landscaping ideas and garden plants.

Keep in mind that sun exposure is the penultimate requirement for some plants, and your neighbor may have the opposite sun available for plants that you have. What looks great next door may not work for your location, so be certain that you also make notes about the site, sun, and other growing conditions.

Colorful Photos

Colorful photos of landscape plants are another useful tool as you plan your landscapes. The pictures and descriptions will let you see which plants will please you, how big they grow, how profusely they bloom, and other details you'll need for your landscape design.

Some catalogs actually have plans of borders, beds, and fragrant and other types of gardens included, with the lists of plants to grow in them. You can copy them or adapt from them as you wish. Naturally, those plant experts have matched their plants well, which gives you other insights for your own designs.

Garden Design Books

Another good idea is to borrow garden books that are filled with dramatic, colorful garden scenes. That will stimulate your thinking and let you see what you can achieve in your home grounds.

Plan books are another good source of design ideas. Most ready-made plans are theme oriented and usually include a site plan with a planting list and drawings or photos that show you what the garden will look like at eye level. You can follow the plan or choose the elements that appeal to you. You can harvest an idea here and there and combine them into your own landscape plans. Creative gardeners read garden design books the way good cooks read recipe books.

Final Planning Thoughts

Once you have drawn your plans and reviewed your wish list of plants from trees and shrubs to flowers, herbs, and other elements for your landscape, make an extra copy. Then cover one copy with plastic so it won't get torn or wet and messy as you use it while doing your various planting projects. With a good plastic cover you also can use a grease pencil or Magic Marker to make changes or sketch what has been accomplished step-by-step.

As you develop your plan and plant accordingly, you can periodically use colored pencils to color in completed features. Show fall foliage in appropriate colors and evergreens in their shades of green. You'll be surprised how that may encourage you to continue on the path to creating even more beautiful landscaping in the years ahead.

If you prefer to take an easier route, and have computer skills, there are several useful software packages available that let you design your gardens and total landscape look on your computer. Some of the advantages are that you can see the relative sizes of shrubs and trees as they grow and mature. That will help you avoid planting too close to buildings or other plants and also save on future pruning to keep plants in line.

Let your fingers do the walking as you plan your home landscape. You'll find a pencil is much easier to move and use than a shovel to dig up plants put in the wrong spot. More importantly, you'll have hours of fun planning, anticipating, and relishing the joys of your more beautiful landscapes to be.

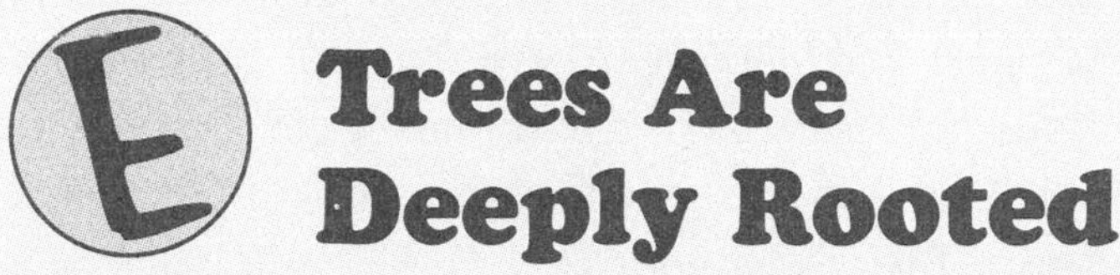

Chapter 3

Trees Are Deeply Rooted

Now that you have an idea, and possibly even a plan, for your landscaping venture, it's time to start digging in to the details. You should start with trees. This chapter will help you choose which trees to include in your design, where to put them, and how to plant them.

The Many Values of Trees

While designing your landscape, you surely had several ideas for trees. And if not, you should start thinking about them now. Trees add an elegance and beauty that no other plant can compete with. Many veteran gardeners recommend you begin your landscaping venture with trees, due to the growing time and permanence of the trees. However, because trees are a permanent part of the landscape, several people hesitate to make those final decisions necessary to plot and plant trees. If you are a part of this group, perhaps the following facts can help you put your fears aside and understand the value of trees.

- The net cooling effect of a young, healthy tree is equivalent to ten room-size air conditioners operating 20 hours a day, according to the U.S. Department of Agriculture.
- Trees can boost the market value of your home by an average of 6 or 7 percent, according to one national real estate survey.
- Landscaping, especially with trees, can increase property values as much as 20 percent, according to Management Information Services.
- There are between 60 and 200 million spaces along our city streets where trees could be planted. This translates to the potential to absorb 33 million more tons of carbon dioxide every year and save $4 billion in energy costs, according to the National Wildlife Federation.
- Trees properly placed around buildings can reduce air conditioning needs by 30 percent and can save 20 to 50 percent in energy used for heating, according to the U.S. Forest Service.
- Trees can be a stimulus to economic development. Commercial retail areas with trees are more attractive to shoppers, apartments rent more quickly, tenants stay longer, and space in a wooded setting is more valuable to sell or rent, according to The Arbor Day Foundation.
- In laboratory research, visual exposure to settings with trees has produced significant recovery from stress within 5 minutes, as indicated by changes in blood pressure and muscle tension, according to Dr. Roger S. Ulrich of Texas A&M University.

Assets of Specific Trees

There are several species of trees to choose from. There isn't a "best" species, so your decision relies heavily on what appeals to you. However, not all trees are created equal, and each has its own assets to consider. This section will highlight some of the more popular trees, but don't stop here. Continue your research until you find the tree(s) perfect for your landscape.

Some trees, such as locusts and pines, grow quickly. Others mature slowly. Here you'll find a list of good basic trees. Some work well as street trees. Others are better for backyards, shade, decorative accent, or their blooming beauty.

Norway maple (*Acer platanoides*) is a European native that grows well in the eastern United States. Some are columnar, which means they grow more upright than the typical spreading type. They have a shallow root system, which makes it difficult to grow grass or other plants around them.

Red maples (*Acer rubrum*) flower in early spring with tiny red buds bursting against smooth gray bark. If you are interested in finding trees with brilliant red fall foliage, consider the red maple.

Silver maples (*Acer saccharinum*) are fast growing. Be aware that they also tend to clog septic fields, but their graceful leaves and tree shape are two points in their favor.

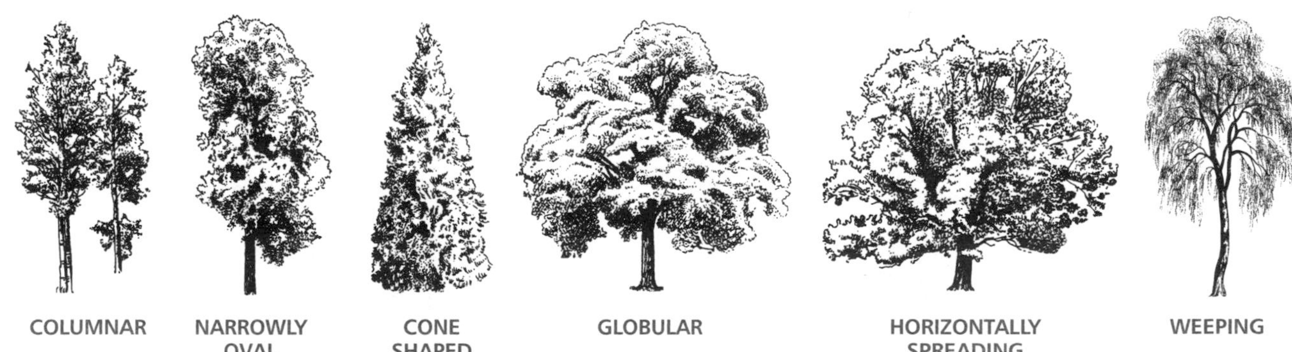

▲ Different shapes of trees, from columnar to weeping.

Sugar maples (*Acer saccharum*) are strong trees that hold up well in wind or ice storms. However, they grow rather slowly. You can make your own homemade maple syrup from the sap that will begin to flow in the spring!

Ash trees (*Fraxinus*), green and white, grow rather quickly. The green ash develops a broad crown, and the leaves turn bright yellow in fall. White ash becomes a larger tree, which is hardier and good for home use.

American sycamores (*Platanus occidentalis*) have bark that flakes off as the tree grows. This tree grows fast and big. Though it can tolerate urban air pollution, it is susceptible to diseases.

White oaks (*Quercus alba*) are majestic. They have thick branches and offer a rounded outline that will complement any landscape.

Red oaks (*Quercus rubra*) are faster growing and develop a broad, round-topped look with deep red fall color. These, too, withstand city conditions well.

Pin oaks (*Quercus palustris*) are useful. Their upper branches are horizontal while the lower ones droop close to the ground. You can prune away low branches if you wish. These trees will do well in moist or soggy areas.

River birch (*Betula nigra*) has salmon-colored bark that peels off in thin layers. It, too, thrives in moist or soggy areas, and it makes for an attractive landscape feature.

Lindens (*Tilia*) are best known as shade trees. They also produce beautiful small flowers in the spring, but since the flowers attract bees, it's best to plant them away from doors, windows, or populated areas.

Crabapples (*Malus*) are splendid in bloom and versatile, too. There are more than 200 different varieties, so check local nurseries at blooming time or mail-order catalogs. Look carefully at flowering crabapples. They offer dazzling beauty in bloom and fruits for feathered friends in summer and fall. Even summer foliage can be attractive, ranging from pure green through crimson.

Flowering cherry trees (*Prunus*) are available in many sizes and shapes. Some have single and others double white to pink to red blooms. Keep in mind that cherry trees don't like wet soil.

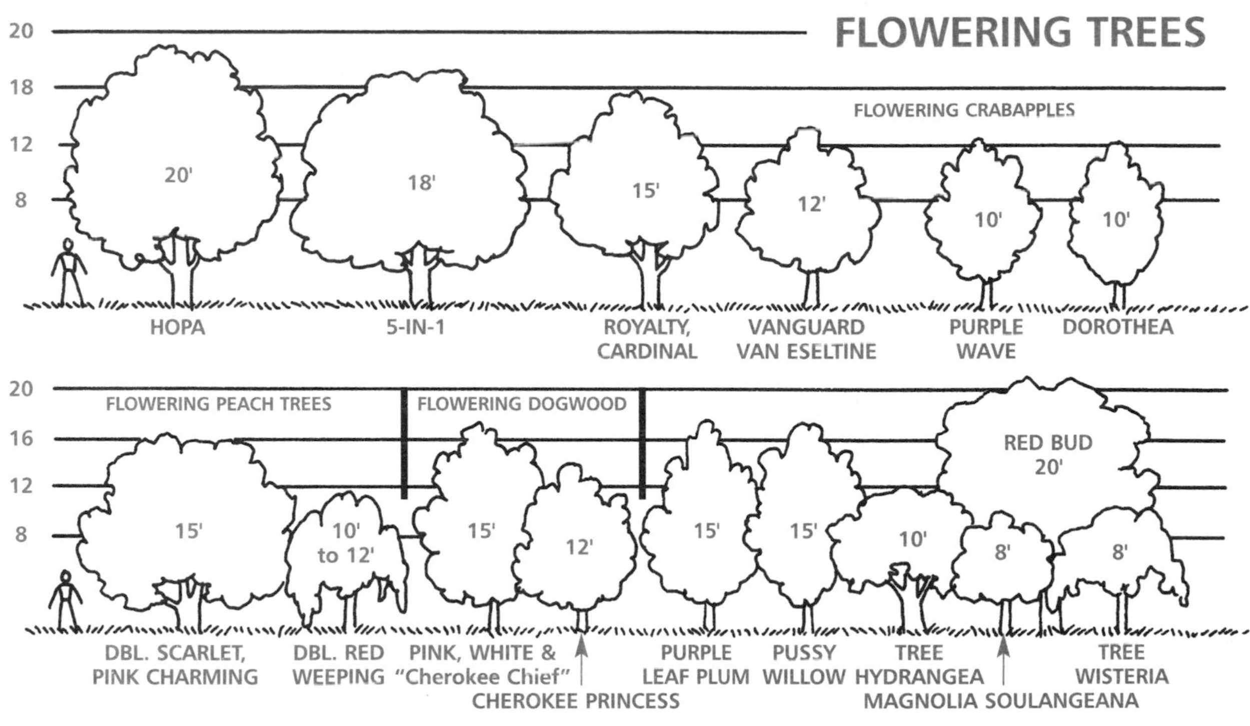

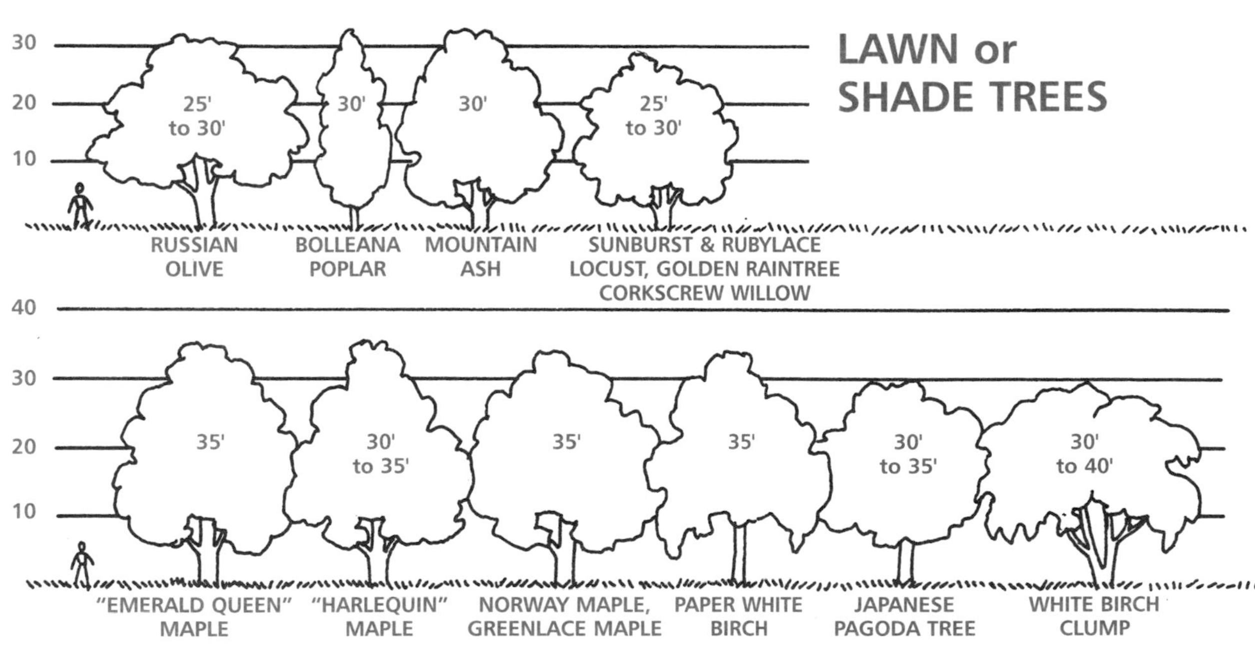

▲ Examples of flowering tree shapes and sizes, and examples of lawn/shade tree shapes and sizes.

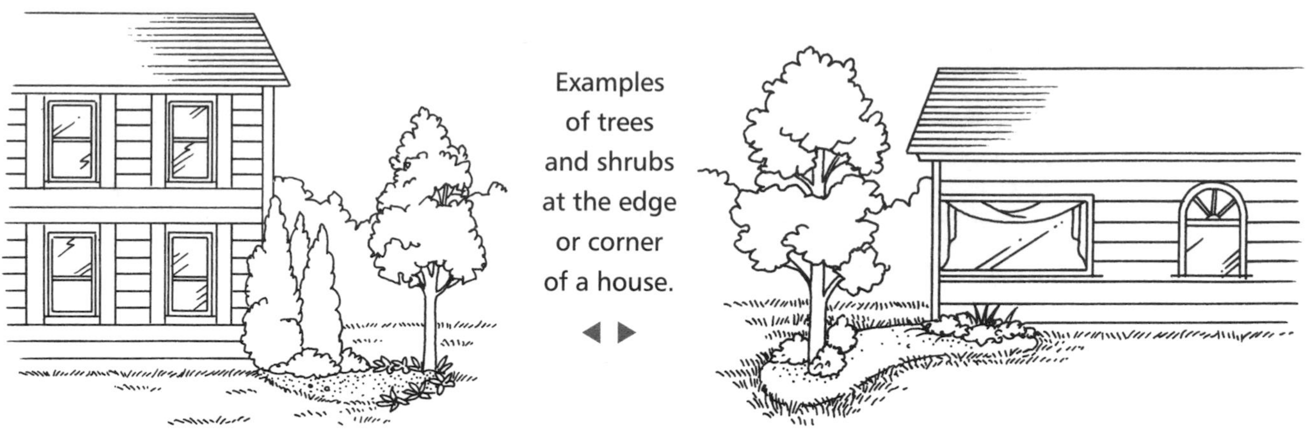

Examples of trees and shrubs at the edge or corner of a house. ◀ ▶

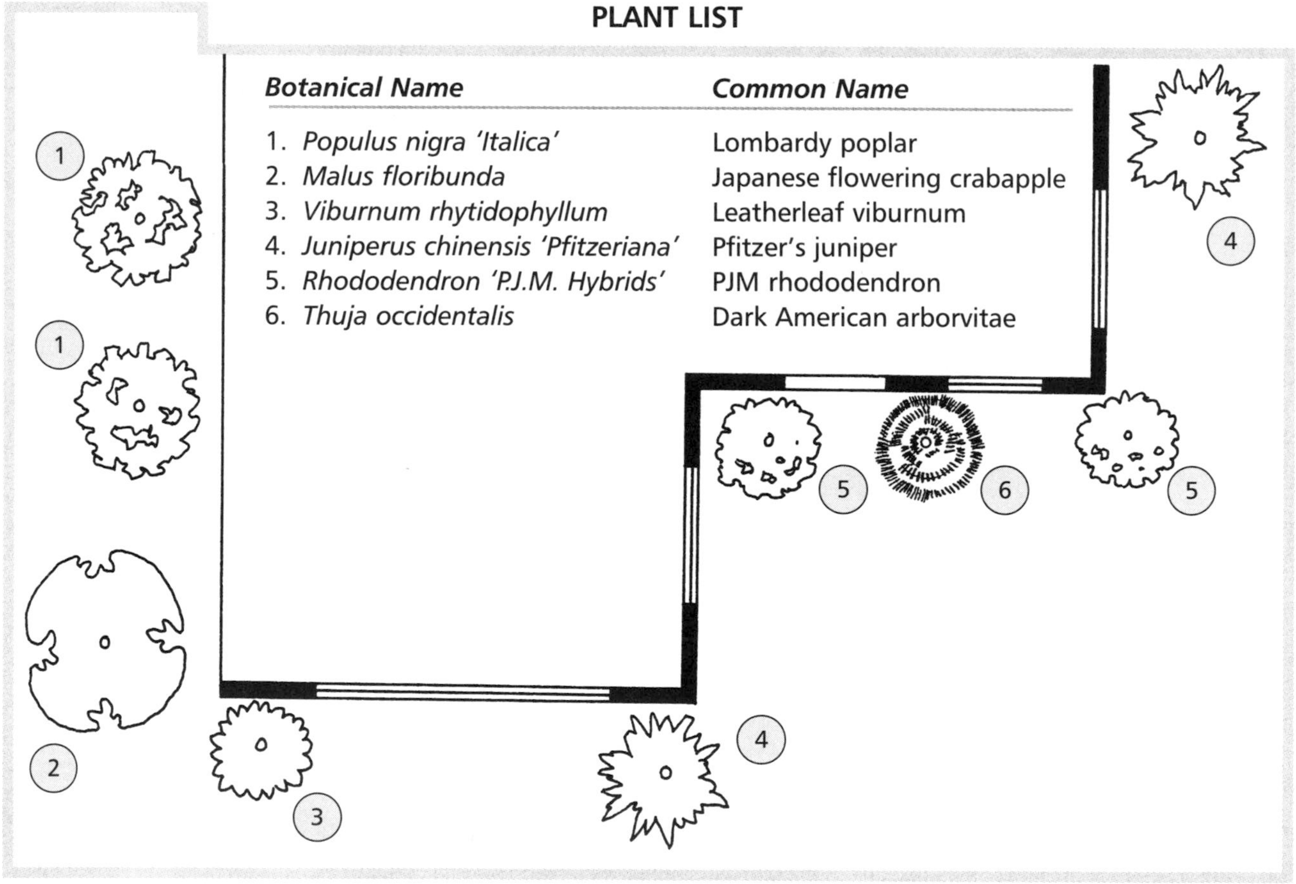

PLANT LIST

	Botanical Name	***Common Name***
1.	*Populus nigra 'Italica'*	Lombardy poplar
2.	*Malus floribunda*	Japanese flowering crabapple
3.	*Viburnum rhytidophyllum*	Leatherleaf viburnum
4.	*Juniperus chinensis 'Pfitzeriana'*	Pfitzer's juniper
5.	*Rhododendron 'P.J.M. Hybrids'*	PJM rhododendron
6.	*Thuja occidentalis*	Dark American arborvitae

▲ Examples of small trees of different shapes around a house.

Visit local nurseries in the spring to see which flowering trees appeal to you. Review catalogs to find other more exotic and distinctive trees such as hardy Silk trees, flowering peach, or Oriental, or American dogwood trees. Your choices seem almost limitless. Just be sure you match the tree to the growing conditions your area provides.

Eight-Step Planting Plan

If you carefully follow these eight simple steps, you can significantly reduce the stress placed on the plant at the time of planting and get your trees off to a strong, fast, healthy start. That is the most important part of a tree's new life on your home grounds. Once it takes root, it will grow with minimal care to reward you with shade and beauty for your lifetime.

Always check with utility companies before you dig to plant trees, especially along streets and in front of your home. Also, before you choose trees to plant near utility lines, determine the mature height and width of your choice to prevent future conflicts.

1. Dig a shallow and broad planting hole, three times the diameter of the root ball and only as deep as the root ball. Loosen the surrounding soil somewhat to give the roots room to expand and establish themselves easily.
2. Identify the trunk's flare. This is the point where the roots spread at the base of the tree. When planting, keep the trunk's flare partially visible. You don't want to cover it completely with soil.
3. Place the tree at the proper height. This means that you don't want the tree to be planted too deeply, since most of the roots will develop in the top 12 inches of soil. It is better to plant the tree a little high (1 to 2 inches above the base of the trunk flare), than to plant it at or below the original growing level.
4. Carefully straighten the tree in the hole. Before you begin backfilling, look at the tree from several directions to confirm that your tree is straight. If not, straighten it.

5. Fill one third of the hole with soil, and gently but firmly pack the soil around the base of the root ball. If your tree is balled and burlapped, cut and remove all string and wire from around the trunk and the top one third of the root ball. Be careful not to damage the trunk or roots in the process. You can leave the burlap on the bottom, to hold the soil in place. It will eventually rot down in the soil.
6. Fill the remainder of the hole. Carefully pack the soil to eliminate air pockets that may cause roots to dry out. Add soil a few inches at a time and settle with water. Continue until the hole is filled, with the tree firmly in place. Don't add fertilizer at this time.
7. If staking is necessary for support, now is the time. Stake only those trees that call for it. Ask your local nursery if you are unsure. To support your tree, use two stakes on either side and a wide, flexible tie material. (Check with your local nursery for the best material to use to stake a tree.) Don't forget to remove the stakes after the tree has established a firm roothold (usually after the first year).
8. Finally, mulch the base of the tree. Mulch serves as a blanket to hold in moisture, protect against harsh soil temperatures, and deter grass and weeds. Be sure that the actual trunk of the tree is not covered with mulch. Mulching in a circle 18 inches in diameter also gives you a safety zone so you don't mow lawns too close to trees and risk damaging the trunks. Leave a mulch-free area,1 to 2 inches wide, at the base of the tree to avoid moist bark conditions and prevent decay.

FACT

Once you have completed these basic steps, your tree should do well in its new home. If you have any problems or questions about the care of your tree, be sure to consult your local certified arborist, tree care nursery staff, or garden center professional for assistance.

After planting, keep the soil moist but not soaked. You should water the trees at least once a week and even more often during hot weather.

Check the soil around newly planted trees periodically. If soil is dry below the surface of the mulch, it is time to water.

Tree-Planting Tips

First key point for all trees: Never plant trees in spaces too small for their mature size. For major landscape shade trees, it is important to provide them with adequate growing room for their mature size. They need it for their root systems, which will eventually expand rapidly and extensively.

The best time to plant trees is during their dormant season, which is in the fall after leaves drop or early spring before buds break. Cool weather conditions allow trees to establish their roots before warmer weather stimulates new top growth. However, if you miss the dormant season, you can plant container-grown or balled and burlapped trees any time during the growing season.

Fruit trees, trees in landscape beds, and specimen ornamental trees are grown for different reasons and are not planted the same way as shade and street trees. Consult your local nursery or arborist for planting instructions for these types of trees.

Whether the tree you are planting is balled and burlapped or bare rooted, it is important to understand that the tree's root system has been reduced substantially from its original size during harvesting. Because of this, trees may exhibit what is known as transplant shock, which is indicated by slow growth and reduced vigor following transplanting. You can prevent this problem by proper site preparation before and during planting and good follow-up care.

Tree-Planting Programs

Trees are attracting more attention every year. As a result, tree-planting programs are springing up around the world. Ask around in your community and explore the Internet. You'll uncover much worthwhile knowledge, plus be able to dig up bits of history, heritage, and hands-on growing advice.

Project Learning Tree

Project Learning Tree (PLT) is an innovative environmental education program designed for educators who will be working with students from kindergarten through twelfth grade. The program emphasizes teaching students how to think, not what to think, about environmental issues. It is a program complete with curriculum materials that help students understand all aspects of the natural world and environment from the carbon dioxide and oxygen cycle to the movement of pollutants and more.

For more than two decades, PLT has been working with diverse groups to develop and implement a useful environmental education curriculum. At this point, an estimated 25 million students worldwide have participated in PLT activities. There is a network of nearly 500,000 trained PLT educators. More than 30,000 new educators are introduced to PLT each year through daylong workshops led by trained volunteers. You can obtain more information about Project Learning Tree and opportunities for working together by calling ✆ 888-889-4466.

Global ReLeaf

Global ReLeaf is American Forests' educational program that promotes planting and caring for trees to improve the environment. There are two types of Global ReLeaf projects. In urban areas, trees are planted through the Global ReLeaf Fund. The program encourages people to plant trees around their homes and businesses or join community groups to plant trees that shade, cool, and beautify their neighborhoods. In less-developed areas, trees are planted in ecosystem restoration projects called Global ReLeaf Forests. Many of these areas have been damaged by natural or human causes. The trees planted help clean the air and water, filter polluted runoff, and slow global warming.

If you are interested in learning more about Global ReLeaf, you can get information by calling the Global ReLeaf Tree-Planting Hotline at

800-545-TREE. At this point, the organization reports having planted trees in over 500 projects in every state and province in North America as well as twenty-one countries worldwide.

Before delving into tree planting, be sure you first determine what the selected site offers in terms of sunlight, soil moisture, and height availability. Then, from those facts, you can choose trees that will thrive on your land and are best suited for your desires.

President Eisenhower Ash Trees

Some tree-planting programs have been organized to honor people. For instance, members of the Veterans of Foreign Wars (VFW) and other public figures have planted thousands of Dwight D. Eisenhower Green Ash Trees, the official tree of the National WWII Memorial in Washington, D.C.

"These majestic trees have stood as silent witnesses to history," said Mary Eisenhower, granddaughter of President Eisenhower and chief executive officer of People to People International. "Now they will stand in our cities and towns as lasting memorials to those 16 million soldiers in uniform during World War II, and to all who have served in the military and on the home front to preserve our freedom."

The nationwide effort was organized by the VFW Foundation, American Forests, Wal-Mart Stores, Inc., and The Scotts Company. It provides Eisenhower Green Ash Trees for planting in parks, community areas, and at veterans' memorials. The trees are authentic direct offspring of a green ash tree that grows at the birthplace of President Eisenhower in Denison, Texas. As a tribute to President Eisenhower's role as Supreme Commander of the Allied Forces during World War II, the Eisenhower Green Ash Tree has been named the official tree of the National World War II Memorial.

Eisenhower Green Ash Trees are available for sale at all Wal-Mart stores. Visit *www.americanforests.org* for more information and to order a free Famous & Historic Trees catalogue.

The American Tree Farm System

The American Tree Farm system is another active program that is deeply rooted across America. It is actively promoting the planting of millions upon millions of trees, especially by small lot family tree growers. Their mission is to promote the growing of renewable forest resources on private lands, while protecting environmental benefits and also increasing public understanding of the benefits of productive forestry.

The American Tree Farm System's goal is to reach the 9 million forest landowners who are not actively managing their land in a sustainable manner and persuade them to join other individuals who share a unique commitment in protecting watersheds and wildlife habitat, conserving soil, and providing recreation for their neighbors while at the same time producing the wood America needs.

FACT

Trees take in carbon dioxide that humans exhale and give people oxygen back in return. They are a vital part of our environment. As trees are cut in America and around the world, there is a natural need to replace them with new trees. You can do your part by re-treeing America!

Get Involved!

If you want to get involved planting trees to better the environment, you may want to consider starting locally. For instance, check with your town about planting trees along the street. There may be incentive programs that can help defray costs. The trees near the street, and often between the sidewalk and street, are probably city-owned. The city should have a program for planting and caring for these trees. Ask at city hall.

There is a national program for cities called Tree City, USA. Check into it. This program offers much useful information about helping cities become better homes for people by planting more trees. Encourage your town to fully fund a quality community forestry program.

Pollution can cause problems for many trees. Fortunately, some trees are better able to withstand the highway fumes, dust, glare, and smog.

In fact, they'll help clean the air in your neighborhood and soften city noises, too. The following trees are deemed "clean" trees, and they are relatively resistant to pests and disease.

- London plane trees grow fast, produce high shade, and are an excellent "see-under" tree that does not obstruct signs. Grows 50 to 75 feet tall.
- Norway maple is fast growing, with dense foliage that turns bright yellow in fall. Grows 50 to 75 feet tall.
- Sugar maple is a splendid shade tree with symmetrical shape and orange fall foliage. Grows well set back from highways, and mature height is 60 to 70 feet tall.
- Ginkgo is also called Maidenhair tree and is pest and disease free. Erect forms are excellent for narrow places on city streets. It is slow growing and reaches a mature height of 30 feet.
- Honey locust has rather thin, airy foliage but grows well, is graceful, and matures to about 30 feet tall.
- Red oaks are the fastest growing of the oaks and the handsomest of all street trees. Lustrous foliage turns deep red in fall, and the tree grows to 50 feet tall.
- Columnar Norway maple is an upright form of vigorous Norway maples. It leafs out early and holds yellow autumn foliage late. Grows to 40 feet tall.
- Red maple is another native tree well adapted to dry or wet areas as well as street sites. Grows to a graceful tree 40 feet tall.
- The Washington hawthorn has dense shiny foliage and white flowers in profusion in June, with small, red fruit in fall. Good for under wires on poles, it matures to 20 feet tall.
- Hopa crabapple is another excellent small tree with upright, vigorous growth. It is covered with rose-colored flowers in May and small red fruit in autumn, and it matures to 20 feet tall.

You may also want to take part in another program: replanting elm trees that once graced and lined streets throughout America. The Dutch elm disease killed millions. Now a disease-resistant variety has been developed. You can check with local nurseries or the state arborist about this program and help re-elm America.

Chapter 4

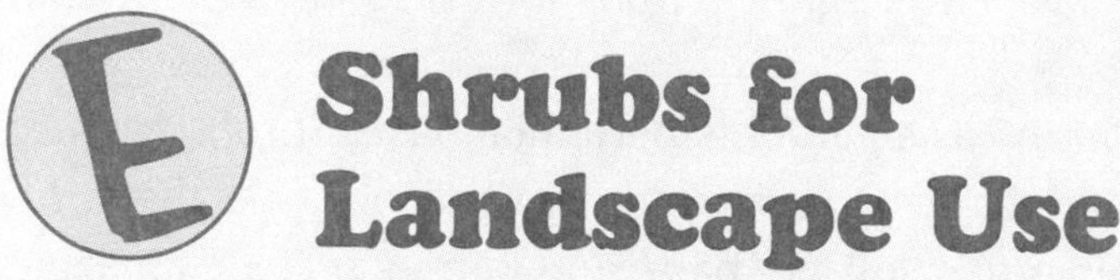

Shrubs for Landscape Use

Shrubs of all types, shapes, sizes, and blooming habits are available to grace your landscape. This chapter will give a brief overview of several popular shrubs for your consideration. Use this chapter, shop at the local nursery, and peruse mail-order catalogs to find those shrubs that will please you most and grow well in your area.

Top Ten Shrubs

If you have chosen to add shrubs to your landscape, you may have noticed that there is a wide variety available to you. This could create a problem (and certainly some frustration!) when it comes time to make a decision. Luckily, in a recent poll, veteran gardeners came up with ten reliable, decorative, easy-to-grow shrubs for seasonal excitement in your landscape.

Think of shrubs as a garden's perennial base. Shrubs can define and outline your outdoor living areas and garden spaces. As they grow and bloom, their blossoms, foliage, bark, and berries provide amazing diversity. Try reading through mail-order catalogs and you'll discover many worthwhile shrubs that could be perfect additions to your home grounds.

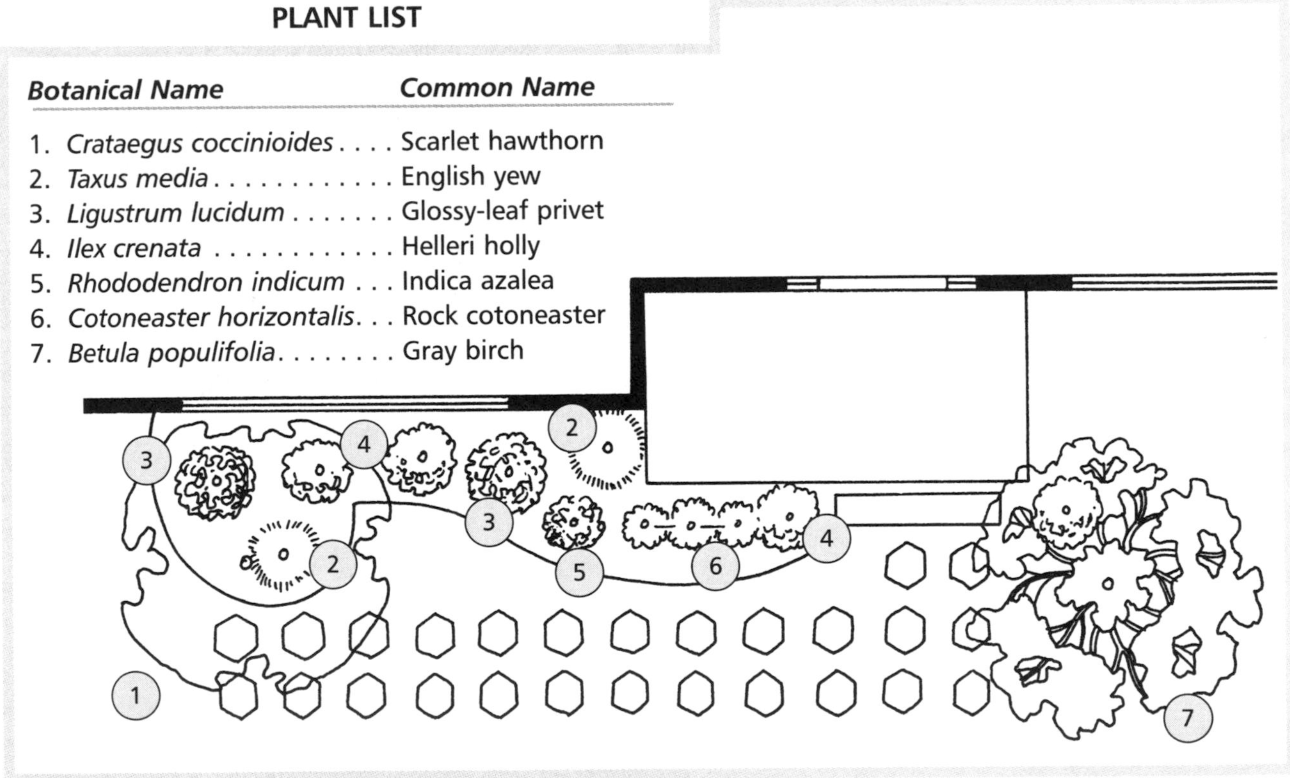

PLANT LIST
Botanical Name
Common Name
1. Crataegus coccinioides . . . . Scarlet hawthorn
2. Taxus media . . . . English yew
3. Ligustrum lucidum . . . . Glossy-leaf privet
4. Ilex crenata . . . . Helleri holly
5. Rhododendron indicum . . . Indica azalea
6. Cotoneaster horizontalis. . . Rock cotoneaster
7. Betula populifolia. . . . . Gray birch

▲Examples of shrubs and trees landscaping for porch area.

A careful selection of shrubs guarantees the beauty that changes from season to season. Here are ten shrub favorites that can grow in most parts of the country. They are easy to grow and have something to offer year-round.

1. **Viburnum** (*Viburnum*). A genus of some 150 species, viburnums can be evergreen or deciduous. The blooms are fragrant and beautiful. They also produce colorful berries favored by birds. Viburnums need well-drained soil and a location that is sunny to part shade. Viburnums grow in zones 4 through 8 and can be semi evergreen in the South.
2. **Flowering quince** (*Chaenomeles*). Depending on the cultivar, the colors of the cup-shaped flowers of flowering quince can fall anywhere from white or pale peach to bright coral. You can cut twigs as they bud out and force them into bloom for indoor bouquets. The hybrid Cameo has the largest blooms of the genus, nearly 2 inches across with double blossoms that resemble tea roses. These last longer than other varieties. The delicate color of its petals ranges from peachy pink at the edges to rosy pink in the center. It is hardy, grows about 5 feet tall, and is almost completely thornless.
3. **Butterfly bush** (*Buddleia*). Cultivars like Dubonnet, Pink Charming, or Argentea offer masses of nearly foot-long, trumpetlike flowers that suggest lilacs, which gives it the other name, summer lilac. The slender, distinctive gray-green leaves have a silverish sheen. Butterfly bushes typically bloom for much of the late summer, so they are a great choice for a sunny spot that has fertile, well-drained soil.
4. **Walking Stick** (*Corylus avellana*). Harry Lauder's Walking Stick sprouts a witch's broom of upright twigs that will not grow straight but twist and curl instead. Its foliage is as handsome as the straight members of the filbert clan, also known as hazelnut. No doubt it is an attention-getter. It grows in zones 4 through 8.
5. **Flower Carpet roses** (*Rosa*). These new marvels are now available in pink, white, apple blossom, and red. The unique Flower Carpet is a radical innovation in the breeding of the rose, a much-hybridized

worldwide favorite, and America's national flower. Flower Carpet thrives on 4 to 5 hours of sun per day and produces clusters of blooms nonstop from spring to fall. More colors are being developed in response to early popularity of this new type of rose. They grow in zones 5 through 10.

6. **Mock orange** (*Philadelphus*). This shrub is a fast grower that can grow up to 10 feet in a few years, but at half of that height starts yielding immaculate white flowers with the unforgettable scent of orange blossoms. Mock orange needs annual pruning. For fragrant garden delights, mock orange is a winner. Good in zones 5 through 8.
7. **Heavenly bamboo** (*Nandina domestica*). This shrub has leaves similar to bamboo, hence the name. It can reach 6 feet tall with beautiful foliage all year long. The white flowers become clusters of red berries, which stick around during winter. Heavenly bamboo will thrive in sun or shade but only a location in full sun will inspire bumper crops of berries. Grows in zones 7 through 10.
8. **Spirea** (*Spiraea*). This shrub is a dense and delightful bloomer in spring to summer and makes a flowering hedge. The cultivar Shibori produces both pink and white flowers in the same cluster. The cultivar Anthony Waterer starts out with reddish foliage that turns blue-green in the summer and purple in the fall. It thrives in zones 4 through 9.
9. **Siberian dogwood** (*Cornus alba*). Siberian dogwood is a delight that features leafless bright red twigs that liven up the winter landscape. These shrubs are at their most dramatic when snow covers the ground. Also known as red-twigged dogwood, its vigorous, sturdy upright shoots can reach 10 feet tall. This shrub works nicely as a thicket or as a fence and can be a real attention-getter. In the spring, clusters of ¼-inch white flowers appear and the berries that follow are white flushed with blue. They attract birds of all kinds and grow in zones 2 through 10.
10. **Lilac** (*Syringa*). Lilacs provide old-time romantic fragrance for all. New lilac hybrids are marvelous and produce even more flowers with

elegant fragrance. After lilac blooms are gone, the foliage remains and the heart-shaped leaves make a nice bushy display. Some lilacs tend to sucker, which gives you more plants for elsewhere in your landscape or to share. If the shoots are unwanted, they must be dug out and removed periodically. Lilacs do well in zones 3 through 7.

LEFT: Sweet Bay *(Laurus nobilis)*

RIGHT: Lilac (*Syringa*)

LEFT: Fuchsia *(Fuchsia triphylla)*

RIGHT: Mock orange (*Philadelphus*)

Favorite Flowering Shrubs

To help you pick shrubs that will be dramatic and useful, here's a list compiled from veteran gardeners who responded to a survey about their favorite flowering shrubs. Check out mail-order catalogs for photos to see which will please you best, and also which will grow well in your area.

Beauty bush (*Kolkwitzia amabilis*): This shrub grows large, with an upright spreading habit and has showy pink flowers from late May to June. It likes full sun in borders and is best as a specimen plant.

Cotoneaster (*Cotoneaster*): This has a creeping or spreading habit and offers a wide selection of types. Inconspicuous pink or white flowers in dense foliage are followed by attractive red berries.

Flowering almond (*Prunus glandulosa*): The flowering almond is a low-growing small shrub with a round top. It has double pink or white flowers in May and prefers sunny spots.

Forsythia (*Forsythia*): Forsythia is an old-time favorite blooming shrub that is available in many new varieties. It provides profuse blooms and vivid yellow color early in spring when daffodils are blooming. You can select either upright and weeping or flowing patterns, depending on varieties. Forsythia prefers sunny spots.

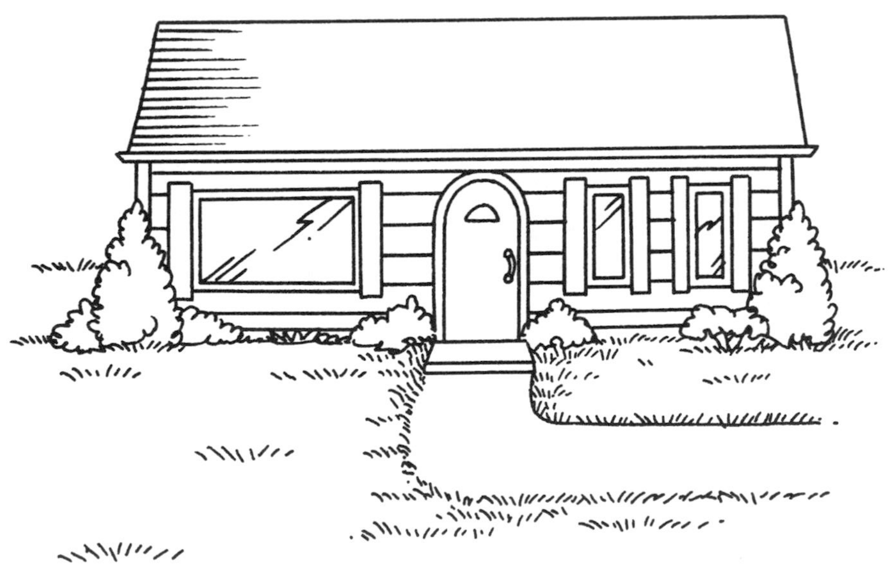

▲Illustrations of shrubs and trees at entrance or front of home.

Hydrangea (*Hydrangea*): Also known as snowball plant, hydrangea is known for its large white flowers. But newer, improved blue and red varieties provide colorful, massive accent plants for gardens. Blooms can be 6 to10 inches across.

Good Evergreen Shrubs

Evergreen shrubs also have a place in most home landscape plans. They can serve as windbreaks to stop icy blasts against home foundations and also provide dense, dark green backgrounds for garden flowers. Here are some popular evergreen shrubs that may fit your garden well.

Japanese yews (*Taxus cuspidata*): These shrubs have dark green leaves, stand shearing well, and make fine hedges or specimens in foundation plantings. Pruned branches also provide useful foliage for holiday decorating.

Junipers (*Juniperus*): The low Andorra or Sargent and the ground-hugging Blue Rug are low evergreens, take full sun, and require less care in general than do yews or other junipers.

Mugho pine (*Pinus mugo*): This is a broad, round shrub with moundlike dwarf forms available for rock gardens or low border plantings. Other types grow taller and need periodic pruning every year or so.

Chinese holly (*Ilex cornuta*): Chinese holly makes a dense shrub, 8 to 9 feet high, and grows in shady locations. Many fine varieties are available, some even with variegated leaves. Hollies are versatile in middle and southern states, usually thriving in climate zones 7 through 10.

Pyracantha (*Pyracantha coccinea*): Also called firethorn, this shrub grows rapidly and can be trained easily. As a shrub with dark green leaves and bright orange-red berries in fall and winter, it deserves your attention.

"Wow Power" Shrubs

If you love butterflies and hummingbirds, plant shrubs that attract them. Or, if you just want dramatic, colorful shrubs with what veteran gardeners call "Wow Power," here are some to consider.

The Buddleia Species

Honeycomb is considered to be the finest yellow buddleia. Its golden blooms are easy to see, and it has a strong fragrance that attracts butterflies. You also gain a long bloom season from June to November

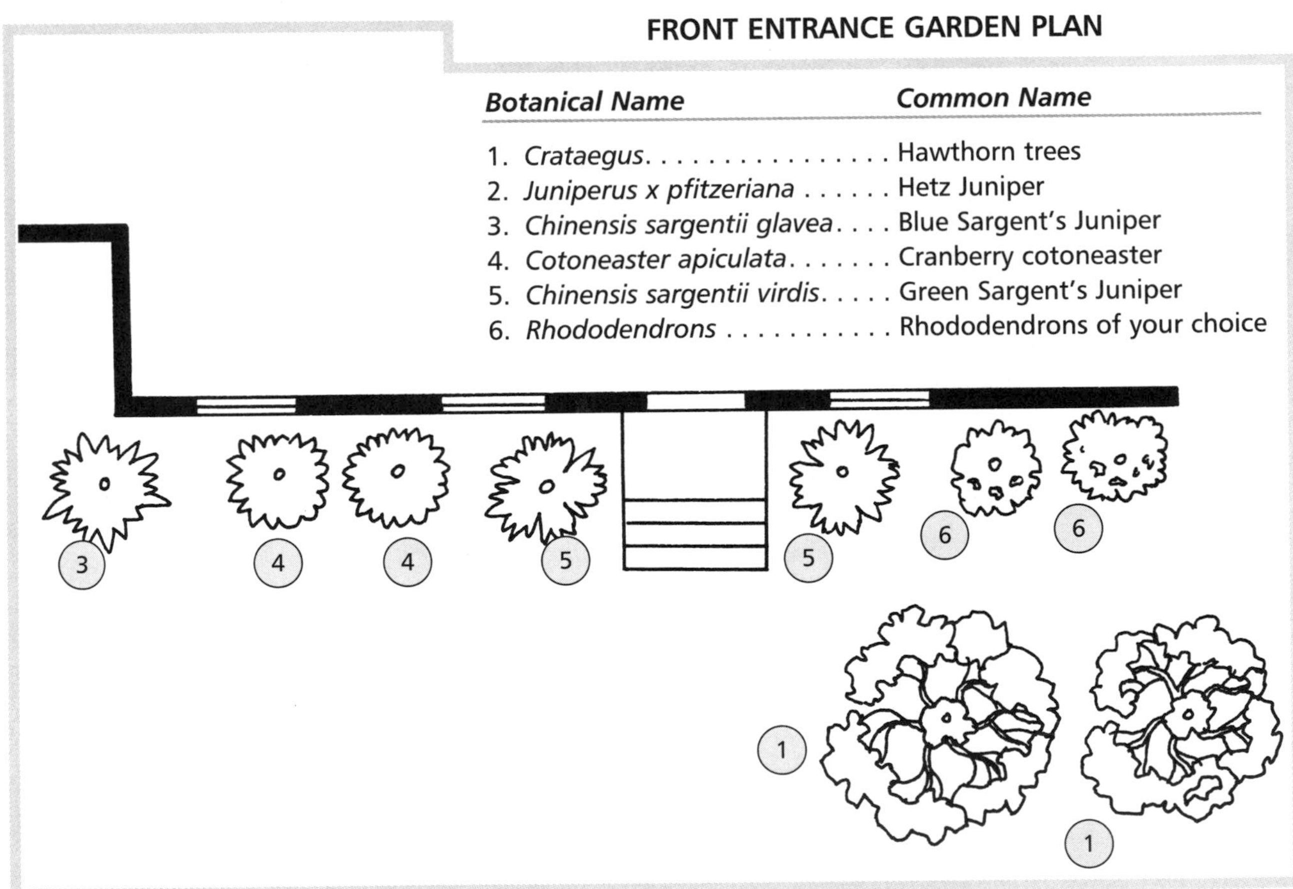

FRONT ENTRANCE GARDEN PLAN
Botanical Name
Common Name
1. Crataegus. . . . . Hawthorn trees
2. Juniperus x pfitzeriana . . . . . . Hetz Juniper
3. Chinensis sargentii glavea. . . . Blue Sargent's Juniper
4. Cotoneaster apiculata. . . . . . . Cranberry cotoneaster
5. Chinensis sargentii virdis. . . . . Green Sargent's Juniper
6. Rhododendrons . . . . Rhododendrons of your choice
3
4
4
5
5
6
6
1
1

▲ Front entrance design example with small trees and shrubs.

in many areas. With a carefree habit that does require a hard spring pruning, Honeycomb reaches 8 to 12 feet in warmer areas. It is resistant to drought, pests, and disease.

The Salix Alba Species

Coral Embers Willow has been a favorite in Europe for more than a century. This lovely selection of the white willow stands out against the dark colors of winter with its bright orange-red stems. Its bright green foliage has silvery undersides, and in many locations turns yellow in fall. This vigorous shrub grows 4 to 5 feet in a single season but should be cut back to 12 to 15 inches in late winter.

Britzensis is very hardy and easy to grow in well-drained soil in full sun. It is tolerant of poor growing conditions and even thrives in wet soils.

The Hydrangea Species

Among hydrangeas, Nikko is a super blue beauty. This blue hydrangea sports consistent blue flowers in various soils with pink flowers joining the blue in neutral soil. You can enjoy a wealth of attractive, deep blue, globe-shaped flower heads all summer with Nikko Blue. Nurserymen say that this is the most reliable of the blue-flowered selections with exceptionally large blooms that are truer blue in a wide range of soils.

The most striking, consistent blue color of Nikko Blue is achieved in acid earth. In neutral soil, both pink and blue flowers appear. By adding acid mulch, pine needles, and similar materials, you can help it stay true blue.

Hydrangeas are among the showiest of summer and autumn-flowering woody plants. They are shade tolerant so they grow well under trees or on the shady side of a building. Plant them singly as focal points or mass together for stunning borders.

The Hibiscus Species

Hibiscus are making a comeback. You can enjoy a super hibiscus this year and turn your landscape into an ocean of color with Hibiscus Blue Bird. Blue Bird bears a profusion of huge, azure blue flowers all summer on bushy plants with handsome cool green foliage. These stately deciduous plants are so beautiful that it's easy to forget their tough, carefree nature.

Hibiscus grows best in full sun in ordinary soil and reaches 8 to 12 feet tall. To increase bloom and to shape, prune to two buds per branch when dormant. It grows in zones 5 through 9.

Gardenias

For those who want something special and are willing to dish out tender loving care, gardenias do well in southern states. Follow the special care they need for truly fragrant, beautiful plants.

Specimen Shrubs

Special accent or specimen shrubs are plants chosen to stand alone in the landscape to provide a specific accent or interest. They will give your landscape that very special look that catches people's attention. Fortunately, a variety of dramatic plants, smaller trees, and shrubs enable you to have appealing highlights in your landscape. Because most of these are smaller than typical large landscape trees, they are included in this chapter. Call them minitrees if you wish, but do consider their potential for your landscape.

Golden Chain Trees

Golden Chain trees (*Laburnum*) are something special indeed. In late spring, 18- to 24-inch racemes of golden yellow flowers resembling wisteria transform the Golden Chain tree into a sparkling cascade.

Growing 12 to 15 feet high by 9 to 12 feet wide, the Vossii cultivar is one of the best choices for smaller gardens. Magnificent in bloom, it is handsome all season long with its smooth, bright green bark and lower leaf foliage. You can grow this cultivar in a well-drained, sheltered site with partial shade.

Weeping Higan

Weeping Higan cherry (*Prunus* "Plena Rosea") is a rare, double-flowered, extremely early-flowering cherry that has cascading flowers in early spring. Its full weeping habit sports profuse, fully double, rosy pink flowers that mature to white with fine-textured foliage. The Weeping Higan cherry can reach 10 to 15 feet high and wide.

Weeping Sally

The Weeping Sally willow is truly unusual and rare and worth considering as a specimen plant. This spectacular small weeping tree is the female form of the Kilmarnock willow. Its long branches bear silky silver catkins that appear before shiny foliage in early spring. Its graceful form, foliage, and flowers create year-round interest. Weeping Sally grows only 6 to 8 feet tall and 4 to 5 feet wide.

When choosing shrubs, keep two key points in mind. First, select plants that are suited to your area and will perform in your climate. Second, consider the total look of your landscape scene. All plants should harmonize and blend together, rather than become a hodgepodge of specimens that don't seem to fit together.

Shrubs with Winter Fruits

Here's a handy shopping list of shrubs bearing fruits that will serve as food for birds during the fall and winter. Look up their specific growing needs in catalogs and think how nicely some may fit into your landscape dreams.

- Korean Barberry (*Berberis koreana*)
- American Bittersweet (*Celastrus scandens*)
- Thornless Cockspur Hawthorn (*Crataegus crus-galli inermis*)
- Russian Olive (*Elaeagnus angustifolia*)
- Winterberry (*Ilex verticillata*)
- Highbush Cranberry (*Viburnum trilobum*)

Shrub Size Checklist

When you begin reviewing the variety of different shrubs that may have a place in your landscape plans, it is sometimes difficult to determine sizes at maturity. Therefore, the following lists will provide you with the shrubs that will fit your sizing needs.

Large Shrubs—8 Feet and Higher

- Amur Maple (*Acer ginnala*)
- Pagoda Dogwood (*Cornus alternifolia*)
- Red-twig Dogwood and its cultivars (*Cornus sericea* or *alba*)
- Winged Euonymus (*Euonymus alatus*)
- Common Witch Hazel (*Hamamelis virginiana*)
- Mock Orange and its cultivars (*Philadelphus*)
- Mugho Pine (*Pinus mugo*)
- American Elderberry (*Sambuvus canadensis*)
- Common Lilac and its cultivars (*Syringa vulgaris*)
- Upright Japanese Yew (*Taxus cuspidata*)
- Sargent Viburnum (*Viburnum sargentii*)
- American Cranberry Bush and its cultivars (*Viburnum trilobum*)

Medium Shrubs—5 to 8 Feet Tall

- Gray Dogwood (*Cornus racemosa*)
- Hedge Cotoneaster (*Cotoneaster lucidus*)
- Many-Flowered Cotoneaster (*Cotoneaster multiflorus*)
- Forsythia and its cultivars (*Forsythia ovata*)
- Panicled Hydrangea and its cultivars (*Hydrangea paniculata*)
- Winterberry and its cultivars (*Ilex verticillata*)
- Mock Orange cultivars (*Philadelphus*)
- Dwarf Flowering Almond (*Prunus glandulosa*)
- Nanking Cherry (*Prunus tomentosa*)
- Hardy shrub roses (*Rosa*)
- Van Houtte Spirea (*Spiraea x vanhouttei*)
- Arborvitae shrub cultivars (*Thuja occidentalis*)
- Weigela hybrid cultivars (*Weigela*)

Small Shrubs—3 to 5 Feet

- Japanese Barberry and its cultivars (*Berberis thunbergii*)
- Red Leaf Japanese Barberry and its cultivars (*Berberis thunbergii atropurpurea*)
- Smooth Hydrangea and its cultivars (*Hydrangea arborescens*)
- Dwarf Ninebark (*Physocarpus opulifolius*)
- P.J.M. Hybrid Rhododendron (*Rhododendron* "P.J.M.")
- Rugosa Rose and its cultivars (*Rosa rugosa*)
- Garland Spirea (*Spiraea x arguta*)
- Common Snowberry (*Symphoricarpos albus*)
- Japanese Yew (*Taxus cuspidata*)

Very Small Shrubs—Under 3 Feet

- Dwarf Japanese Barberry cultivars (*Berberis thunbergii*)
- New Jersey Tea (*Ceanothus americanus*)
- Cranberry Cotoneaster (*Cotoneaster apiculatus*)
- Dwarf Bush Honeysuckle (*Diervilla lonicera*)
- Smooth Hydrangea and its cultivars (*Hydrangea arborescens*)
- Creeping Juniper and its cultivars (*Juniperus horizontalis*)
- Russian Cypress (*Microbiota decussata*)
- Japanese White Spirea (*Spiraea albiflora*)
- Blueberry hybrid cultivars (*Vaccinium*)
- Dwarf European Cranberry Bush (*Viburnum opulus* "Nanum")

Chapter 5

Bulbs Are Beautiful

Bulbs should be a basic part of every home landscape. Veteran gardeners and landscapers love bulbs because most are perennial. Once planted, they reward you with blooming beauty every year and require very little care. With thanks to the Netherlands Flower Bulb Information Center, in this chapter you'll learn all about bulbs and how to grow them.

What Is a Bulb?

Actually, a flower bulb is an underground flower factory. Everything the plant needs is contained within the bulb, including a food supply, flower, and leaves. If you cut a bulb in half, you will be able to see the underground flower factory, and even the flower itself.

All gardeners need to do for success is place the entire bulb into the ground at the correct depth, cover it with soil, and give it sufficient water. Eventually, the miracle of the bulb will appear above the ground and provide its blooming beauty for all to enjoy.

Bulbs, Corms, Tubers, and Roots

Many flowers advertised as bulb flowers, aren't really true bulbs. For instance, crocuses are actually corms, though you will see them placed alongside the bulbs. Corms look a lot like bulbs (albeit a little flatter) but store their food in an enlarged basal plate, whereas bulbs store their food in the scales.

Also often sold with bulbs are tubers, such as begonias and dahlias, and roots. The inside of a bulb is protected by a thin layer of skin called a tunic. Tubers and roots do not have a tunic, and are essentially enlarged stem tissue.

Now that you know the difference, you needn't worry yourself too much about it. From here on out, you will see all referred to as bulbs. The flowers will be just as beautiful whether they are true bulb flowers, tubers, corms, or roots.

Two Groups of Bulbs

Bulbs fall generally into two groups. Spring-flowering bulbs are planted in the fall and their flowers bloom in the spring. Summer-flowering bulbs are planted in the spring and produce blooms in the summer. Most gardeners divide bulbs into two categories: hardy, the ones that you plant in the fall that stay in the ground to bloom in the spring, and tender, those that you must dig up to store indoors for replanting next year.

As a general rule, spring-flowering bulbs are hardy, meaning you plant them in the fall and they survive the winter weather to bloom in the

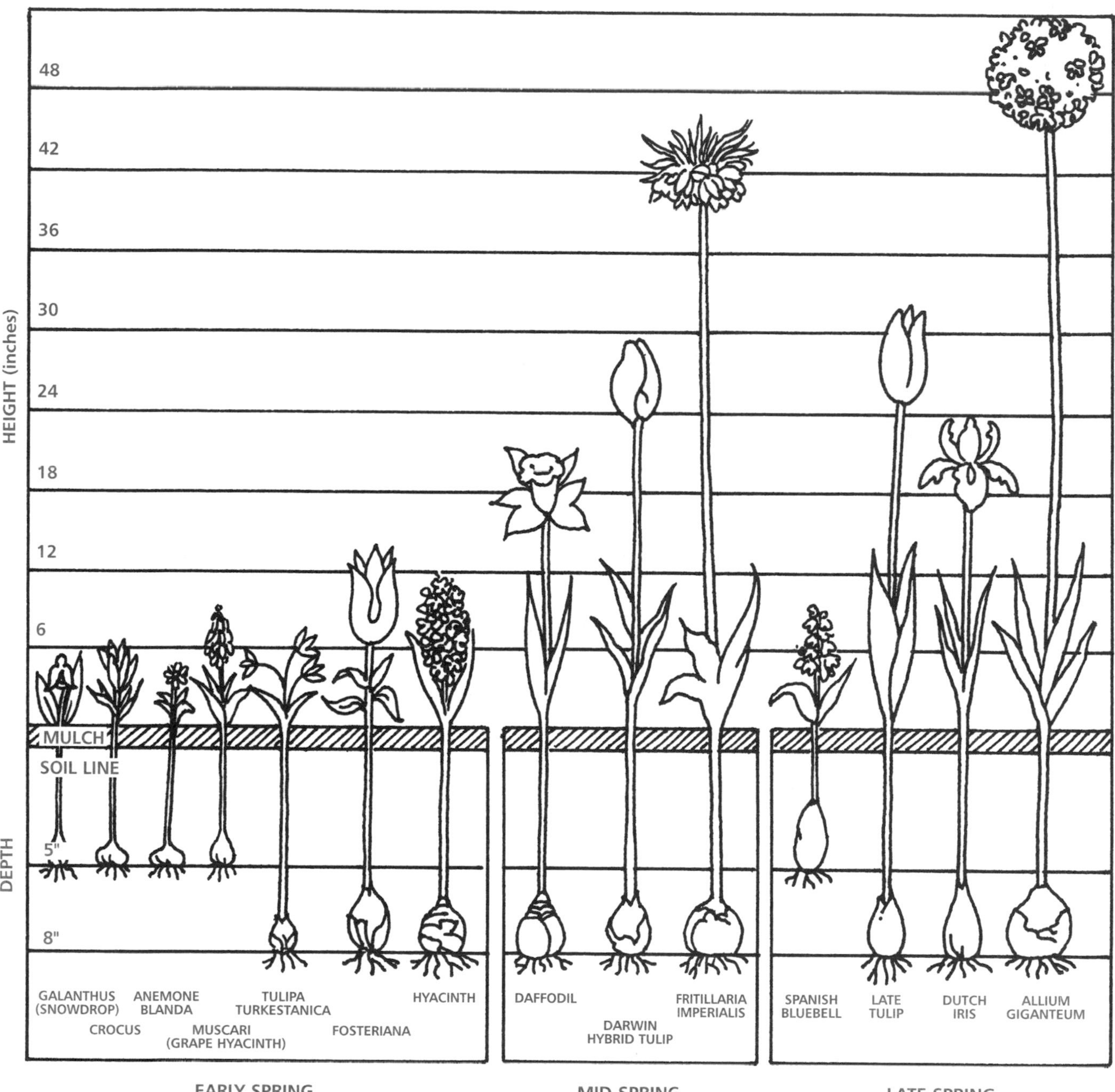
54
48
42
36
30
24
18
12
6
HEIGHT (inches)
MULCH
SOIL LINE
DEPTH
5"
8"
GALANTHUS (SNOWDROP)
CROCUS
ANEMONE BLANDA
MUSCARI (GRAPE HYACINTH)
TULIPA TURKESTANICA
FOSTERIANA
HYACINTH
DAFFODIL
DARWIN HYBRID TULIP
FRITILLARIA IMPERIALIS
SPANISH BLUEBELL
LATE TULIP
DUTCH IRIS
ALLIUM GIGANTEUM
EARLY SPRING
MID-SPRING
LATE SPRING

▲ Planting guide for bulbs.

spring. Spring-flowering bulbs include crocuses, daffodils, tulips, and similar plants.

Typically, most summer-flowering bulbs are tender, meaning these bulbs wouldn't survive the winter, so you must dig them up, store them indoors, and replant them next spring. Summer-flowering bulbs include dahlias, gladiolus, and begonias.

Buying Bulbs

Bulbs are sold in many places from garden centers and nurseries to mail-order catalogues, supermarkets, home centers, mass merchandisers, and the Internet. Some mail-order firms even specialize in rare and heirloom varieties that are truly special. When you buy bulbs, try to check them out first. It is worth keeping these three points in mind:

1. Bigger is better. Bigger bulbs produce bigger blossoms. Often bulb catalogs will note that their bulbs are "double-nosed." This translates to two blooms per bulb. In some cases you can divide these bulbs to start two different plants.
2. Avoid soft, mushy, or moldy bulbs and those that are heavily bruised. If you have a problem with a mail order, report it immediately and offer to return the bulbs to verify the poor condition. Sometimes bulbs can be damaged in transit if placed next to heat or crushed, and your supplier will most likely replace these.
3. Bulbs have a papery outer skin, or tunic, just like an onion's, which may become loose or torn. This condition does not damage the bulbs and may actually promote faster rooting after the bulb is planted, according to veteran bulb gardeners.

Remember that the photographs in catalogs, on packages, or on the Internet show blooms at perfect conditions. The hot pink, brilliant yellow, or bright orange colors may not be quite as vibrant and produce the same effect in your grounds.

Spring-Flowering Bulbs

To enjoy spring flowers such as daffodils, hyacinths, crocuses, tulips, and others, you must plant their bulbs in the fall. The dormant period of cold temperatures stimulates their root development.

Be sure to check with your local garden center or mail-order firm for specific planting details regarding a particular type of bulbous plant. Generally speaking, however, spring-flowering bulbs are often planted before the ground freezes, usually in September.

Colorful Temptations

In addition to tulips and daffodils, you'll also want to plant other exotic "Dutch" bulbs, such as spring-flowering scilla, muscari, fritillaria, and allium. In this context, consider "Dutch" the usual name for bulbs produced in the Netherlands, which is the world's largest producer of bulbs. True, bulbs are grown elsewhere, including the United States, but the majority of bulbs are still grown in Europe.

FACT

The USDA publishes a climate zone map covering the entire United States. You'll find it at *www.usna.usda.gov/Hardzone/ushzmap.html* to help you determine your own horticultural zone for guidance in selecting plants that are appropriate for your climate. You can also consult your local garden center to learn which bulbs thrive in your area.

Spring-flowering bulbs offer a wide variety of colors, heights, and flowering periods. Let your imagination run wild. Easy-to-grow bulbs allow you to concentrate on garden design in myriad ways and displays. All the key planting information you need to know about specific bulbs is usually provided on the package your bulbs were purchased in or in flyers included with your bulbs from mail-order firms.

Top-Selling Flower Bulb Varieties

Top Ten Tulips			
Rank	Variety	Color	Classification
1.	Tulip Parade	red	Darwin hybrid
2.	Tulip Oxford	yellow	Darwin hybrid
3.	Tulip Angelique	blush pink	Double Late
4.	Tulip Apricot Beauty	salmon	Single Early
5.	Tulip Pink Impression	rose	Darwin hybrid
6.	Tulip Red Emperor	fire red	Fosteriana
7.	Tulip Queen of Night	darkest maroon	Single Late
8.	Tulip Shirley	white, edged purple	Single Late
9.	Tulip Attila	purple	Triumph
10.	Tulip Purissima	white	Fosteriana

Top Ten Narcissi			
Rank	Variety	Color	Classification
1.	Narcissus King Alfred	yellow-yellow	Trumpet
2.	Narcissus Salome	white-pink, yellow	Large-cupped
3.	Narcissus Ice Follies	white-white	Large-cupped
4.	Narcissus Teta a Tete	yellow-yellow	Cyclamineus
5.	Narcissus Minnow	yellow-yellow	Tazatta
6.	Narcissus Fortissimo	white-yellow	Trumpet
7.	Narcissus Tahiti	yellow-red	Double
8.	Narcissus Las Vegas	white-yellow	Trumpet
9.	Narcissus Barret Browning	white-orange	Small-cupped
10.	Narcissus Mount Hood	white-white	Trumpet

Landscaping Tips

To plan for landscape harmony and design delightful displays, consider these key points:

- The color of the flower
- What months it will bloom
- How high it will grow
- What months to plant
- How deep to plant

Plant low-growing bulbs, such as grape hyacinths, in front of taller flowers such as tulips. Always plant bulbs in groups of three or more. Single plants can look rather strange standing alone. It is interesting to plant scattered clusters of early-flowering bulbs such as crocus or daffodils throughout your lawn, especially in hard to mow areas, to achieve a "natural" look.

Also, plant clusters of daffodils around a woodpile or in a meadow area that is not mowed often. Be daring and experiment. You know which flowers you like. Plant them. Also, pick a flower bulb variety on a whim and try a small planting. If it does well for you, add more next year.

Cut out pictures of bulbous plants from mail-order catalogues, magazines, or bulb packages, and plan your dream garden on paper right in your own living room!

Planting Tips

Since your bulb gardens are likely to be a permanent part of your landscape, it pays to dig or till the areas deeply and prepare the soil well with composted organic matter to provide bulbs with the best possible growing conditions. Most spring-flowering bulbs prefer well-drained soil and do best in full or partial sun.

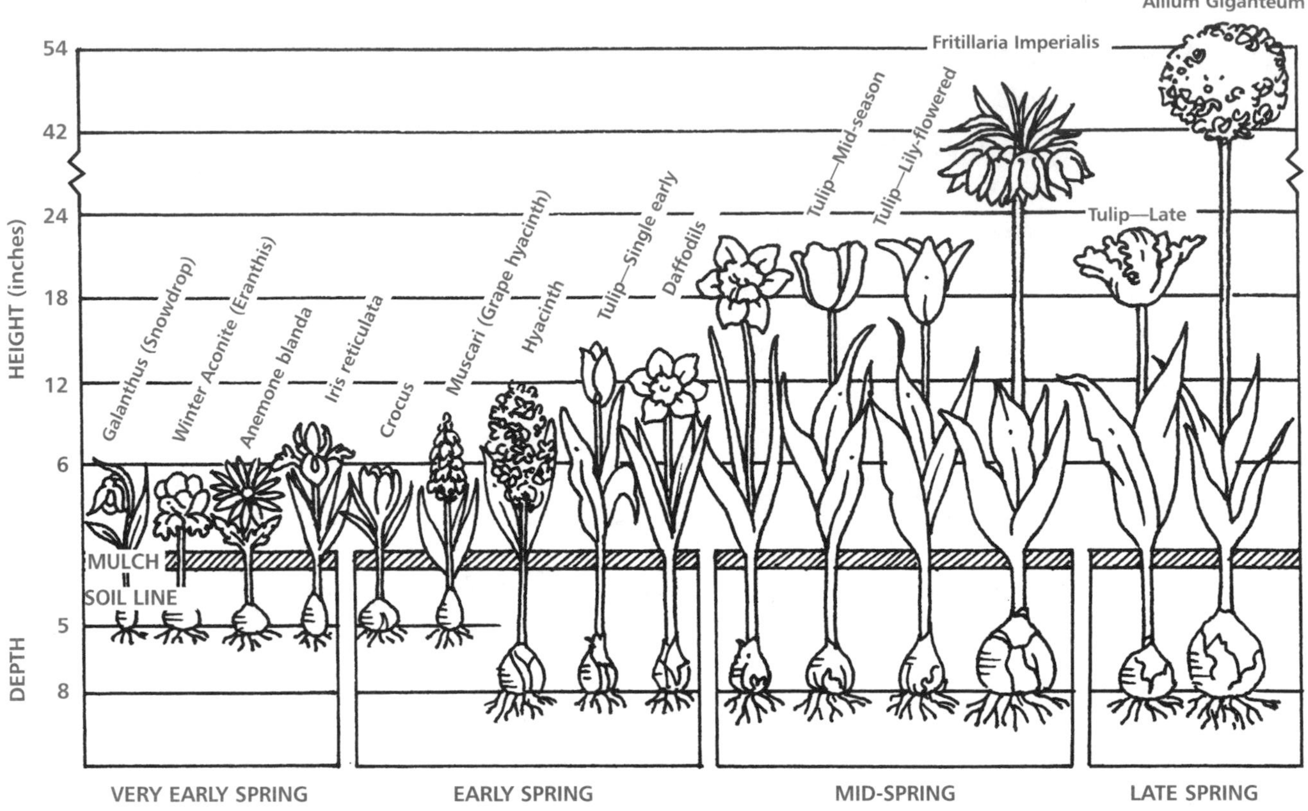

▲ Bulb planting chart.

After choosing the planting site, follow this checklist:

- ❑ Prepare a trench for a bed planting or dig individual holes for single bulbs or clusters. Naturally, a cluster of blooms will be more dramatic and striking. Large bulbs should be planted 8 inches deep and smaller bulbs 5 to 6 inches deep. Always check the bulb-planting chart that comes with your bulbs or is available from your garden center each year.
- ❑ Dig at least 8 inches deep to loosen soil and turn it. Remove weeds and stones.
- ❑ Mix in compost you have made or that you obtain from your garden product supplier. Peat moss is good to loosen soil. It also tends to lower soil pH and adds to the soil's organic matter content and

water-holding capacity, too. You may also add bulb booster soil amendments. Ask your local garden center if lime and phosphorous should be added to soil in your locality.

- ❑ Next, gently place, do not push, the bulbs firmly in the soil with the pointed side up. Space large bulbs 3 to 10 inches apart and small bulbs 1 to 2 inches apart, depending on how massive a display you want to have.
- ❑ Cover the bulbs with soil and water generously. Add 2 to 3 inches of mulch—pine bark is fine—on top of the garden bed. This will provide added protection from soil heaving the first year. Plus, it thwarts weeds and keeps the soil from drying out.

FACT

Consider your local growing conditions. Not every type of bulb performs everywhere so check to be sure that those you prefer will perform in your area. Local garden center specialists and County Extension Agents are two key sources for reliable information.

Basically it all boils down to these key facts: buy the best bulbs, put them in the ground properly, and then dream all winter of the glorious blooms of spring that will reward your efforts.

Summer-Flowering Bulbs

Summer-flowering bulbs originate from subtropical regions such as South Africa and South America. They like warm temperatures and humid conditions. Most are not winter hardy. Generally speaking, summer bulbs fall into the category of tender bulbs, which do not perennialize in zones that experience frost in winter. However, they are well worth adding to your gardens, at least as test specimens to determine how you like them. They can provide bright color and dramatic displays, so it is worth the extra work of digging up and storing bulbs in the fall for replanting next year.

What You Need to Know

Here are key considerations.

- Summer-flowering bulbs need sufficient water and humid conditions.
- Summer-flowering bulbs should be planted when the soil temperature is approximately 13°C or 55°F. If planted before this temperature is reached, the bulbs will not begin active growth, which can cause the bulbs to rot.
- Summer-flowering bulbs are generally planted close to the surface at 3 to 5 centimeters or 1 to 2 inches deep, where the soil is warmer. Check planting depth charts available at stores where you buy bulbs.
- Most, though not all, summer-flowering bulbs such as dahlias and begonias should be harvested before the first fall frost, depending on the climate zone.
- If your winters are not severe, you can perennialize the bulbs by leaving them in the ground and covering them when there is light frost. Very often these bulbs will bloom better the following year. If you have doubts about your area, ask veteran gardeners or garden center specialists.

Landscaping Ideas

Traditional summer-flowering bulbs can greatly enhance gardens and landscapes. Dahlias, gladioli, and tuberous hybrid begonias are readily available. Here are some ideas for using these bulbs in your garden.

- In perennial beds and in combination with ornamental grasses and hosta varieties
- In rock gardens and in combination with low-growing ground-cover plants such as ivy, myrtle, and juniper
- As underplantings and border plants in combination with shrubs and trees

When making decisions about using bulbs, think about the overall design you wish to create. This includes factors such as flowering periods and length of season, flower colors and sizes, and use of companion plants that fit the sunny or shaded growing locations of your landscape.

Summer-flowering bulbs have several useful applications. Consider them for use in their own beds for maximum focal display. Pick a large or small area solely for the purpose of growing these ornamental flowers. That might be a border, a small strip of land along other parts of your landscape, walks, or driveway. Or, create a special showcase garden for the most dramatic ones.

Summer-flowering bulbs also are useful as cut flowers, providing floral spikes suitable for use as either fresh cut or dried flowers. Glads are favorites and truly dramatic in the garden or on the table for dazzling displays in many colors and hues.

FACT

You can camouflage or reduce the negative impact of dying bulb foliage by planting bulbs with other perennials that will mask the bulb foliage as it matures and yellows or by planting taller flower-bulb plants behind lower-growing foreground shrubs and other perennials.

Keys to Successful Summer Bulbs

The key to successful planning for almost all summer-flowering bulbs is site selection. Consider two major factors: drainage and light.

The soil must be well drained. This is a critical factor for planting flower bulbs. One method of determining if the site drains well is to observe the proposed planting area the day after an intensive rainfall. If water remains in the selected spot, then the soil does not drain adequately and you should pick another spot. Alternatively, you might choose to simply improve the drainage.

Also, check for proper light conditions. Depending on the genus, flower bulbs perform optimally under five different light conditions. Check light needs for the summer-flowering bulb flowers you wish to grow. Determine if they fit these light categories. (With thanks to expert horticulturists, these details are listed precisely as provided for proper guidance.)

1. **Full Sun**—Plants that perform satisfactorily when exposed to full sunlight for the entire day.
2. **P.M. Sun**—Plants that perform satisfactorily when exposed to full sunlight from noon to sunset.
3. **A.M. Sun**—Plants that perform satisfactorily when exposed to full sunlight from dawn to noon.
4. **25% Continuous Shade**—Plants that perform satisfactorily when grown consistently under a 25% reduction of full sunlight.
5. **50% Continuous Shade**—Plants that perform satisfactorily when grown consistently under a 50% reduction of full sunlight.

Perennials, Annuals, and Bulbs

Here are some points to consider when you think about annuals, bulbous flowers, and perennials. Your perennials, which come back every year, provide the garden with its basic "foundation," according to professional landscape horticulturists. Plants such as hostas, liatris, irises, peonies, phlox, astilbes, black-eyed Susans, Asiatic lilies, Shasta daisies, and daylilies are some good ones that provide continuity in your landscape year after year. Their rewarding performances can be counted on to peak at different times of the summer.

It's best to plant bulbs as soon as possible after bringing them home. If you are unable to do so, store them in a dry, cool area (between 50 and 60°F).

Basically, some will come in full glory in the early summer, others later. Your task is to create ongoing color panoramas where perennials that bloom at the same time are teamed up to create fantastic flowery displays. A midsummer blaze of a mass of brilliant yellow lilies can be made more dramatic by adding a trellis or frame pyramid covered with vines of rich purple clematis.

Adding Annuals

Once you have determined your perennials "foundation," you can add annuals, which last for only one summer. Among your choices are such fast-growing flowers as petunias, zinnias, geraniums, marigolds, and impatiens, which will provide quick color input and all-season performance. Many bloom nonstop all summer.

Here Come the Bulbs!

Plant hybridizers and breeders are creating remarkable remakes of old-time flower favorites. New hybrids of coleus and petunias have been introduced in garden centers. Today you also can find many new varieties of summer-blooming flower bulbs, including such superstars as lilies, canna, dahlias, begonias, gladiolus, and caladiums. These glories are treasured for their exotic and dramatic appearance and their ability to add splashes of color at critical times in summer. Summer bulbs excel as perennial partners along with annual flowers. Consider planting some summer bulbs for dramatic effect and to add more summer color to established perennial plantings.

Establish Goals

The secret to any garden is to follow your inner gardener insights. Be curious, experiment, try something new each year. Let your imagination run wild at times. Gardening is truly a growing experience in many ways. You may discover that you can be a landscape artist, painting pictures with colorful blooms that beautify your home grounds, and an interior decorator, too, creating bouquets that grace your indoors.

Goal 1: Try something new every season. Maybe it's a new lily this year, or begonias or oxalis or new roses. Be flexible. If you like what you've done, make it a basic part of your landscape. However, consider mixing things up periodically for a daring new look. Your ingenuity may surprise you.

Goal 2: Be ruthless with yourself and your garden. If a plant or planting isn't working, dig it out. Give it away or just dispose of it. Annuals and flower bulbs are easily moved. Perennials can be moved also, but with a bit more work.

Goal 3: Trade with friends and neighbors. If you have admired someone's special plants, offer to swap with some of yours that they like. That's a good way to harvest garden knowledge and make new friends, too.

Goal 4: Be flexible. Don't ever set your garden plans in cement. Gardens should have a life of their own. Let your plants speak to you. Then express yourself and create changing scenes.

Frequently Asked Questions

For some reason, new gardeners have always seemed to have more questions about bulbous plants than most other types of plants. From surveys of garden centers and mail-order firms that specialize in bulbs, these are the most frequently asked questions and the best answers from experts.

Q: Why can't I plant tulips in the spring?

A: Spring-flowering bulbs such as tulips and daffodils must be planted in the fall or early winter to bloom in spring. That is because they require a long period of cool temperatures to activate the biochemical process that causes them to flower. They also need time to develop strong roots.

Q: It's February and I just found a bag of bulbs that I forgot to plant. Do I save them till next year?

A: No! If they are still firm and plump, plant them now. Bulbs are living plants, not seeds. They cannot wait; they will dry out. Your bulbs will try their best to bloom no matter how late it is in the season.

Q: What should I do after tulips and daffodils fade in the spring?

A: After tulip flowers have faded, "deadhead" them. That means clipping off the faded blooms so that they won't use energy going to seed. (Narcissi do not require deadheading.)

Q: Should I fertilize bulbs?

A: If you're planting bulbs for only 1 year's bloom, you don't need to fertilize. For bulbs that you will naturalize or perennialize, no fertilizer is need at fall planting time for the first year's bloom. For naturalized bulbs after the first season, you have three good options:

1. Work a good organic compost or well-rotted cow manure into the soil when planting, and add a mulch of this material.
2. Use a slow-release bulb food, 9-9-6 NPK (see Chapter 9). Refer to specific instructions on the package for best results.
3. Use an 8-8-8 or 10-10-10 NPK, fast-release soluble fertilizer, about 1 tablespoon per square foot. Refer to specific instructions on the package for best results.

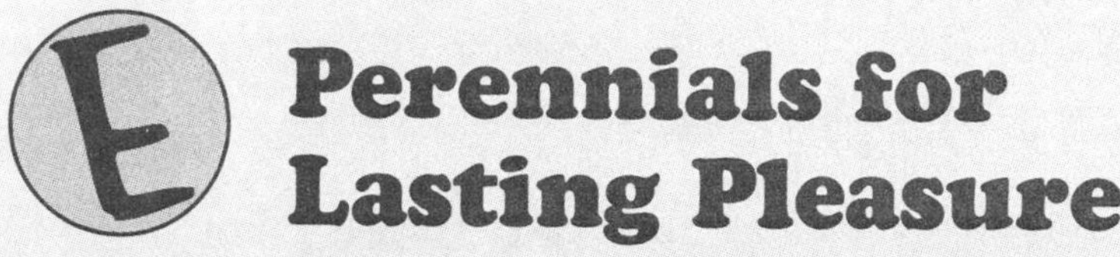

Chapter 6

Perennials for Lasting Pleasure

Perennials provide permanent pleasure for your landscape. You need only plant them once, and then every following year you will see their blooming beauty make its mark in your gardens. This chapter will show you how to make the most of perennials and offers tips and suggestions for the most popular and tried-and-true perennials.

Getting Started with Perennials

As you know, you must plant annuals every year because they cannot withstand the winter temperatures. Perennials, on the other hand, are perfectly comfortable in the cold climate and are able to survive well enough to come back year after year, without your ever having to replant them.

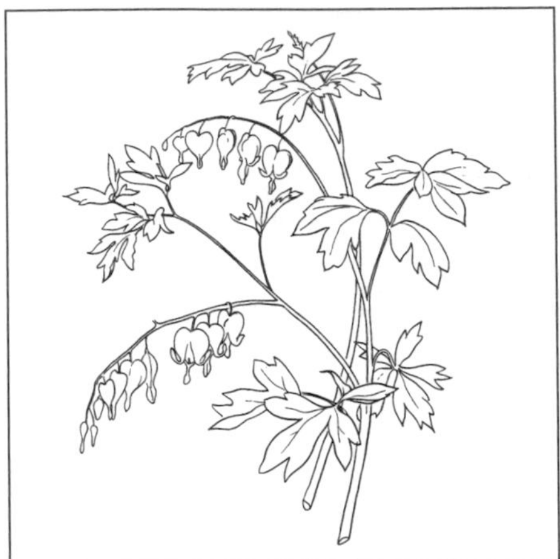

Bleeding Heart (*Dicentra spectabilis*)

Planning for Perennial Gardens

Most flowering perennials prefer 6 to 8 hours of sun per day. Some perennials are adaptable to different situations, but few do well in poor clay or wet soils. In fact, soil quality is probably the most important factor for success of a perennial flower garden. The soil needs to be moist during the growing season, but it is very important that the soil not be excessively moist during the winter dormant season, to avoid rotting roots. For best results, the soil should be slightly acidic with a pH from 6.5 to 7.0.

You can buy perennials as bare root plants or in containers. Be sure plants are healthy. Bare root plant roots should not be dried out, nor should the young shoots be wilting. It pays to check that roots are white and are not tightly coiled in the pot.

Give Them a Good Start

You can plant container-grown plants throughout the season. Most gardeners prefer to plant in the spring. However, early fall planting of perennials promotes development of roots before winter begins. You will need to water both container-grown and bare root plants when planting them. When planting container-grown plants, they should look the same in the soil as they did in the container, with the same amount of plant above ground. Be sure to spread the roots of bare root plants when planting and pack soil gently but firmly around the roots.

Once they get a roothold, perennial flowers require only routine maintenance or regular watering. Watering needs can vary with different perennials. Your best bet is to check with your garden center specialist or refer to the directions that come with mail-order plants. A basic rule of thumb is 1 inch of water a week for plant establishment. Once well rooted, many perennials will require watering only during prolonged dry periods.

FACT

Generally, perennials damaged or killed during the winter are not injured directly by cold temperatures but by frost heaving, which occurs when the soil alternately freezes and thaws. That damages the dormant crown and root system. To protect perennials, apply mulch in late fall to help stop frost heaving.

While not required, you may also want to use a starter fertilizer to help get them started. For established plants, an annual application of a balanced, slow-release fertilizer can be helpful. Use balanced fertilizers because excess nitrogen will produce excess foliage instead of desired flowers. Simply follow the directions for the type of fertilizer you prefer to use. Mulching is helpful to preserve soil moisture and suppress weeds. Apply about 2 inches of mulch material around perennials.

Types of Perennials

There are hundreds of perennials to choose from. Flip through mail-order catalogs and magazines and browse your local garden center. You will undoubtedly find several that jump out at you. Don't be shy. Plan your landscape for those that strike your fancy. If you are having trouble deciding among all the beautiful perennials, read on about some of the different varieties to get you started. For example, you may want to try some cultivated perennials from seeds in August. You can try Shasta daisy, purple coneflower, lupines, Oriental poppy, and columbine. Globe thistle and common globeflower are also useful plants for decorating gardens.

LEFT: Columbine (*Aquilegia*)

RIGHT: Globe thistle (*Echinops ritro*)

Good Perennials for Shady Areas

Many gardeners have trouble making shady spots sparkle. Hostas offer distinct advantages with their multicolor foliage. Wayside Gardens, a mail-order firm, has focused on this plant and offers a range of hostas. Northern Exposure has a wide yellow-green-to-cream margin on large, flat, blue-green leaves. Blue Angel has heavily textured leaves that are 12 inches across and 16 inches long. Great Expectations offers irregular blue-green margins and creamy centers that add interesting color and pattern to the round, puckered, broad leaves. Night Before Christmas forms a neat, dense clump of velvet-textured, thick leaves 8 inches long and 3 inches wide.

FACT

Other firms are promoting hostas, too. They are being offered today at many chain garden centers. The blooms are not dramatic but are favored by hummingbirds. After bloom, merely snip away the long flower stalks and add to compost piles.

Consider coleus, too, for shady spots. With these striking coleus plants, the color is in the foliage. A big advantage is that they spread and thrive in shade where many other plants fail to perform.

White Trumpet lilies are one of the more dramatic plants for woodland gardens. The blooms are white with green tints and purplish red coloring on the inside. This giant lily produces huge flowering stems as much as 10 feet tall, each carrying twenty or more enormous 9- to 12-inch trumpets in early to mid-summer. A bonus is their intense, sweet fragrance that perfumes the entire neighborhood. Plant in full to part shade in rich, well-drained soil high in humus, and be patient. It takes a year or so for them to begin their dramatic displays.

Hellebores Are Winter Treats

It took more than 50 years of dedicated English breeding to produce an exciting new winter-blooming rose, according to Wayside Gardens specialists. They believe Royal Heritage hellebores are destined to supplant even hostas as the premiere carefree perennial for shade and partial sun. That could prove very true.

These new hellebores come in a range of colors including purple, red, white, green, pink, and even yellow, in 2-inch flowers with overlapping petals. Even better, these new hellebores produce flowers for nearly 5 months, from winter through spring.

According to botanists, these plants are very permanent, low-maintenance, and disease- and pest-free. They develop into sturdy, long-lived clumps 18 to 24 inches high and 2 to 3 feet across. They do best in well-drained, moisture-retentive soil and can even thrive in clay. That's a big plus for gardeners who are cursed with clay soils in low-lying areas.

Sun-Loving Perennials

Most perennials, from irises to peonies and phlox, prefer sun. You'll find more about them later in this chapter. Because more gardeners are looking for different types of plants for distinctive landscapes, some of these special plants are worth considering. As you shop for permanent perennials, keep in mind where you will want to grow them and match plants to the garden soil, light, and location conditions. Sun-loving perennials offer long-lasting color for many years, combining beautifully with annuals and shrubs.

One special plant worth consideration is the new climbing clematis, Blue Light, that offers huge fully double flowers on a dwarf plant. Blue Light blooms from spring through early summer, and then again from late summer through fall. It is compact enough for container culture, growing only 6 to 8 feet tall.

Heirloom Perennials Make Comeback

In the past few years there has been a big swing toward heirloom and antique plants. Most major mail-order firms now feature them. Other firms specialize in the rare, exotic, and hard-to-find varieties. Check out catalogs and have some fun with those rarities that can be real eye-catchers in your garden. More mail-order firms now are featuring pages of heirloom flowers. Nostalgia is gaining ground in gardens it seems.

One old-timer is gaining new friends. Hollyhocks are in vogue again. Sometimes it is easier to shop by collection. Old Barnyard mix hollyhocks, discovered at an old farm in Vermont, are old-fashioned single-flowered blooms that sport some of the darkest, richest colors known to the Hollyhock family. As with these standbys, blooms are studded with a prominent yellow center and arise profusely on sturdy 4- to 6-foot stems in summer. They attract hummingbirds by the dozens as well as make dramatic displays.

Mums Are a Perennial Pleasure

Fall mums have often disappointed gardeners. Often offered as perennials at garden centers, many end up being like annuals because they don't survive the winter. However, plant breeders have tried and succeeded at perfecting mums. In fall 2001, gardeners across North America had a new fall delight, a carpet-style perennial mum. It is a true cold-hardy garden mum that will return year after year and increase in size as it matures.

By its third fall, one My Favorite mum can measure up to 22 inches high and 45 inches across, with a canopy of red daisylike flowers adding up to more than 1,000 per plant. This very different mum is the first in a series to be introduced by the newly formed My Favorite, a joint venture of Ball Horticultural Company of the United States and Anthony Tesselaar International of Melbourne, Australia.

FACT

An additional treat is that the My Favorite mum is a huge hit with Monarch butterflies, which add to any butterfly and hummingbird special garden.

The new perennial mum is exceptionally cold hardy and has thrived in climate zones as cold as USDA horticultural zone 3 and Canadian equivalents. Its cold hardiness has been proved in sustained winter poundings of –30°F in central Minnesota. Happily it also can be grown successfully in warm climates up to zone 9. This new mum lends itself to a variety of garden uses, including hedges, borders, and large containers. It is now available in five colors: red, coral, pink, yellow, and white.

Daylilies Are Multipurpose Perennials

Daylilies are one of the most adaptable plants and are now available in an amazing number of cultivars. They are quite versatile and can thrive in full sun or shady areas, and moist or dry soil. Today you can purchase single- and double-flower forms. They are well worth a trial because they take root so well that they actually crowd out weeds. That's a happy plus! There is one drawback though: As their name says, all daylily flowers routinely last a single day.

New Breeding Breakthroughs

Many daylilies today flower for several weeks during early, mid-, or late summer. Two very specific trends in daylily breeding have resulted in some exciting breakthroughs. First, the Altissima types were derived from a Japanese species of the same name. They are noticeably distinct and often send up a flower stalk that is 6 to 8 feet high. Foliage, on the other hand, is hardly unusual and grows to 2 feet.

The second breeding trend is the development of so-called ever-blooming daylilies. This is good news indeed and nothing short of a minor phenomenon for residential and commercial landscapes. Selections include the popular Stella D'Oro, Song Sparrow, Happy Returns, and Mini Stella.

Why do people plant daffodils with daylilies?
Daffodils and daylilies are perfect companions in a perennial garden. Both require full sun to bloom to their full potential, and they take turns in the garden. The daffodils emerge and bloom early. As the daffodil foliage matures and yellows, daylilies grow rapidly, hiding the daffodil leaves.

All-American Daylilies Named

Not surprisingly, with the growing popularity of daylilies today, there is an All-American selection that honors the best of the new varieties. This All-American title is granted only to those rare daylily varieties that have shown superior performance across at least five USDA hardiness zones.

The three new winners for 2002 join a select group of cultivars that have been awarded the honored All-American title since the All American Daylily Selection Council (AADSC) test program began in 1985. The 2002 All-American varieties are tried and true cultivars whose test scores earned them the top honor. Each winner in a respective category offers a blend of beauty and performance, according to daylily enthusiasts.

Bitsy was the winner in the landscape category as one of the longest-blooming varieties encountered in 12 years of testing. Leebea Orange Crush is one of the rare daylilies exhibiting such balanced performance that it won honors in both the landscape and exhibition categories.

Finally, Judith, with its profusion of glowing pink blossoms, was the exhibition category winner.

FACT

There are more than 48,000 registered daylilies that are being bred in at least twenty-five states by hundreds of individual hybridizers. New daylilies are tested for at least 2 years. Then All-American finalists are grown for another 3 to 5 years in open field conditions before being announced.

Hail the Classic Irises

Irises are among the easiest of perennials to grow and provide an abundance of beauty with minimum care. To enjoy them, it helps to know more about the different types so you can evaluate those that appeal to you and will do best in your garden.

Basically, irises used as garden plants fall into three main groups: Aril Irises, Bearded Irises, and Beardless Irises. Frankly, a collection including representatives from each group will provide a great variety.

Identifying the Groups

Bearded irises are identified by thick, bushy "beards" on each of the falls, which are the lower petals of the blossoms. Most were native to central and southern Europe. The bearded irises have been divided into groups by the American Iris Society: the miniature dwarf bearded, standard dwarf bearded, intermediate bearded, border bearded, and miniature tall bearded.

Aril irises are two very different types of irises grouped together under the term *aril.* These are the oncocyclus and regelia irises of the Near East. Aril irises aren't as easy to grow as the bearded irises, and they prefer warm, dry regions. However, recently hybrids were produced from crossing the arils with the more common bearded irises, making them easier to grow while still maintaining their striking features.

Beardless irises came from Asia. They all bloom after the early types of irises, which extends the iris season even longer. Among the beardless irises are Spurias, Siberians, Japanese, Louisianas, and Species types.

Some bearded irises are "rebloomers," which means they bloom again in the summer, fall, or winter. Additional water and fertilizer applied during the summer months encourages them to bloom again.

Iris Planting Tips

Irises can reward you for many years with their spectacular displays. For best results, match your garden conditions with the needs of the type of iris you prefer. Then prepare your ground and plant well. Pick a sunny spot in well-drained soil and prepare the soil thoroughly by spading or rototilling to a depth of at least 10 inches. Spread fertilizer and work it into the top of the soil. If possible, this should be done two to three weeks before planting. Irises prefer lighter soil. If you have heavier clay soil, add very coarse sand and humus. Bone meal and a balanced flower garden fertilizer that is low in nitrogen are good for irises.

Iris roots must be buried firmly to hold the plant in place, but the rhizome should be near the surface. This is important. If you bury the rhizomes, they won't grow right and could actually rot.

An easy way to achieve this proper planting depth is to dig two trenches with a ridge between them. Then place the rhizome on the ridge and spread the roots carefully in the trenches. Firm the soil and allow for settling to keep the rhizome above any possible standing water. When you fill the trenches with soil, be sure to keep the rhizome near the surface of the soil.

Set several plants at least 1½ feet apart with rhizomes "facing" the same direction. This keeps them from crowding out each other as they grow. Adding a mulch of old hay or straw helps prevent frost heaving.

Beardless irises should be transplanted in the fall or in early spring. These irises should be set slightly deeper than the tall bearded types.

All irises are heavy feeders and need to be fertilized regularly. Follow directions on the package of the type of fertilizer you use. Remember that flowering plants produce excess foliage if you use the higher nitrogen fertilizers that you use on lawns. Balance of NPK is needed for flowering plants.

Be prepared to divide to multiply irises. In about 2 or 3 years, rhizomes will begin to crowd each other. You will need to divide the plant, which is easy. Simply cut the newer parts of the rhizome free and discard the old parts.

Peonies Are Hardy Classics

Peonies are among the classics of American gardens and are making a comeback. Few plants rival them for floral display and foliage. The two most popular types of peonies used in landscaping are Paeonia hybrids (garden peony) and Paeonia suffruticosa (tree peony).

By selecting and planting early-, mid-, and late-season bloomers, you can extend the flowering season for 6 weeks. Peonies grow from 2 to 4 feet in height. Support is often required for tall, double hybrids, or heavy blooms could fall over. These beauties thrive in sunny locations and well-drained soils. Though peonies can survive in several soil types, they do best in soil with a pH range of 6.5 to 7.5, deep and rich in organic matter. Most varieties are hardy from zone 8 to zone 2.

Peony Planting Tips

Peonies thrive in any well-drained, good, rich garden soil and prefer full sunlight. When peonies are planted in poorer soil, dig a hole 2 feet deep and 2 feet wide and fill with rich topsoil for each plant. Plant or divide peonies in early fall, but you can do it in spring as soon as the soil is workable.

Give each plant an area about 3 feet in diameter. Dig a generous hole that is big enough to accommodate the roots. Place the peony in the prepared hole so that the eyes—those small, red buds—are 1 to 2 inches below the soil's surface. Then, fill in with soil and water well. Mulching is also a good idea. That's all there is to it. Peonies are one of the easiest plants to plant and watch grow without much other work at all. Actually, peonies will grow well, if undisturbed, for many years.

FACT

Ants on peony blossoms are neither beneficial nor harmful to the plants. It is common. The ants are simply attracted to the sugary liquid secreted by flower buds. Just ignore them.

If you note a decline in bloom, overcrowding is usually indicated, so you must divide the clump. Carefully lift the clump and wash away soil to expose the eyes. Using a clean, sharp spade, divide the clump into sections with three to five eyes each and good roots. Replant immediately.

Goldenrod (*Solidago*)

Don't Forget Goldenrod

One of the most overlooked perennials is Goldenrod. Many think it is a weed, but it is a valued plant in gardens in England and Europe. Sometimes gardeners tend to overlook the obvious, and this is one plant that deserves reconsideration, especially for natural wild landscapes.

Collections Are Helpful

Sometimes it pays to let experts do the testing and evaluating, and come up with what they find are the best combinations of plants for a perennial border. The Bluestone Nursery worked on that idea and perfected what they call the Bluestone Perennial Border.

Bluestone Perennial Border

This border is designed for those interested in the joy of perennial gardening but in need of some help planning a border. The following garden is designed for an area 5 feet by 30 feet. Also included is an optional island layout. There are twenty-four varieties and fifty-nine plants in the collection. The layout includes:

- 1 Phlox David
- 3 Boltonia Snowbank
- 3 Gloriosa Daisy
- 1 Coreopsis verticillata
- 3 Echinacea White Lustre
- 1 Echinops ritro
- 3 Aster Alma Potschke
- 1 Kniphofia Flamenco
- 3 Rudbeckia Goldsturm
- 3 Achillea Coronation Gold
- 3 Armeria Dusseldorf Pride
- 3 Aster Frikarti
- 1 Liatris Kobold
- 3 Shasta Daisy Alaska
- 3 Mum Grandchild
- 3 Sedum Autumn Joy
- 3 Viola Blue Perfection
- 3 Mum Golden Regards
- 3 Campanula Blue Clips
- 3 Heuchera Bressingham
- 3 Gaillardia Goblin
- 3 Mum Drummer Boy
- 1 Nepeta Walker's Low
- 3 Veronica Giles van Hees

LEFT: Barberton Daisy (*Gerbera jamesonii*)

RIGHT: Coreopsis (*Coreopsis grandiflora*)

Preselected Shade Garden

The Bluestone plant enthusiasts also came up with a design for a beautiful shade garden for an area 4 feet by 20 feet. You can buy directly from that firm, or use this collection as a guide to pick a few starters and expand your shade garden in future years. The layout includes:

3 Ajuga Silver Beauty
3 Lamium Shell Pink
3 Thymus serph. Coccineum
3 Lobelia cardinalis
3 Aruncus dioicus
6 Asperula odorata
3 Tiarella wherryi
3 Alchemilla mollis
3 Brunnera macrophylla
6 Aquilegia Hybrids
3 Lamiastrum Herman's Pride
3 Viola Queen Charlotte
3 Polyanthus Pac. Giant Mix
3 Anemone robustissima
3 Geranium Biokovo
3 Adenophora lilifolia

Chapter 7

Annuals Are Appealing

As you plan your landscape, perennials are a base. However, look over the wide variety of types, colors, and shapes of appealing annuals. They grow quickly, provide summer color when early perennials have passed their prime, and also give you a marvelous amount of blooms for cut flower displays indoors.

Pick and Plant Your Beauties

Annuals provide prolific displays of blooms, and several new hybrids of different flowers with brighter colors and larger blooms make annuals sure to please. The All-America Selections organization has been testing new varieties for years in comparison with old favorite annuals. From those tests have come some of the most dramatic and best blooming annuals you'll ever see.

LEFT: Canterbury Bells (*Campanula medium*)

RIGHT: Sweet William (*Dianthus barbatus*)

Annual Popularity

Annuals have retained their fair share of popularity for several reasons.

- **Color.** Annuals deliver joyous color of almost every shade of the rainbow, including black, which can have a significant visual impact in gardens.
- **Dependability.** Constant blooming assures continuing beauty in the yard, a steady supply of cut flowers, and welcome visits from butterflies and birds to please all.
- **Diversity.** Annuals feature flowers in dozens of distinctive shapes and sizes, some with colorful foliage, too.
- **Versatility.** Annuals do well to edge beds, punctuate borders, climb

arbors, carpet the ground, hang from the porch roof, and even overflow containers of all kinds.

- **Self-reliance.** With adequate water during dry periods, mulched annuals require little care.

You will love the fervor of annual flower plants that bloom as furiously as they can for as long as they can. That's a blessing for every gardener.

Easy to Sow and Grow

One big benefit is that annuals are easy to grow from seed right in your garden. If you sow them by early spring, you'll have annual flowers all summer long for indoor bouquet displays and beauty right in the garden.

Direct outdoor seeding is easy. As soon as soil has warmed in the spring and has dried from spring rains, dig or till down 8 to 10 inches to loosen it. Then mix in some organic matter. Adding a slow-release fertilizer is also a good idea. Slow-release fertilizers feed plants over a period of time to provide steady nutrition as they grow and bloom. Rake soil level and smooth before planting.

Some annuals, such as flossflower and snapdragon, need light to germinate. Therefore, you should not cover these seeds. Be sure to check the seed packet to determine if you need to cover your seeds with soil.

Sowing for the Natural Look

If you want to create an informal, natural look in your garden, just scatter a handful of seeds, sprinkling them around randomly, and then rake the soil to cover them. If you are using tiny seeds, such as petunia or portulaca, it pays to mix the seed with sand for a more uniform distribution. Follow directions on the seed package, of course. If seeds are tiny, you may want to water them lightly or cover them with a soil-less mixture to ensure they don't blow away before they can sprout.

Formal Sowing

You can opt to plant annual flowers in more formal rows. Simply use a stick or trowel tip to trace straight, shallow furrows or designs and circles in your prepared seedbed and plant away.

Marigold (*Calendula officinalis*)

Just sprinkle or dribble a handful of seeds slowly between your thumb and forefinger as evenly as possible along the furrow. For larger seeds such as sweet peas, poke holes with a pencil and insert the seeds into the holes. Remember that most annual seeds need to be covered with a bit of soil to germinate properly. Follow seed packet instructions.

Although most seed packets say that a furrow should be about twice as deep as the seed is thick, practically speaking, most seeds are so small that a ¼- to a ½-inch-deep furrow is fine.

Caring for Annuals

Annual seeds can germinate and set roots themselves rather well as long as they have enough moisture. Sprinkle water periodically during that important first few weeks of the germination period. Then, keep them moist to ensure healthy development of the sprouts into seedlings. During heat spells, you can help germination and early sprouting by spreading a shade cloth or cheesecloth on the soil so it doesn't dry out while tiny plants are forming and taking root.

Thinning is your next important step in direct seeding. When planting annuals, it is very easy to overseed, causing the seedlings to become crowded. All you have to do to thin them out is follow the directions on the seed packet and pull out the extras.

Give Seedlings Enough to Eat

Young seedlings need nourishment to perform their best. You can use either pelleted fertilizer or liquid fertilizer. Whichever you choose, just be sure to read the directions on the package. You don't want to overdo it.

Occasional Trimming

The only other care that annuals may need is occasional trimming. Simply pinch or prune off faded flowers and broken or leggy stems so flowers stay neat and compact. Consider using stakes for tall annuals such as cleome, also called spider flower, and larkspur. These plants may tend to flop or break when hit by winds or heavy summer rains.

It pays to save seed packages and refer to them periodically since many now give tips for growing throughout the season, including notes about proper feeding of some plants that like extra fertilizer for best growth.

Self-Sowing Annuals

As perennials have become popular, some gardeners have neglected annuals. That's a mistake. They deserve wider use. You'll soon discover that many annuals practically grow themselves. Annuals die with cold and frost, but some are called hardy annuals because they can handle some cold and usually reseed for next year. Try out some of the self-seeding annuals and see how they perform in your garden. Keep in mind that not all hardy annuals self-sow reliably every year; you'll just have to experiment a bit.

To encourage self-sowing, stop deadheading faded flowers as the summer ends, and let plants develop seed heads and drop their seeds around the plants. Better yet, pick a few stems with dried seeds and shake them or bury them where you want new plants. For example, reseed daisies and black-eyed Susans by shaking old seed heads onto the ground in new areas, then cover with a light layer of soil. By next year, you may discover new beds arising.

It is important to wait until after a hard frost assures that winter is truly on the way before shaking or burying seed heads. To ensure a good crop of seedlings next year, do not disturb mulch in areas where self-sower annuals cast their seeds.

Be aware that some self-sowing annuals can become nuisances. Their seedlings reappear in profusion and may monopolize areas you want for other plants. Watch for these seedlings and pull them up while they are young. Here are a few of the easiest annuals to grow from seeds that tend to be self-sowing for another year.

Alyssum
Baby's Breath
Calendula
Coreopsis
Cosmos
Larkspur
Morning Glory
Portulaca
Rudbeckia
Johnny-jump-ups—Viola

All-America Selections is a system of testing new hybrid varieties of flowers and vegetables in comparison with old-time favorites. Those that measure up and demonstrate superior characteristics of bloom, flower size, disease resistance, and other attributes are awarded the prestigious All-America honors.

New Varieties Appearing Annually

America's gardeners are looking for new plants every year. Here are some of the newest and best flowers that were featured in recent mail-order seed catalogs, seed packets, or as bedding plants at garden centers.

Abutilon F1 Bella Red is exceptionally floriferous and compact, delivering great branching, and is perfect for garden containers or as an indoor houseplant. Also now available in coral, apricot, and salmon shades.

Ageratum Leilani Blue produces clusters of blue flowers and grows to be about 14 to 16 inches tall. It likes full sun or partial shade.

Asclepias Garden Leader Scarlet prefers a warm, sunny, well-drained location and is useful to attract butterflies and hummingbirds. Nice as a cut flower or patio plant.

Begonia F1 Dragon Wing has large pendulous flowers that combine with glossy green leaves in a showy display. It is heat tolerant.

W Begonia F1 Queen Pink consistently has roselikc double blooms. It has a spreading habit and can thrive in all weather conditions.

Impatiens Dazzler Blue Pearl is compact with uniform habit and generates masses of bluish lilac blooms.

Impatiens Garden Leader Sun & Shade Lipstick was new for 2002 and is the most complete series available, including thirty-five colors plus twelve designer mixes.

Pansy F1 Happy Face Purple Smile has been quite improved. Flower stems have been shortened so garden height is only 4 to 6 inches.

Petunia Double Madness Satin Pink is an outstanding double floribunda petunia that is compact, with plants delivering masses of 3-inch flowers all summer. It thrives in pots, baskets, and landscapes.

Petunia F1 Explorer Rose Pink is among the earliest to flower in the spring and continues to flower under short fall days. It has tremendous flower power and quick recovery after a storm.

Petunia F1 Lavender Wave is an AAS Flower Winner with large, 2-inch, rich deep lavender blooms on ground-hugging 5- to 7-inch-tall plants spread up to 4 feet. An exceptional garden and container performer, it blooms freely all season and tolerates heat and cold conditions.

Petunia F1 Tidal Wave Silver is another AAS Flower Winner with a distinct bicolor flower: silverish white with a deep purple center. It is a unique hedgiflora type.

Petunia Ramblin Peach Glow, another new Petunia series, offers a fascinating crawling habit. It grows 8 to 10 inches high and crawls 2 to 3 feet, and is best grown in full sun or partial shade. Also good in containers, window boxes, or hanging baskets.

Rudbeckia Cherokee Sunset, an AAS Flower Winner, has double and semidouble blooms in sunset colors. Mature plants are 24 to 30 inches tall.

Scabiosa S. columbaria Nana is a compact and long-flowering Scabiosa that produces blue-violet flowers.

Snapdragon Crown Red are semidwarf with lots of secondary branching for the most color on a full plant. Additional new color is Crown Yellow (*Syngenta*).

Sweet Pea (*Lathyrus odoratus*)

Sunflower F1 Double Dandy is the first-ever dwarf, double-flowered red sunflower. It has a well-branched habit, reaches only 1½ to 3 feet tall, with 4- to 5-inch velvety, wine red blooms.

Sweet Pea April in Paris is the perfect match of fragrance, form, and color. It brings intense scent into exhibition blossoms, is long-stemmed, vigorous, and prolific.

How to Start Annuals Indoors

There are many reasons for starting seeds indoors. One is that many parts of America have short growing seasons. Starting plants such as tomatoes, peppers, petunias, and others indoors gives gardeners extra weeks of growing time. That's important for the timely ripening of fruits such as tomatoes and melons when they are transplanted and growing in the outdoor garden plot. Of course for most gardeners, young and old, novice and veteran, there's the magic of watching a seedling push up above the soil surface that creates a bond between you and nature.

Indoor Seeding Materials You Need

To gain a jump on spring and win extra weeks of growing time, here's a checklist of what you need.

- ❑ Containers. Any shallow container that holds soil, such as flats with or without individual cells, peat pots, or paper pots, will do.
- ❑ Germinating mix, either commercial or homemade. Mix your own with a 50-50 combination of fine sphagnum peat moss and vermiculite.
- ❑ Seeds of annual flowers, plus perennials, vegetables, herbs.
- ❑ Plastic bags or plastic wrap.
- ❑ A spritzer or water mister.
- ❑ Transplanting mix. A good potting soil will do, but a mix specifically formulated for young seedlings is better.
- ❑ A balanced all-purpose fertilizer.
- ❑ Plant labels, which can be Popsicle sticks.
- ❑ Heating cable or mat as an optional but useful way to speed up plant growth.

Care and Cultivation Tips

Once you have all your supplies, it's time to get down to basics and plant the seeds. First, wet the germinating mix thoroughly and let it drain. It should be moist but not soggy. Next, fill flats or individual pots with the mix to within about 1 inch of the top. Then, make shallow row indentations in the flats with a ruler or your finger. Sow thinly so you do not waste seed. In pots, set three to four seeds in shallow holes and cover with mix.

Most seeds need darkness to germinate, but some need light. Be sure to read on the package what each needs, and give each variety the tender loving start it needs in your care.

Next, mist the surface with water to settle the seeds. Then, cover flats with a sheet of plastic wrap or set them in a plastic bag as a mini-greenhouse, or set pots in plastic bags and close with twist ties. When you begin to see the seedlings emerge, take away the plastic covering. (This usually takes about 7 to 10 days, though some take several weeks.) In the meantime, keep the mix evenly moist, not soggy.

Transplanting

The first leaves on a seedling are cotyledons, not true leaves, and don't look like the leaves shown on the seed package or that you would recognize on the mature plant. When you see the seedlings growing at least two sets of the leaves you see on the seed package, transplant them into pots.

Make a mental note or write this down and keep it handy where you store your fertilizer: Read and follow directions for the type of fertilizer you purchase. Extra isn't better. It could overfeed and burn your tender plants.

1. Moisten the transplanting mix and let it drain.
2. Fill 2¼-inch pots about ¾ full.
3. Carefully pick each seedling out of the flat and hold each by the leaves, not the stem. Remember that plants readily grow new leaves but not new stems.
4. Set the seedling in its pot and use more mix to fill in around the roots. Firm the mix down. Sprinkle with water after transplanting.
5. Place the pots on a south-facing windowsill that gets a lot of sunshine. Be careful not to set them too close to the glass as they could receive excess reflected heat.
6. Water transplants regularly from the bottom until they grow 3 to 4 inches tall. Then you can begin to water from the top.
7. Feed as you water by diluting a water-soluble fertilizer to half the strength recommended on the label. Or, feed at regular strength every

week to 10 days. Watch your plants to see how they are enjoying and prospering from their diet.

Key Points for Annuals

Read and heed the directions on seed packages. You'll note that some varieties prefer being seeded directly in the outdoor garden. Others will give you a longer growing season if you start them indoors in pots or flats and then transplant them into the garden when the weather is right. Some seeds germinate best when not covered with soil, including ageratum, begonia, coleus, columbine, impatiens, nicotiana, petunia, Oriental poppy, and yarrow.

Mind These Four Key Do's

1. Do know the average date of the last spring frost in your area. You'll need to start most plants indoors a few weeks before that date. Seed packets include that information.
2. Do give your pots on windowsills a quarter turn every week so plants grow straight instead of bending toward the light.
3. Do opt for the easiest flower plants to start indoors if this is your first attempt. These include coreopsis, dianthus, gaillardia, gloriosa daisy, marigold, yarrow, and zinnia.
4. Do remember to label your seed containers as you sow. Little seedlings may look alike, and you'll want to know which plants you have in which containers when it is outdoor planting time.

Observe These Key Don'ts

1. Don't combine different varieties of seeds in one flat unless they germinate in the same number of days.
2. Don't let seedlings in flats grow large before you transplant them, or their roots may become so tangled that it will be hard to separate them.
3. Don't overwater seedlings. Soggy soil promotes fungus and root rot.

Light Requirements

Most seeds don't need light to germinate but do require light when they sprout. If they don't get adequate light they become tall and "leggy," which is a condition that is almost impossible to correct. Most seedlings require 12 to 14 hours of direct light each day for proper growth.

If you do not have a south-facing window, you should consider using some artificial lights. When growing seedlings under lights, you can use a combination of cool and warm fluorescents, or full-spectrum fluorescent bulbs. Seedlings need a high intensity of light. The bulbs should be placed very close to the plants, no more than 3 inches away from the foliage, and should be left on for 12 to 14 hours per day. If you are growing your seedlings on a windowsill, you may need to supplement with a few hours of artificial light, especially during the winter months.

FACT

To give seedlings in pots or a planter flat indoors adequate light, you can place aluminum foil on a sheet of cardboard, place it behind the seedlings, and let it reflect more light on them.

Keep Moisture in Mind

Sometimes it pays to reinforce key points about gardening. Starting seeds can be a tricky project until you get the feel for it. Make a permanent mental note: Proper seed germination requires consistent moisture! It is important that the soil be kept moist but not soggy to prevent the seeds from rotting. Check the soil every day to ensure that it is moist, not wet. Be aware that seedlings prefer room temperature water rather than cold water. Some gardeners cover their flats with clear plastic until the seeds germinate. Once seedlings sprout and begin to grow, you should remove that cover to reduce excess moisture.

Focus on Hardening Off

Once weather has warmed up it's time to start "hardening off" your seedlings—gradually introducing them to the outdoors. Early spring weather outside will not be as kind to your plants as you were. Place your plants outdoors for 1 hour each day on a protected porch or under the shade of a tree. Gradually increase the amount of time they spend outdoors.

Be sure that you water well so the roots establish good soil contact. Once you have them planted, give yourself a much-deserved pat on the back. Your gardening skills will pay off as the season unfolds and your annual flowers grow bigger and burst forth in beautiful profusion for you.

If you have chlorinated city water, it helps to fill some pots or gallon jugs with water and let the water sit overnight or for a few days to let the chlorine dissipate.

Easier Gardening Ahead

In 2002, the Ball Horticultural firm began introducing nationwide a unique, consumer-friendly line of flowering plants in garden centers. Called Simply Beautiful, this line is designed to simplify the gardening endeavor so anyone, from beginner to veteran gardener, can create a beautiful garden easily.

An interactive consumer Web site, *www.simplybeautifulgardens.com*, groups all varieties by sun and shade and suggests different garden uses such as beds, hanging baskets, and mixed containers.

The Ball Company realized that many new gardeners don't know the difference between various flowers. Therefore, they named these folks "dabblers." These people make up probably 85 percent of the market for plants. Rows and rows of plants, flowers, shrubs, soils, and potting equipment seem to fill garden centers. That can be mind-boggling!

"Most shoppers feel lost and don't know where to begin when they enter a garden center," says Jeff Gibson of the Ball firm. "We wanted to simplify the selection process and make it easier for them to have a beautiful garden that thrives all season."

Ball is the leading breeder of annuals in the world. They carefully researched to find out how they could help the gardener feel more confident and be more successful. Average gardeners told them they wanted beautiful and reliable plants that perform without a lot of fuss, and simple-to-understand information for the plants they purchase for their gardens. Thus the Simply Beautiful line was born. Ⓔ

Chapter 8

Entranceways and Outdoor Living Rooms

In this chapter, you'll learn how to give your front door a colorful, pleasant landscape smile. You'll also get tips and advice for color coordinating your home grounds, using portable color, and giving yourself some great views out of your home windows. Put these useful landscaping ideas to use and you'll enjoy a more glorious outdoor living experience for years to come.

Focus on Your Front Door

As you begin landscaping, first focus on your front entranceway. This all-important feature will say a lot to guests and passersby. You can make your front entrance welcoming to others by dolling it up with your newfound landscaping skills. If you are still unsure of what you want to do with the entranceway, take a look at others around you. Drive or walk around town and take notes on those that you like. You'll soon find your own style and preferences.

Container gardens offer the fastest way to dress up an entry, emphasize a path, or dress up a patio or deck with lively splashes of color. As you look around to upgrade your landscaping, think about your front door. Medium-sized trees can flank one side of the door while lower-growing shrubs greatly enhance the entranceway.

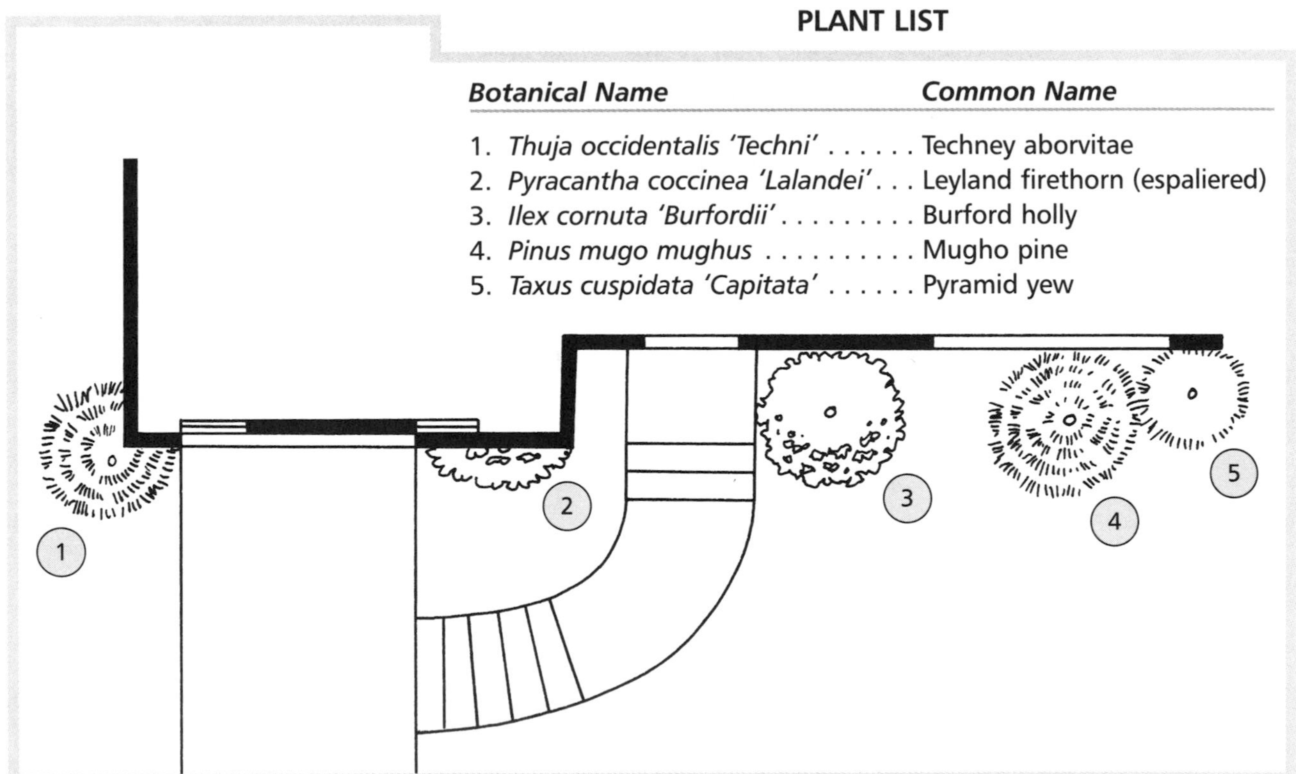

PLANT LIST
Botanical Name
Common Name
1. Thuja occidentalis 'Techni' . . . . . . Techney aborvitae
2. Pyracantha coccinea 'Lalandei' . . . Leyland firethorn (espaliered)
3. Ilex cornuta 'Burfordii' . . . . Burford holly
4. Pinus mugo mughus . . . . Mugho pine
5. Taxus cuspidata 'Capitata' . . . . . . Pyramid yew
1
2
3
4
5

▲ Examples of entranceway trees.

Combine Plants for Appeal

Landscaping a sloping entrance can be no problem. A firethorn will thrive at the side of the drive. Holly, yew, or dwarf mugho pine can be used at the doorway, with a grouping of shrubs. If the slope is steep from door to drive, consider a rock garden or several terraced levels. New cascading scarlet or white Meidiland landscape roses will carpet the ground, hold the soil, and provide hundreds of dazzling blooms for weeks on end. Daffodils can be naturalized for early spring bloom.

When planning for entranceway excitement, don't get overzealous and use plants that are known to attract bees! Your guests won't think the entranceway is very welcoming if they have to brave a swarm of bees.

Simply Fun Trials

You can doll up your entranceway quickly and easily with hanging baskets of Misty Lilac petunias. Then fill a tub with purple rose designer geraniums, sun-loving periwinkle, and blue lobelia. Finally, flank entry walks with 10-inch pots filled with purple Starlett minipetunias for sunny exposures, or if the area is shady, use Fiesta Ole Stardust pink double impatiens. See, landscaping doesn't have to be all that difficult. In just a few minutes you can create a beautiful and welcoming entranceway.

Plan Outdoor Living Rooms

You can create a healthy, low-maintenance landscape if you follow some simple steps in preparing your outdoor living rooms, entertaining areas, and your planting beds. To avoid disappointment, begin with small garden beds or a manageable section of your yard.

The first thing you'll want to do is prepare the ground and improve the soil. Peel back sod and get rid of any rocks. Use peat moss, compost, or manure to improve the soil. If you have large trees in the area, you'll want to create a raised bed or just build up the soil around them. This is done so you can avoid the tree's roots. However, don't raise the soil level more than 4 to 6 inches over a tree's root system since this can affect the roots' oxygen exchange and actually suffocate the tree.

Water and Weeds

Install drip line or soaker hoses to ensure that new plants survive the first summer. Aim to keep your watering chores to a minimum.

If you're planting shrubs or regular perennials, lay a fabric weed mat on the prepared soil. You can find them locally. You'll have to create spaces in the mat where you want the plants to go. Weed mats allow water and air to penetrate the soil but suppress weed growth, which makes beds easy to maintain.

Incorporate a granular fertilizer into the soil around each plant to provide a slow-releasing source of nutrients. With this type of timed-release fertilizer, you'll need to fertilize only once or twice during the growing season.

Mulch to Finish

Once planting is done, mulch over the weed mat or between creeping plants with compost, old leaves, or bark mulch. Any small weeds that do germinate will be growing in the top few inches of organic mulch and can be easily pulled out and composted. To give beds a demarcation, you can use vinyl edging, brick, or stones to achieve an edging definition and keep plants in their place.

Move Your Garden Around

You can enjoy an instant garden on the deck, patio, or in a corner of the yard by filling different-sized containers with flowers of related colors. Set plants close together in pots for a dramatic cascade of color look. For another look, vary the heights of the container plants. Consider the value of mixing leaf textures and plant shapes, too.

It's best to keep your selection of plants down to three types when you want to mix and match in one large container. Keep it simple and use complementary hues and tones. Landscape advisors suggest you use no more than three. For example, use Angel Mist summer snapdragon for height, Double Wave petunias for mass, and Aztec trailing verbena Lavender to cascade.

Try lighting up a shady spot with a combination of Fiesta Ole Stardust double impatiens, silvery nicoletta, and the new light lavender Fanfare trailing impatiens. A combination of three varieties is attractive yet easy on the eye and simple to arrange. If you have shady areas, look up other shade-loving plants in catalogs or ask your local supplier about ways to brighten otherwise dull areas.

You can use almost anything for containers—baskets, urns, pots, tubs, boxes—but make sure they have holes for proper drainage. If you have decorative containers you would like to use but they don't have holes, you just need to get creative. Place your plant in a smaller container that does have holes for proper drainage, put some pea gravel in the bottom of the decorative container, and then place the smaller container inside the bigger, decorative one. Be sure to drain the decorative container occasionally. (See Chapter 17 for tips and suggestions on container gardening.)

FACT

According to the Pennsylvania-based Conard-Pyle Company, one of the world's largest growers of roses and hybrids, there is a renewed interest in the famous Peace Rose, introduced at the end of World War II, and any of its hybrids. These roses, combined with the new World War II Memorial Rose, Bronze Star, and Silver Star roses make a wonderful statement in a peace or memorial garden.

Watery Accessories

Fountains and water accessories are becoming more and more popular with gardeners. Fountains offer an eye-pleasing feature and an ear-pleasing sound to any outdoor corner. Softly splashing water is a soothing symphony in any garden, creating peace and tranquility. A water feature can add fun and playfulness or elegance and grandness to any landscape.

When installing a fountain, the first rule is to make sure that it is on a level surface. If need be, the ground can be leveled with small pebbles. Next make sure that it is near a properly grounded 110-volt AC-only GFCI protected receptacle for your pump. Many pumps are submersible and must be underwater to function properly. You can find many types of fountains at fine garden centers throughout the United States and Canada. For more information, visit *www.campaniainternational.com.*

Other Garden Accessories

Get creative with your outdoor living rooms. You can add birdbaths, various pieces of sculpture, and similar accessories to your garden. Even the venerable elves and trolls so famous in European—especially Scandinavian and Irish—gardens are gaining popularity in America. Garden accessory manufacturers are producing excellent copies of birdbaths, planters, and ornaments that represent a particular historical design style.

If you are interested in old-favorite garden accessories, you can find more details about American Heritage garden accessories at *www.campaniainternational.com*.

According to the National Gardening Association, container gardening products are the fastest-growing category of the entire lawn and garden market, with retail sales increasing from $558 million to $783 million in 1998. The major growth in this category has been in outdoor plant containers. Here are some unique products for landscape use.

Prairie-Style Urn is cast from a period original. The prairie style of architecture emerged in the American Midwest in the early part of the twentieth century. Large, yet simple, cast stone planters graced porches and terraces.

Bucks County Cherub was rescued from an old garden in Bucks

County, Pennsylvania. This graceful cherub was originally manufactured in Philadelphia circa 1910–1920. The cherub's graceful form and sweet countenance bring an old-fashioned charm to the garden. The pebbly texture of the cast stone original has been preserved.

Haskell birdbaths reflect the Victorian era's appreciation for nature that most likely inspired the creation of the classic American garden ornament: the birdbath. According to manufacturers bringing back old-favorite garden accessories, these pieces are designed to bring to mind an America full of front porches and rocking chairs, spacious green lawns surrounded by blue hydrangeas, grand old shade trees, and, not surprisingly, that old-fashioned birdbath that was always the centerpiece of Grandmother's garden.

Good Lawns Make Great Landscapes

The lawn is a beautiful and integral part of the American home landscape. You'll spend less time maintaining your lawn if your grass is healthy. A thick and healthy lawn suppresses weeds, resists pests and disease, and keeps maintenance to a minimum. If you pay attention to several key points you can save work and grow a better-looking lawn! *The Everything® Lawn Care Book* has hundreds of great lawn growing tips. Here are just a few key points.

- **Mow high.** Mowing high leaves more leaf surface so plants can make more food. Mowing high also helps to reduce weed problems. Most weeds need light to germinate and taller grass will help shade them out.
- **Mulch lawn clippings.** Leave your lawn clippings on the ground to help nourish the soil. However, if your clippings are thick, wet, and smothering the lawn, you should sweep or rake them up and compost them.
- **Use slow-release fertilizer.** Slow-release fertilizer stimulates moderate growth over a longer period of time, and in turn, your lawn doesn't require as much mowing.
- **Reseed patchy areas with the best seed for a particular area.** Most

grass varieties, including fescues, Kentucky bluegrass, and perennial rye grass, require full sun to remain lush and green but will tolerate some shade. If your yard is partially shaded all day, you should plant grass varieties that are specially suited to shade.

Go for Natural

Try the natural look. A formal yard is usually comprised of a wide-open space with strategically placed plants to create order. A natural yard has order as well, but is designed for a more chaotic, free-flowing look.

FACT

You can make your yard more natural and sustainable by incorporating a diversity of plant materials into the landscape. Add stately trees, native shrubs, evergreen ground covers, and ornamental grasses. Don't forget flowering trees; flowering multipurpose shrubs; and blazes of color from bulbs, perennials, and annuals.

The plants used in a natural yard are often native to your area, so they generally will require less fertilizer and water than some of the introduced plant species that are commonly used in home landscaping. You can utilize native plants to create a more natural ecosystem like the creation of a bird or butterfly sanctuary. Or, you can allow sections of your yard to simply "go wild." Check with your local nursery or Gardener's Supply Company for help with a natural yard.

Adopt Ground Covers

It does require a little work to establish ground covers, but their year-round color makes it well worth the effort. They form a ground-hugging companion for taller plants and protect soil from erosion as they spread. When they're mature they keep weeds and other unwanted plants out.

Shaded areas can be troublesome. For these areas, try vinca minor, or periwinkle, lily of the valley, ferns, and pachysandra. For sunny, dry areas, daylilies are excellent, easy, fast-spreading, perennial ground covers.

They are gaining popularity thanks to the many exciting, dramatic new varieties being introduced.

Of course, there are several other options. Juniper, creeping thyme, creeping phlox, astilbes, and euonymus all are good ground cover. Your local garden expert will be able to tell you which will thrive in your area.

Consider Neat Paths

Sometimes gardeners wear a path through their lawn. That signals a need for a pathway that reduces mowing and adds its own neat look. If you have a worn footpath in the lawn, consider creating a wide stone or gravel bed path between the two areas.

▲ Path design examples.

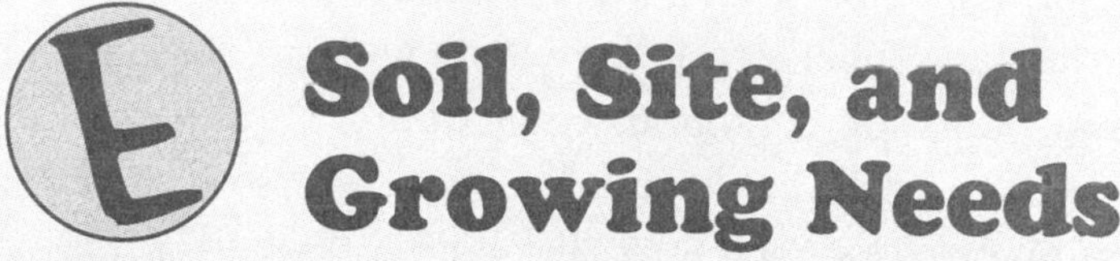

Chapter 9

Soil, Site, and Growing Needs

As veteran gardeners know and advise, if you pick the right site, improve your growing ground by adding organic matter regularly, and apply the proper amounts of fertilizer that your various plants need, you can be a top gardener. Even better, you can enjoy the glorious flowers, tasty herbs, delicious vegetables and fruits, and the best-looking landscape around.

What Is Soil?

It sounds like a silly question. Soil is the dirt in your yard, right? Well, to plant and landscape effectively, you need to know a little more about soil than just that. Soil is what provides the nutrients and structure your plants require.

The basic principle for productive gardening is improvement of the soil. It is your first essential step in knowledge and in growing plants. The better the humus and soil conditions you can build, the healthier your plants will be. Also consider this fact: The insects that destroy your plants dislike healthy plants! They prefer sickly, undernourished plants. The healthier the soil, the less harmful insects you have.

QUESTION?

What's in the soil?
Soil has not only organic matter, air, water, and weathered rock, it also has a "magic" ingredient: organisms. These include small animals, worms, insects, bacteria, and microbes that are beneficial to your plants.

It is important to understand soil basics to improve growing conditions wherever you live and garden. No matter what you have, from clay to sandy soils, from backfill around a new development home to soggy spots in your land, soil can be improved. You can make it productive with a simple, careful, and continuing improvement plan. The emphasis is on continuing. Don't expect instant results. Do what you can to improve the soil today, and then continue on with that natural soil-building process month after month, year after year. The results will astound you.

Soil for Landscape Plants

One productive gardener worked for several years to improve several beds. It was interesting to drive by and see the results, year by year, in more productive flower crops. He worked on improving several 6-foot wide, 125-foot garden rows every year on his poor, streamside, clay soil areas. Every year he added leaves, manure, and organic matter. His improvements are now obvious in the healthy plants, larger vegetables, and superior blooms of the flowers.

Get to Know Your Soil

Soil comes in various types and qualities. An understanding of basic soil formation and composition is essential to your efforts to work with nature in creating an optimum growing environment for your plants.

Don't let soil color fool you. Color doesn't necessarily indicate quality of soil. Many novice gardeners believe that rich soil is dark. Not necessarily! Dark, black soil can be low in nutrients. Reddish, sandy soils actually can be good growing soils. Soil comes in a variety of colors. It may be red, as with the soils of Hawaii and the red shale soils of the Mid-Atlantic states. It may be black, like the soils of the Dakotas. In coastal areas and certain portions of inland states, it may be quite sandy, the result of deposits from glaciers eons ago. In some parts of the country, you'll be confronted with clay soils as thick and sticky as Louisiana gumbo soils. No matter where you live or what soil you find there, you can improve it, rebuild it, and upgrade your growing conditions immensely.

Elements of Soil

All soils have several things in common. They contain minerals, organic matter, water, and air. The proportion of these elements varies, but the components remain essentially the same.

Minerals. Roughly half the soil in your garden consists of small bits of weathered rock that has gradually been broken down by the forces of wind, rain, freezing and thawing, and other chemical and biological processes through the years.

Organic Materials. Organic matter is the partially decomposed remains of soil organisms and plant life such as lichens and mosses, grasses and leaves, trees, and all other kinds of vegetative matter, including decayed mulch or compost you have added.

Organic matter makes up only a small fraction of the soil, about 5 to 10 percent.

Air. About 25 percent of healthy soil will be air. Insects, microbes, earthworms, and all soil life require this much air to live. The air in soil is also an important source of the atmospheric nitrogen that is utilized by plants. Note that well-aerated soil has plenty of pore space between the soil particles. Fine soil particles such as clay or silt have tiny spaces between them. In heavy clay these are too small for air to penetrate properly. Hence, plants don't grow well. Soil composed of large particles, like sand, has large pore spaces and contains plenty of air. Too much air can cause organic matter to decompose too fast. It is important to ensure a balanced supply of air in your soil by adding plenty of organic matter.

Water. Another 25 percent of healthy soil will be water. Water, like air, is held in the pore spaces between soil particles. If the pore spaces are too large, as in sandy soils, the water drains out quickly, causing the soil to dry out.

FACT

Organic matter is essential because it binds together soil particles into porous granules that allow air and water to move through the soil. Organic matter also retains moisture. Humus holds up to 90 percent of its weight in water and absorbs and stores nutrients. Most importantly, organic matter is food for microorganisms that are vital to soil formation.

Know Your Soil Profile

Every soil has a profile. Layers in this profile are called horizons. In the profile you'll find the history of the soil and its formation. Horizons of the profile differ in color, structure, porosity, and consistency. In shallow soils, these horizons may be only 1 inch thick, sometimes less. You also may find soil horizons several feet deep. Usually the horizon will be 1 foot or so thick. You can cut a soil profile with a spade to examine it and learn some basics of what you must deal with in your gardening efforts.

Take a spade and slice the soil in a trench, pit, or large hole. Cut clean on one side to reveal the horizons. You will be able to see the topsoil, subsoil, and below. Try this in different areas and you'll be surprised at the difference you may find just around your home grounds.

Pick Sites That Match Plant Needs

While planning your garden, study the soil so you can match what your plants need to the soil that is available to grow them in. Always remember, soil can be improved, but that takes work, sometimes several years' worth. It pays to find the best sites available and plant landscapes and gardens accordingly.

Soil scientists list the three master horizons simply as A, B, and C. In some cases there is a merged horizon known as an AC profile. When erosion has been at work or where man has misused and depleted the soil, or through a combination of these factors, the upper horizons may be gone.

True soil is the combined A and B horizons that form the major portion of the soil profile. They are the direct result of the soil formation process. In each horizon, you will usually find subdivisions in the A and B portions. In these layers life is moving, for soil is truly alive. Millions of bacteria and fungi, plus plant roots, insects, and small animals, are there, busily at work. Learning to achieve a balance with them, with nature, and with the life processes already in the soil is essential to obtaining the bountiful results you want and deserve.

FACT

Wind, water, and weather all contribute to the initial formation of any soil. Bedrock freezes and thaws. It becomes wet and dries out. In this natural, ongoing process, bedrock cracks and fractures. Over thousands of years, the continual effects of weather and movement result in the first phases of soil formation.

Plants Help Soil-Making Process

Plants add to the process. Bacteria, fungi, tiny lichens, and moss begin to grow. These tiny, primitive plants gain a foothold in the crevices. As roots find their way into cracks, they produce more plants and die. In the process, they deposit the first organic matter.

Over the centuries, this process continues slowly, ceaselessly, positively. As organic matter accumulates, it, too, changes. Rain falls and water carries elements to the lower levels, helping to break down minerals in the parent material. New compounds are formed as air, water, and other elements interact and combine.

If you wish to continue your study of soils, many books are available that provide a depth of knowledge. You may find the subject fascinating. Several gardeners report that they became so interested in soil that they switched careers and became landscaping contractors, and cashed in on their knowledge of the good earth.

Most gardeners are concerned only with the soil they can call their own. Of that soil, the upper portion deserves your closest attention, since it is this level that is the growing medium and that contains the material available for your garden plant use. The upper soil levels are, naturally, subject to the elements. Rain falls and carries carbon dioxide into the soil from the air. It also transports valuable minerals dissolved from humus, sand, and rock particles. The minerals decompose slowly and constantly, reacting with water and other minerals to form new compounds. This process goes on every day, helping to build soil and the needed nutrients for future plants.

In the process, there are additions and losses, too. Clay particles tend to be leached to lower levels, along with minerals and soluble salts. As they move downward, they are deposited in the B horizon, where the roots of plants can obtain these needed nutrients.

Changes in soil formation and depletion occur at varying rates.

In general, organic matter decomposes more rapidly. Minerals decompose more slowly. As plants grow, some of these materials are utilized and returned as the natural cycle of growth, death, and decomposition continues. The plants that grew or grow on the land determine to a large degree the types of organic matter going into the soil.

Your Soil Is Very Much Alive!

Your soil is filled with living organisms, mainly in the upper, plant-growing areas. The action of plants and their roots, insects, worms, animals, bacteria, and fungi help mix soil horizons. Normally, leaves, grasses, twigs, and humus are found at the surface with fibrous roots lower in the horizon. As stronger plant life develops, nutrients from lower levels are picked up by deep-rooted plants and redeposited on the surface in the growth cycle.

Bacteria and fungi in your living soil are vital contributors to soil formation. They live on animal and plant residues. They break down complex compounds into simple forms. Nitrogen-fixing bacteria, for example, in the nodules of legumes, actually fix, or take, nitrogen from the atmosphere and help make it available in the soil for future plants.

You can learn a lot from observing your soil. It helps to have an understanding of the terms used, from groups and types to textures and structures. As you identify what you have, you can better understand the ways to improve your soil as you read this book.

Soil Terms Help Understanding

Texture refers to the size of the majority of particles making up the soil. It ranges from the microscopic clay particles up to the small stones and gravel. Soils are generally categorized with these terms.

- **Clay Soils**—Stony clay, gravely clay, sandy clay, silty clay, clay
- **Loam Soils**—Coarse sandy loams, medium sandy loams, fine sandy loams, silty loams, and clay loams
- **Sandy Soils**—Gravely sands, coarse sands, medium sands, fine sands, loamy sands

To keep your soil alive and healthy there must be pore space, known as porosity. Through this pore space the water, nutrients, roots, and air must move. When you look at a handful of soil it looks like, well, just soil. But about 25 to 50 percent of what you hold in your hands is actually pore space. If there is more, it can mean possible water loss, leaching of nutrients from the upper layers, and excessive nitrogen release.

Too little porosity hinders plant growth because as soil compacts it forms hardpan layers on or beneath the surface. Without pore space, roots can't penetrate to find water and nutrients. Plants won't thrive.

A Balance

All soils can be improved with the proper treatment. Your early goal should be to aim for a balance in structure, texture, and porosity. The word *balance* is important to consider. Nature is a matter of balance, in food chains of animals and in food growing from soils. Excesses are what throw people and plants out of balance in life.

Pick up a handful of rich, warm soil in the spring. Crumble it in your hands. If it crumbles freely in your palm, you are approaching the ideal. Naturally, there are unseen factors, such as nutrient levels, in balance in the soil. But the consistency of the growing medium is of underlying importance.

The closer you have or can rebuild soil to a granular feel, with clusters of soil that easily shake apart, the better your garden will grow. The better the soil, the less chance of erosion, providing that you follow proper cultivation practices.

Soil Conservation

Soil erodes in several ways. Heavy rains on denuded, unprotected sites will carry away topsoil. Left unchecked, gullies develop. Wind can blow away the fine, light surface soil, too.

For practical purposes, water erosion is the main problem confronting home gardeners. That doesn't mean just erosion on sloping garden land. America's proclivity to pave and blacktop driveways, parking areas, playgrounds, and malls denies rain a way to soak into the earth. A heavy rain across asphalt driveways or parking areas can lead to erosion problems on nearby garden areas much faster than you imagine.

Contour farming has proved that soil can be held in place and erosion avoided on sloping or hilly land. If you have a hilly area, you can profit by using contours. Leave a 2- to 3-foot grass strip every 6 to 10 feet, running parallel with the contour of the land. These strips will act as minidams to slow the rapid runoff of surface water. Ground covers such as vetch or clover on steep slopes, and myrtle, pachysandra, or ivy will retard erosion.

Be wary about buying "topsoil" or "loam" as a quick-fix approach to lawn and garden building. Rich-looking topsoil or so-called loam may be offered at low prices by some less-than-honest contractors. On occasion they obtain this good-looking, dark soil from dredging silt in rivers and ponds and mixing it with sand.

Tips for Simple Soil Improvement

Here are some basic tips for improving your soil. They can serve as your quick reference checklist as you dig in to grow better.

To Improve Clay Soils

- Work 2 to 3 inches of organic matter into the surface of the soil. It can be old mulch or finished compost or even peat moss.
- Add at least 1 inch more each year after that.
- Add organic matter in the fall, if possible.
- Use permanent raised beds.
- Minimize tilling and spading.
- Never till or try to cultivate when soil is wet.

To Improve Sandy Soil

- Work in 3 to 4 inches of organic matter such as well-rotted manure or finished compost.
- Mulch around your plants with leaves, wood chips, bark, hay, or straw. Mulch retains moisture and cools the soil.
- Plan to add at least 2 inches of organic matter each year.
- Grow cover crops or green manures.

To Improve Silty Soil

Silty soils contain small irregular particles of weathered rock, which means they are usually quite dense and have relatively small pore spaces and poor drainage. They tend to be more fertile than sandy or clay soils.

- Add 1 inch of organic matter each year.
- Avoid soil compaction by unnecessary tilling and walking on garden beds.
- Consider constructing raised beds, which also are easier to maintain.

Know Soil Chemistry, Too

Yes, you must pay attention also to the acid-alkaline chemical balance, which varies by soil. Different plants need different acid or alkaline growing environments. The addition of manures, minerals, and trace elements plays a part, as does the mechanical treatment of your garden ground. Soil testing is a good idea, especially for new gardeners.

Match Soil pH to Plant Needs

The pH level of your soil indicates its relative acidity or alkalinity. A pH test measures the ratio of hydrogen (positive) ions to hydroxyl (negative) ions in the soil water. When hydrogen and hydroxyl ions are present in equal amounts, the pH is said to be neutral (pH 7). When the hydrogen ions prevail, the soil is acidic (pH 1 to pH 6.5). And when the hydroxyl ions tip the balance, the pH is alkaline (pH 6.8 to pH 14).

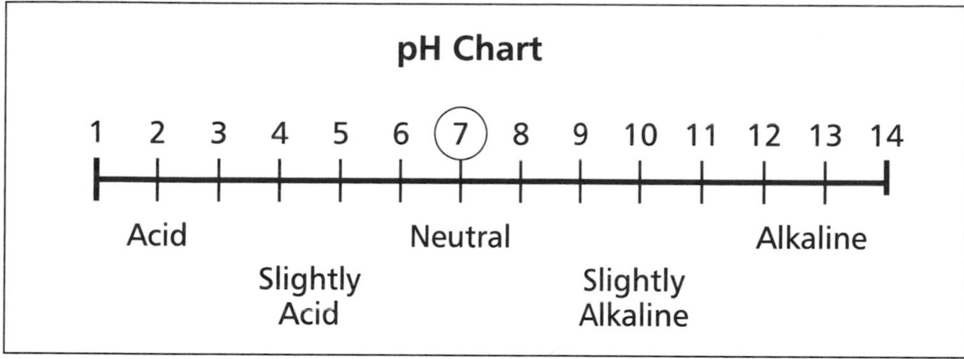

▲ pH chart from acid to alkaline.

Most essential plant nutrients are soluble at pH levels of 6.5 to 6.8, which is why most plants grow best in this range. If the pH of your soil is much higher or lower, plant health suffers because roots can't absorb the nutrients they need to feed your plants.

To improve soil fertility, you need to put the pH of your soil within the 6.5 to 6.8 range. You can't, and shouldn't even try to, change the pH of your soil overnight. It is better to alter it over one or two growing seasons and then maintain it every year thereafter.

Correcting Acid Soil

If the pH of your soil is less than 6.5, it may be too acidic for most garden plants. You should learn what plants need. The most common way to raise the pH of your soil and make it less acidic is to add powdered limestone. Here are some basic guidelines to raise the pH of your soil by about one point:

- In sandy soil, add 3 to 4 pounds of ground limestone per 100 square feet.
- In loam add 7 to 8 pounds per 100 square feet.
- In heavy clay add 8 to 10 pounds per 100 square feet.

Solving Alkaline Soil Problems

If your soil is alkaline (higher than 6.8), you'll need to add acidity. You can do this by adding ground sulfur or acidic organic materials, including conifer needles, sawdust, peat moss, or oak leaves. Here's how to lower soil pH by about one point:

- In sandy soil add 1 pound ground sulfur per 100 square feet.
- In loamy, good garden soil add 1½ to 2 pounds per 100 square feet.
- In heavy clay add 2 pounds per 100 square feet.

FACT

Soils in the eastern half of the United States are usually on the acidic side. Soils in the western United States are usually alkaline. That's just the way it is, and you can blame it on Mother Nature if you wish.

Soil Testing Is Very Helpful

A professional soil test gives you a wealth of information about your soil, most importantly the pH and amount of different nutrients. Your local Cooperative Extension Service office usually offers a professional soil testing service that is low cost, with results specifically focused on your location. If this service is not available, you can also have your soil tested by an independent soil lab. Many garden centers offer soil testing or can direct you to a soil lab that does. Soil test results usually rate the levels of soil pH, calcium, phosphorus, magnesium, potassium, and sometimes nitrogen.

Most labs do not test for nitrogen because it is so unstable in the soil. However, more labs now offer tests for micronutrients such as boron, zinc, and manganese. Trace minerals are important to plants, too. However, unless plants show nutrition problems, you probably won't need micronutrient testing.

To add micronutrients, try adding organic fertilizers or commercial blends that have microelements listed on the label. Organic fertilizers such as greensand and kelp meal usually have micronutrients to help where soil is deficient in them.

To get the most accurate test results, take a soil sample from each garden area, including your lawn, flower garden, and vegetable garden. Each needs different nutrients for the type of plants you grow.

▲ Fertilizing along rows and around plants.

Spring and fall are the best times to do soil tests because soil is more stable. You can also then incorporate any recommended fertilizers your garden ground needs.

Green manures and cover crops planted in fall and turned or tilled under each spring are useful to improve soil and also can add small amounts of nutrients.

Know the ABCs of NPK

You will always see fertilizer expressed in numbers such as 10-5-5 or 10-20-10. Many different types of fertilizer are available today. Millions of gardeners have adopted the liquid foliar feeding system. They simply add fertilizer ingredients into the sprayer that attaches to their garden hose and feed their plants as they water them. It's a great system, easy and foolproof if you follow the directions so you don't overdo things.

The numbers refer to the percentage by net weight of total nitrogen. N, for nitrogen, is always the first number. Next is P, which stands for available phosphorus, and is always the second number. The K, always the last letter, stands for soluble potash. In other words, a 10-5-5 fertilizer contains 10 percent nitrogen, 5 percent available phosphorus, and 5 percent soluble potash.

Basically, that formula means that a 100-pound bag contains 20 pounds of nutrients. The other 80 pounds is made up of inert carriers so the fertilizer ingredients are spread more evenly. Commercial fertilizers can have a wide range of compositions, depending on what the manufacturer puts in the formula. Different plants require different levels of nutrition. The same principle applies to other types of fertilizer formulations.

FACT

Nutrient analysis for organic fertilizers tends to be low, and the nutrients gradually become available to plants over a period of months or even years.

It helps to know what these nutrients contribute to plant growth. Each has a purpose, and when you understand these purposes, you'll be able to make your garden grow better.

Nitrogen

Nitrogen is the key element for vegetative growth. It promotes strong and healthy leaves, stalks, and stems. In fact, it is vital for all green leaf tissue. Nitrogen fosters the development of proteins, called growth builders in plants. Without this essential element, you'll see yellowed foliage and stunted growth.

Too much nitrogen also can cause problems. Oversupply encourages excess leaf and stem growth at the expense of flower and fruit formation. Leafy plants such as corn are big users of nitrogen. So is grass. That's why lawn fertilizers have high first numbers in the formula—16-6-4, 20-10-10. This indicates that nitrogen is high in proportion to the other elements.

Phosphorous

Phosphorus is essential for flower development, good fruit set, and seed production. It is also required for proper development of plant sugars. You do want sweet-tasting squash, tomatoes, and corn, don't you? Then you should pay attention to phosphorus, that sugar-encouraging nutrient in your fertilizer.

Lack of phosphorous is easily spotted. Plants are stunted and have a yellowed look. This may appear similar to nitrogen deficiency, but look again. The distinctive purplish color around edges of leaves and between leaf veins means phosphorous deficiency. Equally important, though unseen, is the retarded root development when phosphorous is insufficient. Leaves may fall and plants may fail to flower. If phosphorous is out of balance with other elements, you can use super-phosphate to adjust the soil nutrient balance.

Fortunately today there are many quality fertilizers in granular and liquid preparations. The labels will tell you which crops to use them on. There are some that are designed for fruits, others for flowering plants, and still others for more general purposes. Ask the specialists at your garden center about them.

Potash

Potash or potassium, the K on the formula, promotes strong, healthy roots. It also aids in seed production. More important to you, it quickens maturity of crops and may help in disease resistance. Potassium deficiency is marked by yellowish mottling. In severe cases, foliage loss occurs and roots won't develop well. Also, fruit set is poor when potash is low.

Chapter 10

Compost and Mulch

The riches held within your garden soil must be unlocked in order to produce the productive, fruitful, bountiful garden that you deserve. As you evaluate your growing ground, do soil tests, and plan your landscape horizons, be assured that you can indeed make that ground come alive and help you grow well. This chapter will tell you how.

The Benefits of Compost

You can use organic materials to make your soil more productive now and improve it regularly without a lot of work. Frankly, nature does most of the work for you. Compost is the key that turns soil into productive land that will yield bountiful harvests of tasty fruits; large and magnificent flowers; and hardy, attractive shrubs and trees. You can make compost easily, and with a little extra effort, speedily.

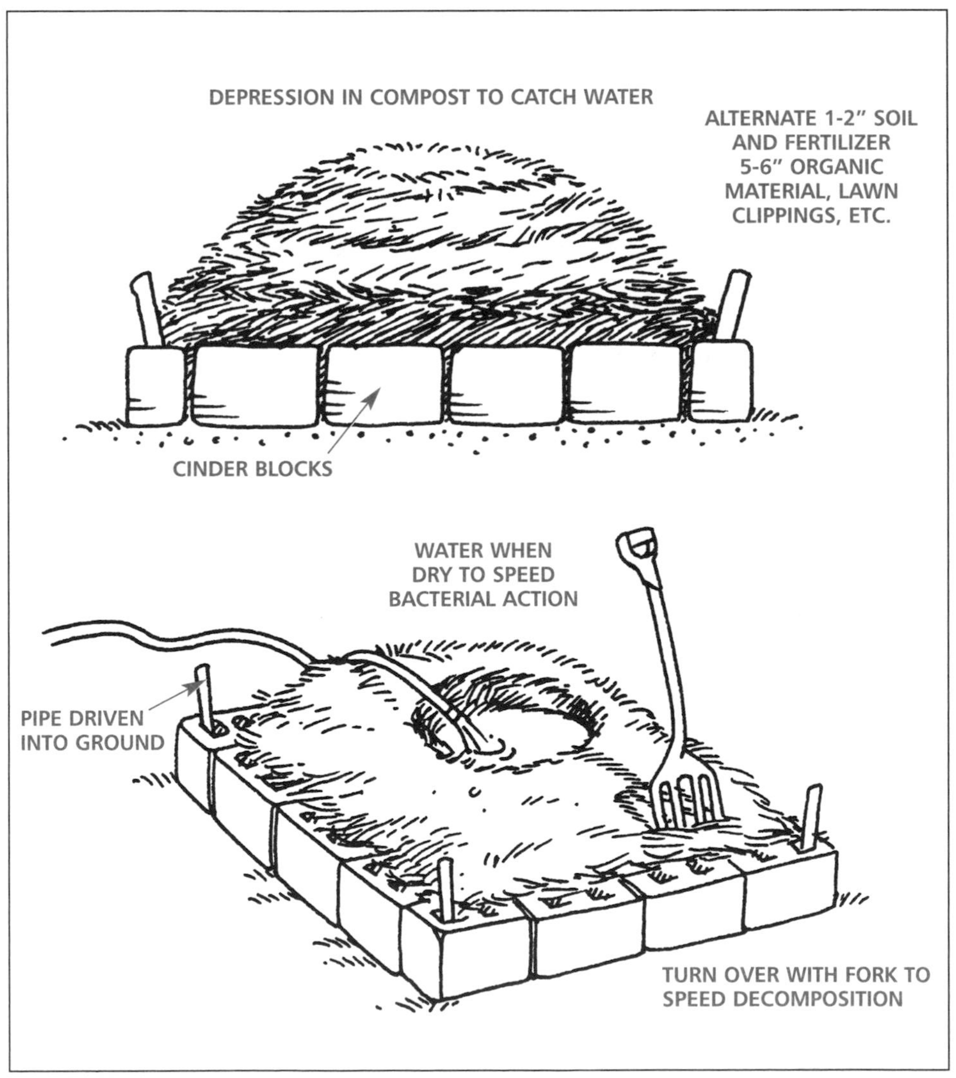

Tiny Animal Life

Using readily available materials, you can actually turn organic matter into usable compost in as few as 14 days. Millions of bacteria, fungi, minute animals, and other microorganisms inhabit organic material. There is a close relationship between the amount of life in the soil and the soil's basic fertility. This tiny animal life reduces complex organic substances such as sugars and proteins to simpler chemical forms. In this way, nutrients are made available for plants again. Your objective is to increase the life and, consequently, the productivity of the soil. The better the compost, the better the soil.

Recycling Organic Material

Compost can be made in many ways and almost any type of organic material can be utilized effectively. Production of compost depends upon the decay or decomposition rate of the various materials used. Bins or pits, in the ground, above the ground, or on wire, plus many other variations have been successfully utilized. You can pick the method that best suits your needs.

Any soil can be improved with compost, even the hard, caked subsoil often found around new home developments. The addition of humus and organic matter through compost provides the best and least expensive way to improve your soil. One nice factor is that soil can never get enough organic matter.

FACT

Good topsoil contains from 2 to 8 percent organic matter by dry weight. You should continue to add organic matter every year in order to keep building your soil bank. The addition of 1 inch of organic matter of humus from compost per 4 inches of topsoil constitutes a good average application.

Avoid using diseased plants for compost. Despite the fact that natural heating in the center of the pile may and usually does kill most disease organisms, there are still some risks.

Preparing Compost

The first thing you need to do is choose a location. Compost pits or piles don't have eye appeal. Consider your nearby neighbors and the appearance and smell of your compost area. Select an out-of-the-way location. You probably will want to screen the area from view by erecting a fence or planting a hedge, shrubs, or perhaps vegetables on a supporting trellis or fence around it. Berry hedges form thick bramble patches, hiding the compost piles and providing tasty berries in the bargain.

▲ Fence compost pile.

Choose a site convenient to water so you can periodically wet down the pile or pit to keep it moist. Moisture is needed to promote faster decomposition. A shady area is good, but avoid low areas in which rain collects and the ground remains soggy. While bacteria that help make compost into good humus require ample moisture, they must have oxygen as well.

The second step in preparing compost is construction of the pit or pile. Remember that air circulation is important. The more air that circulates through the pile and around it, the faster the decomposition. Turning a compost pile with a pitchfork or spade is hard work. Good exercise, but work! It is worthwhile to have at least two piles of compost since it is in flux at all times. In this way, you can begin using the finished decomposed humus in one pile while the other is rotting down for future use as humus.

If you want compost fast, there are a number of ways in which you can build the piles. If you will be satisfied to develop compost over a period of several months, you can use alternate systems. There is no single way. The best way is the method that best suits your needs and garden requirements.

Various Composting Materials

Getting down to basics, almost any organic material can be composted with the simple Indore method. This method was developed in England by Sir Albert Howard, father of the modern organic movement. It is the best, most efficient method used by small and large gardeners.

Layer after Layer

Basically, the Indore method is the simple layering of various materials. You simply begin with a 6-inch layer of green organic material. Do not let the word "green" fool you. Grass clippings or dried leaves may be brown but they are considered "green" matter in the terminology of organic gardening.

Over this first layer of clippings, leaves, and vegetation from the garden, add a 2-inch layer of manure. The objective is to add nitrogen to hasten the decay process. Cow, horse, sheep, and poultry manure will do the job. You can often find bags of manure for making compost at garden centers. If you do not have manure readily available when you are building your compost pile, you can add commercial nitrogen fertilizer that will help break down the organic matter.

The next layer in your compost pile should consist of 1 or 2 inches of garden soil, evenly spread to ensure effective interaction. Then, add another layer of organic matter—old leaves, grass clippings, or other vegetation from the garden—and continue to layer the pile as you began.

With raw manures considered "hot," including poultry and pig manure, use slightly less than you would with cow, horse, or sheep manures. It is best if the manure also includes straw, shavings, or other usual bedding materials used on most farms.

Pile Size

You can build a small pile, just 4 feet wide, 4 feet long, and 4 feet high, or you can increase the dimensions if more material is available. However, as previously recommended, it is desirable to have several smaller piles so they will be in varying stages of action and use as finished compost.

As you apply the layers, sprinkle them with water. The material going into the pile should be moist, especially if dry leaves, grass clippings, and other dry materials are being used.

When you have finished building the pile, leave a depression on the top of it so that rainwater can be caught and allowed to trickle down through the layers. This helps keep them moist. Then, you'll need to apply a few waterings only in dry periods. However, if you are in a drought period, be sure to water the compost pile once or twice a week.

Know Your Bacteria Friends

Two types of bacteria will be at work in your compost. These are called aerobic and anaerobic. The first type, aerobic, needs air circulation in order to do its job. The second type, anaerobic, works more slowly and proceeds without much aeration of the pile. Turning the pile by fork or spade or otherwise providing improved aeration will quicken the entire process. Spading means work, but only two or three turnings are required before the humus is ready.

An alternative to manual aeration is to drive several plastic pipes with holes through them into the pile. This method lets the air penetrate, helps the heat build up as decomposition occurs, and saves your back from the chore of spading. There are many other ways to accomplish similar results; as many, in fact, as there are ingenious gardeners.

Compost Bins and Pits

Elevation of composting material off the ground, thereby allowing freer air circulation beneath, provides one of the easiest ways to speed up decomposition. This can be done in several ways. Cinder blocks are handy, inexpensive, and reusable. Also, they do not rot. Space them around the area on which you will build the pile: one block, one space, one block, et cetera. On this foundation, place a layer of plastic-coated fencing. You can then put a wire fence around the pile or use old boards or even rows of cinder blocks. Be sure to leave spaces for that vital air circulation.

An area 5 × 5 × 10 feet will accommodate one large pile or two smaller ones nicely. Construction materials at hand are just as good, such as stones removed from the garden, old bricks from a dump, coated wire fencing, or even old logs.

One word of caution: Do not use treated railroad ties or attempt to treat the wood with chemical preservatives. Contamination from unwanted chemicals is not good, so why risk outside pollution?

Rate of Decomposition

When you build a pile with the Indore method or variations on that theme, and turn the pile twice or more, you can estimate that the finished compost will be ready in about 2 to 3 months. Several factors influence the rate of decomposition. First is the amount of manure and nitrogen sources, plus moisture, that was included as the pile was built. Next is the amount of aeration that is provided, either through hand turning or by use of a mechanical aeration technique. A third factor is the addition of earthworms. These wiggling helpers can truly hasten the process, but they should not be added until the first heating-up period has ended. The earthworms can be added after this first period, or after the second hand turning.

FACT

As the first phase of decay proceeds in a compost pile, the internal heat of the pile may reach 150°F or more. That serves to kill many weed seeds and other unwanted organisms. You can see for yourself how hot a pile gets by inserting a thermometer into the center of a pile.

Beneficial Bacteria

Bacteria, of course, are the microscopic helpers in any compost building activity. They are beneficial to inoculate the pile as it is built. Soil bacteria cultures may be purchased from various sources, but the easiest way to meet this need is to save the remnants of a previous compost pile. Add the material not quite completely decomposed into humus to the new pile or to the soil or manure layers. The bacteria will thrive and multiply and go right to work with their millions of beneficial bacterial neighbors.

Other Composting Piles

Today, commercially available compost bins and turners are also readily available. With easy hand or mechanical cranking and turning systems, they help you achieve finished compost in a shorter period with less work. Check the back sections of mail-order catalogs to find some examples. Also, ask at garden centers of chain stores or local nurseries that usually carry compost-making materials and sometimes even complete kits.

Field Composting Is Easier

If you have room and can afford to wait for the slower, but easier to make, compost to cure, you will find that field composting is ideal. Basically it is a layering method that needs no building or pit or special pile. As you gather green matter, apply it in layers to the heap. Keep adding more until you have a satisfactory 4- to 6-inch layer. Then add manure or other nitrogen-containing materials such as sludge, tankage, or blood meal. Add on more green matter until there are several sequences of layers. By the following year, you will have good humus even if you do not turn the pile.

FACT

Veteran gardeners recommend screening the finished humus. A 2- by 4-foot frame with hardware cloth across the top is handy for this purpose. In this way you can use the best humus and toss the remainder, including any undecomposed stalks and vegetables, back on the ground or into a compost pile to finish decomposing.

Use Kitchen Parings, Too

Just about any type of vegetation and organic matter can be put to use to make compost. You can turn garbage into humus with little effort—vegetable parings; tops of carrots, radishes, and beets; cornhusks; pea pods; outer leaves of lettuce and cabbage; or any type of household vegetation that is organic.

In a given month, the average family might throw away the makings of a bushel of compost. Why waste it? Especially on small plots of land, leaves and grass clippings are scarce. That's even more true in towns and cities. Many towns now prohibit the burning of leaves and brush and that means a bonus for you. Some towns collect the leaves and dump them at a sanitary landfill or city dump. Then they make compost available for free or at a nominal cost.

ALERT!

Do not use kitchen wastes such as animal fats and bones. They decompose slowly and also attract dogs and other animals.

Help Your Neighbors Help You

You can collect leaves from your own home ground, let the neighbors pile their leaves in your compost heap, or even get the extra supplies you need for compost making from the weekly town leaf pickup. One dedicated gardener watches for people raking their leaves. He stops in, says hello, and offers to truck leaves away in his pickup truck. That provides him with abundant supplies for composting and also plentiful mulching material for his garden beds and borders.

The Values of Mulch

Mulch is a naturally good idea. It is a simple, effective, and practical way to begin a recycling of nature's bounty for better gardening. Just count the reasons to be grateful for this natural discovery. You'll agree with millions of gardeners that mulching pays in many ways.

Important Gardening Activity

Mulch preserves moisture, prevents weeds, improves soil condition, avoids erosion, keeps fruits and vegetables clean, cuts down on disease problems, and, a big plus, adds organic matter to the soil. Mulch is an organic gardening bonanza. Next to composting, mulching is the single most vital, natural gardening activity.

FACT

Basically a mulch is any organic material or ground covering you can use as a protective barrier for the soil that will help retain soil moisture, thwart or stop weeds, protect against frost heaving, and help desirable plants grow better.

Readily Available Materials

Most of the necessary mulch materials are readily and easily available wherever you live. Most are free. The list of materials is endless. Consider for a moment grass clippings, leaves, chopped or ground brush and twigs, and pine needles. Do you have any of these in your area?

Organic mulch includes straw, hay, ground corncobs, peat moss, sawdust, shavings, and composted refuse you or neighbors make. It also includes peanut hulls, ground bark, redwood chips, layers of newspapers covered with grass clippings, and whatever will decompose to add nutrients to the soil.

Black plastic and similar available coverings can also be used as a mulch. So can other materials that stop weeds and help soil retain moisture. Gravel, sand, or stones can be used. Aluminum foil, layers of newspapers, and any other artificial ways to thwart weeds can be used. However, consider appearance. Most importantly, consider your goal: improving the soil and the growing ground beneath the mulch.

Mulch Materials

Focus first on organic materials that add to your total overview of improving your soil for better gardening. Organic materials that break down and recycle into the good earth are primary considerations. Whatever material you use and apply depends, of course, on what you have available and what works into your budget and your natural gardening goals.

Be aware that excessive or overly deep tilling can damage the spreading, underground roots of your valued plants. Many plants are shallow rooted, so hand weeding or hoeing is needed instead of tilling.

If you like to see dark, rich-looking soil around shrubs and trees and along garden rows, you can opt for peat moss, ground sphagnum moss, or chipped bark and wood chips. Redwood chips and pine bark look nice. So do darker shavings and sawdust. There are drawbacks and basic problems with some materials. For instance, woody mulch, chips, and shavings will pull some nitrogen from the soil as they naturally decay. You can correct that by adding some extra nitrogen in fertilizers that you apply to your plants.

Dry lawn clippings are fluffy when first spread. You can gather them abundantly from the bag on your power mower. After a few rains, they tend to form a compact, thin layer. They do decompose, but you can add more layers as you mow your lawn each week. The decomposition has its benefits, of course, as it adds to your soil improvement plan.

Using Mulch Effectively

Hard rains can cause erosion on bare ground. The problem is worse when you cultivate too often. A mulch takes up the shock of pounding rain, letting it seep into the soil below more evenly. Then it holds the water in by preventing evaporation from the sun. A mulch also discourages hardpan from developing on the surface in dry periods.

Balance Soil Temperature

Some plants prefer warm, sunny weather. Others favor cooler conditions. The use of mulches, together with proper planting and culture techniques, can help you extend your gardening season by adjusting soil temperatures. Mulch has been called a lazy gardener's favorite trick. It is indeed, and well worth your adopting, too.

In effect, mulch helps you regulate and balance soil temperature to the desires and needs of your plants. You are, in effect, helping to better control the microclimate around them. Remember that light-colored materials such as pebbles, gravel, straw, and light-colored sawdust will act to reflect light. Darker materials, including peat moss, pine bark, compost, and humus, will absorb light and heat.

Berries Benefit Tastefully

If you grow berries, sawdust can prove a most rewarding mulch system. Research in Canada and the United States has proved that growers can increase yields up to 50 percent when they mulch with 2 to 4 inches of sawdust, top-dressed with appropriate additional manure or other nitrogen sources. That research proved out with blueberries, raspberries, strawberries, and blackberries.

Peat moss is probably the most readily available and common mulch. Your best bet is to buy the biggest bales or bags for cost efficiency. Although peat moss has no nutrient value, most other mulch materials do. For example, lawn clippings provide about 1 pound of nitrogen and 2 pounds of potash for each 100 pounds of dry clippings. Peanut shells yield about 3 nitrogen, 1 phosphorous, and ½ potash in analysis. Compare that to the 5-10-5 analysis of commercial fertilizer, and you'll see that mulch materials do have advantages beyond their weed-control, moisture-retention, and soil-improvement abilities.

FACT

Researchers also have found that leaf mold or shredded leaves can provide a nitrogen content as high as 5 percent. Alfalfa or clover hay are higher in nitrogen than orchard grass or timothy because these legumes have nitrogen-fixing bacteria in their root nodules.

Controlling Weeds

Controlling weeds is an ongoing, tiresome chore. True, you can pull or cultivate or till weeds away, but some are frustratingly persistent. They also have left seeds in the ground, just waiting for you to till. That frees up the weed seeds to sprout, grow, and rob your plants of the nutrients and moisture they need.

No doubt, weeds rob you and your garden. They compete for needed moisture from the soil. Worst of all, weeds also steal nutrients from the soil that could better be used to grow your desired flowers, berries, and shrubs. Happily, proper mulching stops weed growth effectively. Applying it early in the season, and regularly, smothers the seedlings, prevents other seeds from sprouting, and encourages those useful underground allies, earthworms, to work their wonders in the soil around your garden plants. When a few weeds do push through, simply pull them out and discard them or add them to your compost pile.

Some Mulching Cautions

Mulch definitely deserves a place in your gardening plans. However, there are some commonsense precautions to observe. Don't mulch the soil when it is excessively wet. Molds can start to grow below the surface, and the trapped moisture combined with heat can cause hidden mold problems. You may also contribute to damping off disease on seedlings if you mulch too early, before they have true leaves and a strong roothold.

To avoid problems, keep mulches that tend to mat down, such as leaves, spoiled hay, and manure mixtures, away from stems and stalks. Always keep them away from young seedlings. The answer is simple. Avoid mulching until seedlings are well up. You can, however, use a light covering of peat moss, vermiculite, or well-composted, dry humus.

Another good rule of green thumb is to use only peat or vermiculite along seedling rows or around hills. When seedlings are 2 to 3 inches tall, begin adding other mulch materials, but always leave 1 or 2 inches around the stems of young plants. As you plan your landscaping this year, think mulch. It is a time-saver and has many other values that make mulch a key contributing ingredient to your gardening success story.

Chapter 11

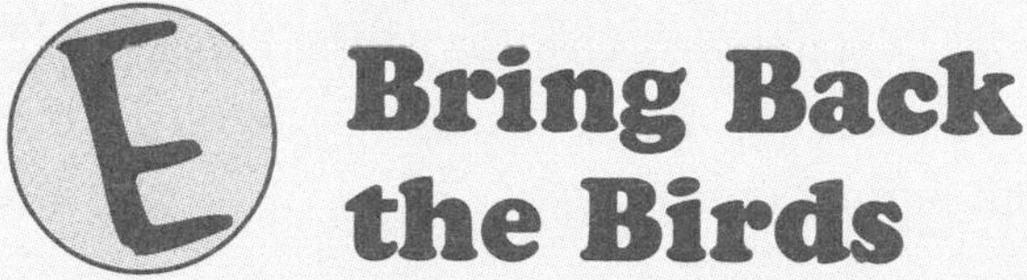

Bring Back the Birds

Whoever said that a person with a small appetite "eats like a bird" obviously never watched our feathered friends at their mealtimes darting, swooping, diving, and catching hundreds of insect pests. Invite birds to your home, and they'll reward you with their singing, flashing color, amusing antics, and hearty appetites, which will help you win the battle with the bugs.

Identify Birds and Their Needs

Old Mother Nature is wise indeed. She designed most songbirds to eat insects. Some species with their enormous appetites can eat several times their weight in insects in a single season. Their capacity to eradicate periodic insect problems is astonishing. Birds have been rightly credited with saving crops, stopping plagues of locusts, and reestablishing natural balance to entire gardens. It stands to reason that the more birds you can attract, the more bugs they will eat. When you help the birds, they will help you, and sing for their supper, too!

Birds Like Variety

Different species eat different things, from seeds to nuts, from weevils to worms. In fact, various species have decidedly distinct appetite preferences. There is no need to become a practicing ornithologist to appreciate our fine-feathered friends, but it helps to know some basics about them, especially their eating habits. It pays to attract birds that eat bugs, not expensive birdseed!

Attend a meeting of a local bird-watching group. Go armed with key questions so you can get answers best suited to your needs and locality, and begin to build your alliance with birds. Some are carnivorous or, more properly, insectivorous. They delight in devouring insects. Other birds are vegetarians. Their diets are made up almost exclusively of seeds and vegetation. Although some are songsters, your focus should be on birds that help you by eating insects, not cost you money for feed. Be pragmatic, unless of course you love all birds!

FACT

Local Audubon Society chapters and nature organizations in your area most likely offer seminars, periodic meetings, and other programs that will give you much more detail about bird populations in your particular area.

Concentrate on attracting the insect-eating birds that repay you best for your hospitality. The incredible appetites of barn swallows, chimney swifts, cliff swallows, house wrens, and flycatchers are notable. You can spot insect eaters by their long, straight or slightly curved bills. Seed-eating birds tend to have stouter, shorter bills for cracking seeds and snapping vegetation.

Watch a swallow or swift aloft. It darts and weaves, swoops and climbs. In a given day, one swallow can gulp a thousand assorted flying and jumping insects on the wing. The ever-busy house wren accounts for hundreds of spiders and caterpillars each day.

Beneficial Birds to Know

Juncos, kinglets, and song sparrows delight in eating scale and other minute insects. Warblers sing for their supper and make quick work of worms and weevils. Scarlet tanagers, vireos, flycatchers, and phoebes are gourmets for moths. Flycatchers and chimney swifts are nature's mosquito-control specialists. Thrashers, meadowlarks, bluebirds, and mockingbirds all do their duty on grasshoppers, worms, caterpillars, and other assorted chewing and sucking insects.

Encourage woodpeckers, too. They will hunt out hidden pests in nooks, beneath bark, or lurking in secluded crevices. They are attracted to suet feeders, which will help you to cultivate their friendship and keep them around your home grounds, busily eating pesky insects.

If you ever see a swarm of grasshoppers on the march, you will likely see a sky full of birds, drawn for a feast. Even the disreputable starling and the cherry-stealing redwing blackbird, as well as others not usually credited with benefits to man, can play a part in pest control. One gardener reports that giant flocks of starlings descend periodically on his lawn, digging up grubs. No birds will eat the adult beetles, but getting rid of the grubs in the lawn means few beetles hatch to destroy valuable roses and berry plants.

Your feathered allies willingly work long hours. With proper encouragement, they will work for you each season. Providing birdhouses, baths, nesting boxes, and shelves is only part of the picture. Habitat is important, too. Hedges, brush piles, and wilderness corners plus wildflower meadows should be part of your bird diplomacy plan.

Look at the total conservation and ecology picture in your landscape as it is now and as you would like it to be. Think with a total environmental improvement plan in mind. Work toward the best balance for the environment in which you live and garden.

Unique Birds Making a Comeback

Purple martins have their own unique requirement: an apartment house. They are picky. It must meet their specifications. Garden centers have these available. Bluebirds also are making a comeback. One of the most beautiful of songbirds, in the past they preferred holes at the tops of old fenceposts, but as farms disappeared, so did old fenceposts. Fortunately, bluebirds now are adjusting, and so are garden centers and bird-watching groups, which have construction plans for bluebird houses or prebuilt ones that have proven successful.

You don't need to be an avid bird-watcher to appreciate the value that birds add to your garden. They please you with music and song in the morning, the antics of fledglings, and a dash of color around your yard. But most important for bird-lovers and pragmatists alike, birds eat bugs by the bushel. Attract them with homes, cultivate their friendship with natural habitats and protection, and they will remain your first line of defense against insect invasions.

Consider Birdbaths, Feeders, and Other Items

Just as we need our homes to raise our families, so do birds. They also like to stay clean and bathe periodically, plus have fresh, clean water even in cold winter weather. Birds naturally look for food and homes and will appreciate your help. When you provide what they need, they'll flock to your home grounds.

Remember that different birds have different habits. Some like to nest

spring

summer

autumn

high. Others prefer low, bushy sites. Hedges are a good starting point. Consider them for borders or property lines, or as screens to hide compost piles, vegetable gardens, garbage cans, or storage areas. Some, like tree swallows, bluebirds, and wrens, like houses. Get to know their needs and you'll win their friendship.

FACT

Hedges and brambles, especially of blackberry bushes and barberry bushes, make good property borders and help keep cats at bay and away from the nests within such thorny hedges. Fortunately, both these bushes grow quickly and thickly.

You have a wide choice of beneficial plants. Most are easily grown in a reasonably sunny location with well-drained soil. Some are quite hardy and thrive despite setbacks of drought or severe winters. You can obtain lists of shrubs, vines, and trees favored by birds from your local County Extension office or state Audubon Society chapter.

Bird-Favored Plants

Aromatic sumac, bayberry, firethorn, and bittersweet are attractive and fruitful for birds. Virginia creeper, barberry, holly, and the American cranberry bush offer abundant food. Of course, some birds will eat your garden berries, but they usually prefer acidic, bitter, or sour fruits.

For specimen planting or groupings, consider autumn olive, mountain ash, ornamental crabapple of all types, and flowering dogwoods. Junipers, yews, and cedars offer refuge and food supplies. Living screens and fences of honeysuckle, roses, multiflora roses, and mulberries are multipurpose, too. They provide privacy, nesting areas, and food.

Remember that birds like variety. Be sure to provide a mix of plantings in your bird-friendly landscape. A few dogwoods against a darker cedar or hemlock windbreak is attractive. Plant low-growing trees and shrubs where they will be set off against a background of taller evergreen trees.

When you plant, aim to achieve the most desirable aspect of good landscaping: a longer season of beauty. Select plants that give you flowering pleasure in spring and summer, plus the bonus of fruit, berries, and/or colorful foliage each fall. Group plants for effects you desire, allowing some specimens to stand alone. Place others in masses or rows.

Birds should be seen as well as heard. Give them some cover near your home, especially near the kitchen, dining room, and bedroom windows. They'll make friends with you faster when you consider their natural shyness. Try vines trained up around windows, or on arbors or trellises, so that the climbing plants can provide a quiet, secluded cover near your house where birds may hide.

Sour cherries, those delights for making cherry pies, are loved by starlings, blackbirds, and catbirds, among others. If you have sour cherries, netting is the only practical answer to stop the birds from eating your pie filling.

Best Bets for Bird Gardening

You have an attractive range of colorful, berried trees and shrubs that look nice and also are favored by birds. Here are some of your potential choices.

American Cranberry

The American cranberry bush attracts thirty or more bird species. This upright, tall shrub has maplelike foliage with showy white flowers in May and June. Glossy scarlet fruit clusters appear in September and may last until May. It likes deep, wet to well-drained soil in sunny to lightly shaded locations. At maturity it will be nearly 20 feet tall.

Autumn Olive

The Autumn olive attracts twenty-five different species of birds and is a valuable addition to your landscaping. Maturing to 20 feet tall, it is a large, spreading shrub with gray-green foliage. The fragrant, small, yellowish blooms appear in May to July. Abundant speckled red fruits ripen in September and may last to February. The cardinal variety is winter hardy in most areas and likes deep, moist soil in sun or light shade.

Bittersweet

Bittersweet is a twining vine with pale green leaves and unique greenish flowers. Bright red berries in yellow husks appear in September and hold through December to attract about ten types of birds. Bittersweet prefers well-drained to dry soil in sun or light shade. In winter, you can cut the stems to create colorful dried indoor decorations.

Crabapples

Crabapples come in many shapes, colors, and sizes ranging from 15 to 25 feet tall. They make a magnificent show in the spring with white, pink, or red blossoms, depending on the variety. Come September, the reddish, orange, or yellow fruits will be available for birds. Choose a moist to dry soil in good sun and you will find that about twenty species of birds will linger on your property.

FACT

To cultivate beneficial birds, get to their needs. The Audubon Society and U.S. Department of Agriculture have useful details about them. Plan to plant bird-attracting shrubs, flowers, trees, vines, and windbreaks. Birds need food, safeguards, and shelter, just as we need our food, clothing, and shelter. Choose flowering shrubs and plants that provide seeds, berries, and/or nuts.

Dogwoods

Dogwood trees, both pink and white, add a profusion of color during spring and fall. They range in size from small shrubs such as Redosier and the Silky dogwood of 10 feet tall to understory trees ranging to 30 feet. Dogwood is a highly ornamental tree with white to reddish blooms from April to June, depending on your area. It thrives in well-drained to dry soil, exposed to moderate sun or shade. By fall, the bunched fruits among the bronze leaves yield a handsome picture and lure more than thirty species of birds.

Holly

Holly is handy for outdoor landscaping and making Christmas decorations, too. Conservationists report some twenty-two bird species are attracted to holly. You have numerous varieties from which to select, in shrub and tree forms, evergreen or the shedding types. Small white blooms appear in spring, with bright red fruits by fall.

Firethorn

Firethorn is a delight. It is a medium-sized shrub with white blooms in June and orange or red berries by September. The berries last until March and add a decorative touch on a wall or side of a garage. Plants prefer moist to well-drained soil with ample sun. You also can espalier firethorn for special effects. Approximately fifteen bird species will frequent these shrubs, which mature to about 15 feet tall.

Hawthorn

Hawthorn has high value for attracting birds. A neighbor counted twenty-five different species visiting his trees, which mature to 20 to 25 feet tall. Pale green toothed leaves make this dome-shaped tree easy to identify. Abundant clusters of white flowers appear from May to June, followed by orange to red fruits in October. Plant hawthorns in deep, moist to dry soil with lots of sun.

You also can add mountain ash, red cedar, and Virginia creeper to your list of desirable trees and vines to attract a host of birds. The red cedar is one tree that has a place for birds but is not usually on birder lists. Often considered a weed tree, the cedar is sometimes found in burned-over areas where grasses and weeds have made a comeback along with sumac and brush of all types.

Ornithologists report that some sixty-eight varieties of birds frequent red cedar. It thrives on moist to dry soil in sun to light shade. The needles of this evergreen tree vary from dense blue-green to light or darker green. Commercial nurseries have several varieties, and they grow rapidly when planted together to make a dense hedge that can screen unsightly views.

Birds like cedar cones, so consider planting a few in a corner of your property where these evergreens can grow to their typical height of 30 to 40 feet.

Birds Like Baths, Too

As you plan bird gardening, remember that birds like to bathe. They also need fresh, cool water to drink. When babies hatch, the parents need a readily available water supply. The closer their food and water supply, the more inclined birds will be to nest and live on your property. Keep water available all season. Place a water tray or bath off the ground with some protection from cats and other predators.

If you have a fountain or sprinkler system that can periodically refresh the water supply, so much the better. Actually, running water attracts birds and it is cleaner than a standing puddle, stagnant birdbath, or other unsuitable source.

Consider Home Sweet Homes

Most birds prefer to build their own nests in bushes or trees where they can hatch and raise their young in seclusion. Yet many other species prefer and will inhabit houses you provide. You can purchase ready-made bird houses, obtain kits to make them, or construct homes with a variety of materials on hand.

Bluebirds, chickadees, flycatchers, flickers, nuthatches, titmice, and wrens are desirable tenants that look for man-made houses. Tree swallows also like houses. Several families will make their homes as a colony in your backyard if you provide sufficient housing for them.

Even owls and the most colorful of all ducks, the wood ducks, can be intrigued into houses that you build. Kestrels also love house homes and will reward you by busily eating their weight in insect pests regularly.

Attract Happy Hummingbirds

Hummingbirds are gaining popular interest. You can help these tiny curious creatures and, with luck, watch their swift, darting flights around the garden. When they come to sip nectar from flowers, they seem almost to hover in place, but their wings beat so quickly they are almost invisible. Garden centers and mail-order firms sell a variety of hummingbird feeders. All that is required is a secluded, sunny area and the time to periodically replenish the sweet sugar solution in the tube. Here's a list of favorite flowers that attract hummingbirds.

Flowers That Attract Hummingbirds

Common Name	Botanical Name
Butterfly Bush	*Buddleia davidii*
Alyssum	*Lobularia maritima*
Bleeding Heart	*Dicentra* "Luxurian"
Butterfly Lily	*Lilum* "Red Butterflies"
Canna	*Canna x generalis*
Delphinium	*Delphinium*
Hostas	Various types
Lilies	Most types
Salvia	*Salvia splendens*
Trumpet Vine	*Campsis radicans*

Other Bird-Attracting Tricks

The more attractive and convenient and safe you make your home grounds, the easier it will be to attract desirable birds. Once you have added some shrubs and trees plus houses for those who prefer them, and have provided access to water, add a few extra welcoming touches.

Hang pieces of twine or old string or slips of torn rags on tree limbs or inside bushes, out of sight. Robins, orioles, bluebirds, and some warblers and mockingbirds will welcome them as nest-building materials. Old wool and hair are favored by wrens, bluebirds, juncos, nuthatches, and some finches.

Leave a puddle around the birdbath before nesting season. Cliff swallows need a source of mud for building their nests. Robins, thrushes, phoebes, swallows, swifts, and grackles also use mud to form their nests.

Barn swallows catch their weight in flying insects daily. It pays to let them nest on a beam inside the garage, shed, or barn. Simply spread a piece of cardboard beneath the nesting spot to catch droppings. When the young have flown away, just add the cardboard and bird droppings to your compost pile.

Once you have convinced valuable songbirds and your flying bug-catching army that you are friendly, they will trust you and raise their young near you. It's up to you to maintain the trust relationship so that they will return from their winter migrations south, to your home bug-hunting grounds generation after generation.

Lure robins with a few nesting shelves around a porch or arbor. A platform 6 inches wide by 8 inches long is sufficient. It helps if it is concealed under a vine, overhanging limb, or the eaves of a building.

Winter Birds

Some birds overwinter in northern areas. The Audubon Society can provide more tips on what special care these species require, so you can help them survive and be ready to nest, raise young, and help you control insect pests next spring. Breadcrumbs and tidbits from the kitchen are often welcomed. Cardinals, chickadees, finches, and juncos will stay around longer if you treat them well. They're also a wonderful sight to behold on wintry days; they add spice and life to the outdoor landscape.

Some birds that stay north in winter need lots of energy to cope with the cold weather. Hang beef suet outdoors when fall weather gets crisp. Chickadees, titmice, and a variety of woodpeckers enjoy this type of hospitality.

Naturally, a supply of birdseed, including a mixture of cracked corn, millet, and sunflower seeds, will keep your bird friends well fed. Place several bird feeders outdoors, either hanging from a branch or on a stout pole or house-mounted rod. Be certain to use a collar around any posts to keep cats, squirrels, and other predators away from the bird-feeding area.

FACT

The new feeders with one-way mirrored reflectors are wonderful on windows. Birds can't see inside, so they will sit and eat busily where you and your family can get some really close-up views of them.

Shrubs with Winter Fruits

Finally, from another veteran gardener and bird lover, here's a handy list of shrubs that bear fruits that will serve as food for birds during the fall and winter.

- Korean Barberry (*Berberis koreana*)
- American Bittersweet (*Celastrus scandens*)
- Thornless Cockspur Hawthorn (*Crataegus crus-galli inermis*)
- Russian Olive (*Elaeagnus angustifolia*)
- Winterberry (*Ilex verticillata*)
- Flowering Crabapple Cultivars (*Malus*)
- European Mountain Ash (*Sorbus aucuparia*)
- Highbush Cranberry (*Viburnum trilobum*)

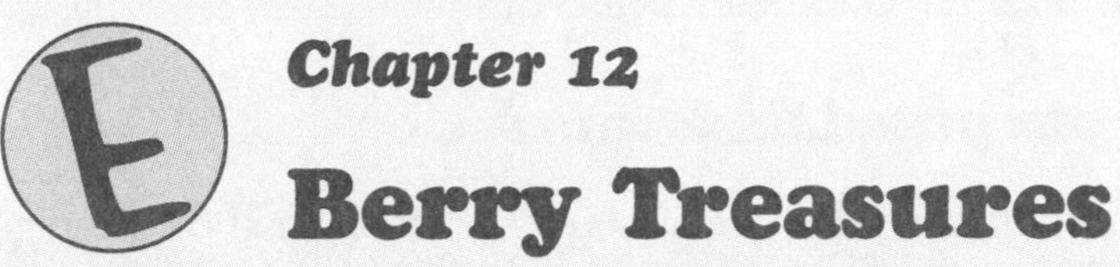

Chapter 12
Berry Treasures

One of the tastiest joys of gardening is the delicious bounty harvested from berried treasures. More gardeners every year are enjoying the mouth-watering goodness of bountiful berries: blackberries, blueberries, grapes, raspberries, strawberries, and even the more exotic elderberries and currants. This chapter will help you harvest buckets of berries from your own land.

Enjoy Berry Tasty Gardens

Dig in today and you can enjoy delicious berries from your own backyard for years to come. It's easier than you think to grow the sweetest strawberries, most bountiful blueberries, ripe red raspberries, and other flavorful treats year after tasteful year. Just a few berry bushes, or rows of strawberries, can yield many quarts of fruit.

Plant Multipurpose Landscapes

You can enjoy the blooms of berry bushes each spring, their fruits in season, and even their fall foliage displays. You also can taste the difference a fruitful landscape makes as you eat your sun-ripened pleasures at their peak of perfection.

Berry bushes offer greater versatility than decorative hedges. Privet hedges may be attractive, but a blueberry hedge can be nearly as dense plus providing its bounty of berries. Where kids, cats, and dogs may wander, a bramble hedge of thorny blackberries may be a perfect property border.

Consider how berry bushes can grace a corner, frame a doorway, or line a path or drive. It has been well said that "good fences make good neighbors." Think how tasteful hedges of berries can be that you share with neighbors as backyard treats. Sharing the cost of planting, tending, and picking can be a neighborly project. If you have a long stretch of wall or fence, try a fruitful planting along it. The natural growth pattern of living hedges breaks up stark lines and adds the tasty advantage of berries in season.

Some veteran gardeners believe that berries should be one of your first landscape investments. Once they're well planted, they'll grow and set permanent, deep rootholds to reward you and your family for many years.

There's no rule that says berries must be planted in a bed. They can do well among other landscape shrubs and trees providing you pick the spot that the various berry plants need to thrive. For example, blueberries prefer acid soil, so they may grow especially well where you have evergreen trees and shrubs.

Strawberries have greater versatility. You can grow them in the ground, in beds, among other flowers, or with vegetables. In addition, they will thrive in barrels or pyramid container planters on porches and patios.

Plant Berries Properly

Prepare soil deeply for your berries since these plants will be permanent parts of your home landscape. Dig or till soil 10 to 12 inches deep. Add compost or composted manure and peat moss if you have heavy, clay soil or sandy soil. For bushes, make holes twice as large as the bare root ball or the roots of container-grown plants.

Pour ½ gallon of water into each hole. Place the plant in the hole carefully to avoid disturbing the roots. Fill the hole half full of soil, tamp down, and water again. Then add the remaining soil, tamp well, and water. Leave a saucer-shaped depression around each berry plant to catch rain. Mulch with compost, grass clippings, rotted leaves, or peat moss. All fruit plants need ample moisture and nutrients, especially as they set fruit.

Because blackberries are hardy and adaptable, you may wish to plant them in the less desirable areas of your land and save the best areas for flowers, shrubs, and other plants that need better soil and site conditions.

As you fertilize your berries, follow the directions for amounts to use on the package of the fertilizer you buy. Too much can be as bad as too little. Pelleted fertilizers are especially useful in bands along berry rows or around plants. Many gardeners today have adopted the foliar feeding system of liquid fertilizers applied by garden hose applicators. This system saves time and gives berry plants the nutrients they need to perform well.

Be Patient with Berries

Americans tend to be impatient people. The immense popularity of fast-food chains proves that people want things handed to them quickly.

That won't work with berries. They will indeed reward you well for many years as perennials, but the first few years of growth after planting may try your patience. As you plan your bountiful berry gardens, remember that berry plants and bushes need a good growing year to set their roots. Most will set only a few berries the first year, and many more the next. Be patient. That's the nature of berry plants. By the third and throughout future years, you'll be amazed what prolific crops they'll bear.

Consider Bountiful Blackberries

To enjoy one of the tastiest berries and have a handsome hedge that grows even in poor-quality soil, consider blackberries. They aren't sold in supermarkets as widely as other berries. In fact, some of the tastiest aren't grown commercially, but you can enjoy the sweet treat of nearly thumb-size blackberries from your land.

Most gardeners remember picking wild blackberries and their thorny canes. Some of the old-time blackberries, such as prolific Darrow blackberries, still bear those thorns. Veteran gardeners swear by them both for true blackberry flavor and also as hedges to thwart wandering neighborhood pets. They also provide thorny bramble shelter for birds.

FACT

Thornless good news for blackberry lovers! Plant breeders have created new blackberry varieties that are thornless, yield huge crops, are vigorous, and are winter hardy in northern states. They also have introduced other varieties that perform well in southern areas. Miller and Stark nurseries both offer the newest blackberries.

Easy Growing Blackberries

Few fruits for the home ground are as dependable in production as blackberries. They prefer temperate climates. Almost any type of soil is suitable for blackberries, provided they can get, or you provide, ample moisture, especially at fruiting time for the juiciest, plumpest berries with high sugar content. They do best when given better soil and growing conditions, of course. Sandy loams are ideal since blackberry roots may penetrate 2 to 3 feet deep. Clay soils restrict root growth and consequently the yield.

Try to shelter all berries from prevailing winds. Some types can take more cold than others, but if you have the windbreak of a house, garage, fence, or trees, blackberries appreciate that consideration. As with all fruits, avoid pockets or low areas where frost gathers and water stands in winter. Blackberries love sun but actually can perform reasonably well in partially shaded areas.

You can select either upright blackberries or more trailing varieties. Uprights are superior. They are more productive, respond well to cultivation, and produce vigorous growth and bountiful harvests. Erect bushes have arched, self-supporting canes. You can train them to arbors much as you would train grapevines.

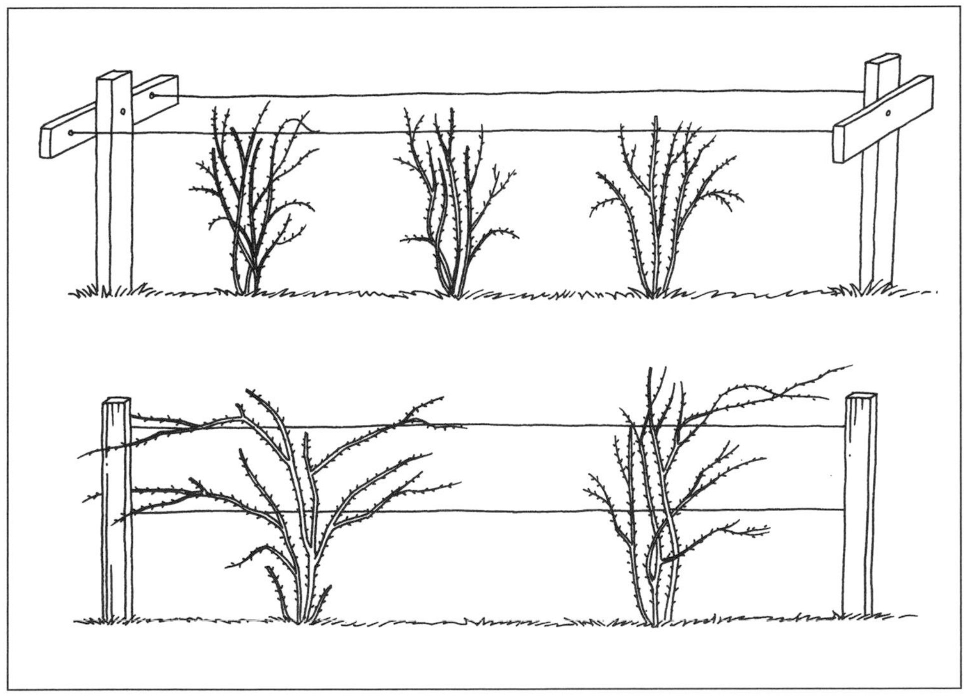

▲ To control blackberries, use two parallel wires or tie canes to wires placed one over the other.

Several other culture methods work well, too. You can allow blackberries to spread into a thick hedge to border a backyard. Or, they can be guided to grow upright between two horizontal wires strung side by side between posts.

Blackberry Varieties

With renewed interest in blackberries, nurseries are offering several excellent varieties. The berries certainly are much bigger and sweeter than wild types. Here are some varieties worth trying.

Alfred was developed in Michigan, is early, and has large, firm, sweet berries on vigorous, productive bushes. It is adapted to northern areas with climates similar to that in Michigan. Darrow has been a standout. It is so superior to the others that some nurseries have dropped old-time varieties in favor of Darrow and other new ones. This variety is particularly noteworthy for its vigor, heavy production, firmness, and quality of the fruit. The plants are hardier, too. Berries may be 1 or more inches long and glossy black. You also will enjoy a long harvest season and may need to pick berries several times over several weeks.

FACT

The Illini hardy blackberry was developed and patented by the University of Illinois and is recommended for northern areas. It is hardier, more vigorous, and more abundant in crops of top-quality fruit than most others. Tests show it fruited 8 years in a row after temperatures to –23°F. It ripens mid- to late July and is easy to maintain.

Chester Thornfree is an introduction from the U.S. Department of Agriculture. Thornfree is a rarity of nature. The fruits are almost replicas of Illini except for their tangy-tart flavor. The nicest part is that you can harvest quarts of berries and not be torn by thorns. Plants will not sucker, and they do best when held upright with stakes. Triple Crown thornless is another flavorful variety with large berries on semierect plants and ripens mid- to late July.

Blackberry Planting Tips

Although blackberries will perform in poorer soils, they welcome additions of organic matter. Nurseries sell rooted cuttings that may be 6 to 8 inches long and 1/4 inch in diameter, but more vigorous rooted plants 12 to 15 inches long are better and root faster. Most varieties send out underground suckers to establish a sturdy, thick bed of plants.

You can plant blackberries anytime during the dormant season, but early spring is best. Most do need room to ramble and spread as they send out their underground runners.

Blackberries become deep rooted, so dig or till the bed 10 to 14 inches deep and add compost or organic matter to improve soil. When the area is ready, set blackberry root pieces 3 to 4 feet apart in the rows. Follow directions from your supplier and the general berry planting tips in this chapter. If you are planting double rows, keep them 6 feet apart to allow for enough space between them to cultivate and pick.

If you have wild blackberry bushes on your property, eliminate them before planting cultivated varieties. Native wild plants may be resistant to diseases but do harbor them, and these can then be transmitted to domesticated varieties.

After planting, tamp soil around rootstocks and water periodically for the first few weeks to be sure the dormant rootstocks set out their roots properly. Try planting blackberries as a corner planting or as part of a meadow garden. Blackberries are one of the easiest berries to grow, so give them a happy start and you'll have years of pleasure from them.

Tips on Blackberry Pruning

To control blackberries and encourage better fruit production, proper pruning is helpful. If you want merely a large bramble patch, forego extensive pruning. Crowns of blackberry plants are perennial. New canes arise from them each year. The canes are biennial. They live only 2 years. During the first year after planting, allow your plants to bush out. The second year you'll find new suckers filling in the open spots and new canes sprouting from the crowns.

During these years, blackberry canes send out laterals, also called side branches. The second year, small branches grow from buds on these laterals, which are the fruiting wood. That makes pruning a simple procedure. Just prune laterals back each spring after the second year to about 12 inches long. Come summer, when harvest is done, cut out the old canes and let the new wood grow because it produces next year's fruit.

When erect blackberry plants reach 40 inches tall, cut off their top tips. This forces canes to branch and become denser plants with more fruit production.

▲ Blackberry bush—unpruned (left), pruned (right).

Try True Blueberries

You can enjoy the best blueberry pie, muffins, and pancakes with true blueberries picked from bushes in your own backyard. Many prolific blueberry varieties are available today. Fact is, blueberries give you more fruit for less effort than other bush berries. They also serve well as ornamental shrubs, producing bell-shaped flowers every spring and clusters of berries each summer.

By choosing early to late-ripening varieties, you can stretch your tastier living season over several months. Some varieties are best for fresh use, others for pies and preserves, while others are conveniently multipurpose. Nursery catalogs provide helpful guides to each variety's uses.

Special Blueberry Needs

Blueberries have special requirements. They prefer loose, well-aerated, somewhat acid soil. It should be about 4.8 to 5.0 pH for best results. You can provide what blueberries need by adding acid fertilizer and mulching with acid-inducing oak leaves, pine needles, rotted manure, and leaf mulch.

Blueberries have a hairlike, fine root filament system, so you should prepare soil a year in advance if possible. Turn under compost, manure, peat moss, oak, and maple leaves to produce a light, fluffy, acid soil condition. Buy 2-year-old stock because this has better root development for a more successful adjustment to your home grounds.

The best planting time is early spring as soon as the ground can be worked. Space plants so they have room to grow to fullest size, about 4 feet apart in rows or groups as part of a landscape design.

FACT

Blueberry bushes can be interplanted among azaleas; rhododendrons; and various pine, fir, or spruce shrubs. As long as they have the acid soil they love, they will prosper and add appeal to conventional landscape shrubbery.

For each new plant, dig an area about 2 feet in diameter and 6 inches deep. Then carefully spread the hairlike roots at or close to the soil surface and cover with topsoil that contains extra organic matter or compost. Mulch with compost, peat moss, pine straw, or oak leaves to prevent weeds and add acidity to the soil.

You may wish to try fall planting with 2- to 3-year-old plants, but be sure to prepare soil well and mulch plants. Always keep their fragile root structure moist. Don't tamp soil as you would for most other plants. Pat it into place, leaving it fairly loose. The fine roots need extra care and protection when planting. Once well rooted, blueberries will give you years of productive yields.

Blueberries are especially thirsty plants. They are grown commercially in sandy soil areas that have abundant moisture, such as southern New Jersey. However, the plants can't abide constantly wet feet. Too much water clogs air spaces and rots roots. Conversely, because they have such a fine, fibrous root structure, they need adequate moisture at all times, especially when setting fruit.

Blueberry Varieties

Some varieties to consider include Earliblue, a vigorous, upright plant that produces clusters of large, firm berries. Blue Ray is vigorous, somewhat spreading, with smaller, tight clusters of firm, light blue berries. Colville is productive, with medium berries. Blue Crop and Berkeley are other midseason varieties. Misty, Jubilee, and Top Hat are three exceptional varieties featured by Stark Bros. Ivanhoe, Atlantic, and Herbert are top-producing varieties from Miller Nurseries that are compact-size plants that have big yields. Herbert is a September-bearing variety.

Northblue and Northsky are two fine varieties developed by the University of Minnesota for northern gardeners. Bluecrop and Jersey are incredible edible hedge-type blueberries. Today you can even use a cultivated version of the Maine wild blueberry as a carpet or ground cover. Brunswick Dwarf is another low grower that forms mats of glossy green foliage and pea-size berries, according to Raintree Nursery.

One drawback is that blueberries are attractive to birds, too. You may find that cheesecloth netting is needed to thwart the birds during the time berries ripen. That's a small price to pay for bountiful harvests of these sweet treats.

Bear with Blueberries, Too

Be patient with your blueberries the first 2 years as they set their roots. Don't expect much of a crop, no matter what variety you plant. Blueberries take their own sweet time to set their roots, but remember that once they do, they'll reward you for decades. You'll be amazed at the blue bounty they'll provide by the third and fourth year—and for years to come.

Grapes Are Great

Grapes fit into just about any landscape plan. You can grow them on a fence, along a wall, or on a trellis. Because they are vines, they'll climb at will to save ground space and let you garden in the sky.

You can grow grapes in almost any part of the country as long as you select proper varieties for your area. Generally they prefer lots of sun, well-drained soil, and good air circulation, which is more important with grapes than with other plants. Your choice of white, red, blue, and green grapes for fresh eating, preserving, and even home wine making seems almost endless. You'll find a wide range of varieties in mail-order catalogs, especially from Raintree, Stark, and Miller nurseries.

Some Southern Varieties

Among blue-black types are Van Buren, with vigorous vines; Fredonia, a Concord-type for midseason; and Mars Seedless, which is high yielding. White varieties include Himrod, Interlaken, and Seneca. Reds includes Carlos, Magnolia, Fry, and Hunt. In the deep south, Flame Seedless and Blue Lake handle heat well and produce nicely.

Some Northern Varieties

For climates similar to the famed Great Lakes commercial grape-growing region, good home varieties include Niagara, with large, compact bunches; red Delaware; blue Concord; and red Catawba. Dozens of other varieties offer taste treats well beyond what you can find in typical supermarket selections. That's another solid reason to add grapes and other fruits to home landscapes. You get a much wider choice of delightfully different flavors than you'll ever find among standard supermarket grapes or other berries.

Pick Grape Site Right

Grapes are sturdy, stubborn, and amazingly long-lived plants. Give them the right location and your family can have grapes for generations to come. Grapes can withstand drought and cold. They can succeed even in quite rocky, seemingly infertile soil. However, if you give them better growing conditions, they'll reward you faster and with more bountiful, tastier yields.

Good full sun and adequate air circulation are basic conditions. Grapes like well-drained soil in an area free from frost pockets. Pick a higher area of your property for growing grapes so spring frosts won't nip buds and ruin a year's crop.

The best, most common use of grapes is along an existing fence or special trellis. They are ideal for a property or boundary marker, adding privacy, screening undesirable views, and even providing a leafy canopy overhead for summer picnics. A 2′ × 4′ or wire fence or support system will provide the support they need for good growth and sunlight for crops.

Grape-Planting Pointers

Once established, grapevines seem to last forever. But they can try your patience in their initial slowness to get started. Prepare your planting spot in the fall. Till or spade deeply because grapes will be growing in that spot for years, and they deserve a well-prepared homesite. Improve the soil by adding compost and well-rotted manure to the soil. If it is heavy clay soil, add sand and compost or peat to improve it. Test the pH and add lime if you must neutralize an acid soil.

Select vigorous 1-year-old plants or order from a nursery. For a much better start, try 2-year-olds; they cost more, but most grape growers say they are worth the investment. Place vines 4 to 6 feet apart along a fence or where you plan a grape arbor or trellis growing system. Spread roots in a 15- to 18-inch-deep hole and place vines at the same depth as they grew in the nursery.

Add soil and firm around roots. Tamp it down well. It helps to shake the plant gently to settle soil around roots. Then tamp down again and add water and more soil. Fill remaining space and leave a saucer-shaped basin around the newly set plant. This lets rainwater collect to help the vine get started right. Water newly planted vines regularly until they are well started. Then, give them 1 inch of water every week, especially at fruiting time, to encourage the plumpest, sweetest grapes.

FACT

Check and plant at the soil mark on the vine and also keep the graft point of grafted grapes above the soil level. Any suckers or sprouts that appear from below the graft union are undesirable and should be pruned off.

Grapes need proper fertilizing, too. Read and follow the directions on the brand of fertilizer that you purchase. It pays to buy fertilizer blended in the proper formulation for fruiting crops. Usually a complete NPK fertilizer that has a higher *P* component is best for flower and fruit production.

Rich, Ripe Raspberries

Raspberry tarts, raspberry jam, and raspberry pie can be yours from the rich, ripe raspberries you can grow productively in your own backyard. You can grow them in beds, berry patches, or along property lines. They thrive in almost any type of soil, so you can grow them in areas not suited for more selective crops. Red raspberries have upright growth and form thickets by sending out underground runners that produce new plants to fill in the rows. They prefer full sun.

Planting Raspberry Tips

Plant rooted raspberry canes by opening soil or digging a hole, spreading roots, and firming soil over them. Space red varieties 3 to 4 feet apart in rows 6 to 8 feet apart. Remove old, dead canes and top

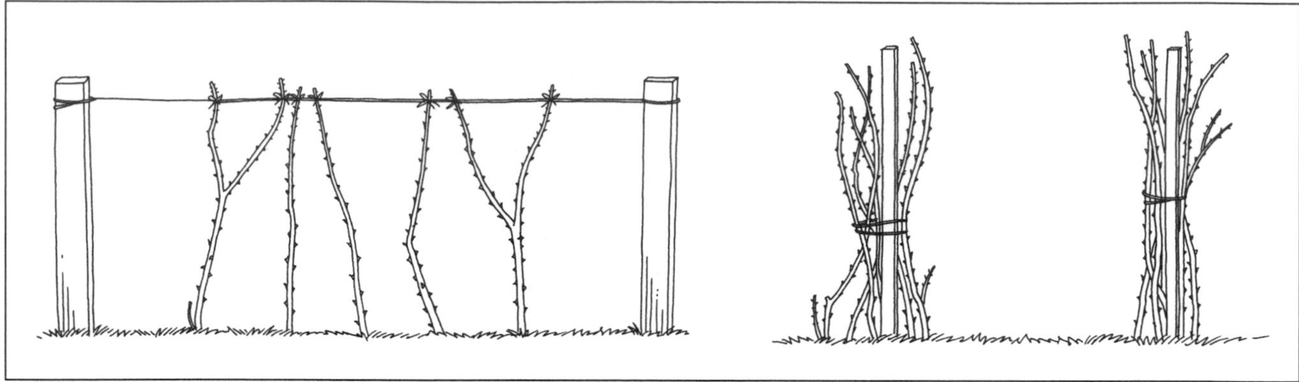

▲ Pruning for red raspberries in hedgerows and in hills.

back tall ones each year to force new side branches that bear the berries that are borne on second-year canes.

Old-time favorite raspberries may bear early, mid-, or late season. Improved new varieties offer two crops a year, one in the spring, another in the fall. Raspberries are shallow rooted, so if you cultivate rather than mulch for weed control, do it lightly to avoid damaging roots.

Never use chemical weed controls on fruit plantings. Not only will this distort the taste, but it can be dangerous to your body. No one would choose to eat chemicals, so why put them on fruits?

Raspberry Varieties

Raspberry plants are winter-hardy and produce moderate summer crops, followed by a prolific fall crop of medium-size berries. Plant breeders have created many disease-resistant and highly productive new varieties. Latham, Sunrise, and Southland are earlier varieties. Citadel and Comet bear later. Hilton is one of the largest, with long, conical, firm berries ripening in midseason. Taylor plants are tall and hardy, with firm, sweet berries. August Red begins producing in July and yields to September. Heritage bears a small late-June crop but a big yield of bountiful berries from September to frost.

Many sweet new varieties are being introduced. A few new varieties begin bearing early and continue right up to frost. Check the latest introductions in catalogs and try different types. Improvements are being made to taste, length of bearing season, and hardiness, so comparisons are useful to find even more productive varieties that keep you well supplied with even sweeter berries than any supermarket can ever provide.

Sweetest Strawberries

Think mouth-watering strawberry shortcake, jam, and strawberry-rhubarb pie. You can enjoy them all with plump, sun-ripened strawberries picked from your own yard. Strawberries are the most productive of any berries. They can be grown in any fertile, well-drained soil with ample sun. Slopes are good. Avoid low areas where frost may settle to nip spring blooms and kill fruit set. You can edge a walk, interplant with flowers, or even grow them in tubs and strawberry barrels on a porch or patio. Space strawberries in garden rows or beds 12 inches apart.

Be careful that the crowns—that point where roots grow down and leaves sprout up—are right at the soil surface. Strawberries are very sensitive to improper planting depth. Too deep or too shallow and the plants just won't set roots right.

Spread roots well. Keep them moist while planting. When plants take root, they will send out runners the first year and parent plants may yield a few berries. They'll bear larger crops the second and third year. After that, cut back or remove older plants. Let new plants, born from runners, become the bearing ones in future years.

Strawberries need periodic renovation. Fortunately, the older plants send out runners to establish young, healthy plants for future, tasty crops. Keep beds well mulched to stop weeds, retain soil moisture, and act as a cushion for a clean berry crop. Remember that all fruit plants need ample moisture and nutrients to perform well, especially as they set fruit.

Plan to add 1 inch of water each week and a bit more during dry periods to ensure plump, sweet fruit.

Using several varieties lets you pick berries very early, in midseason, and late. You may even grow everbearing varieties that begin with small crops in spring and continue producing luscious strawberries right up to frost. Be the envy of your neighborhood. Grow and enjoy tasty strawberries all season long.

Currants and Other Berries

Currants, gooseberries, elderberries, and dewberries are other fruitful options you may wish to try, depending on where you live. Check with local authorities as to whether you can grow these berries in your state. Most fruit catalogs provide such details.

Check mail-order catalogs before ordering currants and gooseberries. Since their cultivation is not allowed by law in certain states, the nurseries won't ship to those states.

Planting Pointers

Currants and gooseberries need a cool, moist, and somewhat shady location. They are bushes, and they can be planted to fill in property borders or as groupings in corners. They also do well interplanted with other flowering shrubs along a shady side of your house. These plants are shallow rooted and prefer moist soil as they set fruit. They grow best in deep, fertile loam and can do well in heavier soils.

Domestic elderberries are now available that far surpass in sturdiness, abundance of crop, and flavor any of the wild varieties that many people had harvested from wild elderberry bushes along streams and lake banks for years. Nova and New York 21 and York are good varieties. More are being introduced, so shop wisely for the best. They do well in moist areas along streams or areas where other plants won't prosper.

Elderberries like sunny locations and will grow rather tall—4 to 6 feet with a spreading habit—so a spot 8 to 10 feet in diameter will accommodate two bushes nicely. Pruning is easy. Just cut back to keep them from outgrowing their allotted area.

FACT

Elderberries are not self-fruitful, so you'll need two different varieties planted near each other to cross-pollinate and ensure good fruit set.

Dewberries Are Nice

Dewberries, called boysenberries in some areas, have a trailing habit and will crawl along the ground, on slopes, or even climb a trellis with a bit of help. They are relatives of the trailing blackberry. These prefer well-drained soil in a sunny spot. Because they are shallow rooted, plant carefully and mulch to control weeds or just lightly weed so you don't disturb plant roots.

Mail-Order Nursery Notes

Many mail-order nurseries offer a variety of berry bushes. Stark Bros., Miller Nurseries, and Raintree Nursery are the three major firms that provide a wide range of varieties. You may find good berry varieties at local nurseries, and that's helpful because they will have been grown in your area and acclimated to your climate and soil situations.

Get some catalogs from key mail-order firms that specialize in berries and fruit trees. They have many useful tips and bits of advice, plus lots of worthwhile information about different varieties and new, improved types being introduced. Your local nursery may be able to order special varieties for you since these national nurseries continue to expand their distribution to local garden centers and other outlets. This year, plant some berried treasures. They will reward you abundantly year after year.

Chapter 13

Enjoy Fruit Tree Delights

Nothing really beats sun-ripened fruit, plucked at its juiciest from a tree in your own backyard. The varieties available to you are truly treats that you will seldom find in supermarkets. Dig in, start your own orchard, and enjoy more fruitful gardening.

Fruitful Landscaping

Fruit trees are versatile. They can be specimens, growing by themselves or in attractive groups. They add a decorative value as well as tastier living benefits to your home grounds. Realtors report that a home mini-orchard is one of those assets that captures the eye of prospective home buyers. That could be useful if you sell your home someday.

Pick a Size

To enjoy the most naturally fresh flavor, begin to landscape fruitfully this year. You have a choice of standard, semidwarf, or even dwarf fruit trees. These smaller trees fit nicely into limited space, and they do bear full-size fruit.

Tall standard fruit trees, usually maturing at 20 to 40 feet tall, provide shade plus beautiful spring blooms and a fruitful harvest. Semidwarf trees, which grow to 6 to 15 feet tall, are easier to maintain and bear full-size fruits. Dwarf trees, which mature to about 6 feet tall, are grafted fruit trees that take even less space.

Many delicious varieties of apples, cherries, peaches, and pears that you won't find in supermarkets are available for home mini-orchards. They offer flavorful tastes you can't find elsewhere.

Give Trees a Favored Spot

As you plan your fruitful landscape, pick a sunny spot so trees receive 8 hours of sun each day to thrive and produce the sweetest natural sugars in the fruit.

Local nurseries can advise you as to which varieties are best for your area. In addition, you can harvest a wealth of valuable information in catalogs from such top mail-order specialty nurseries as Stark Bros., Raintree, and Miller, which feature berries and fruit trees. The catalogs provide a wide choice of truly tasty fruit varieties for growing more delicious home gardens than you can usually find anywhere else.

Be aware that these leading firms also have begun to make their stock available through local nurseries. If you see something you like in a catalog and wish to work with your local garden center or nursery, ask them if they can order what you prefer. You'll also find the Web sites of these key firms in Appendix B.

FACT

To ensure tastier living all season long, select varieties that ripen early, mid-, and late season. You then can have sweet eating from those early-ripening varieties right through to those that naturally ripen at the end of the summer and into early fall.

Appealing Apples

Apples are as American as apple pie. Instead of common store-bought apples, you have a wide variety of apples you can grow in your home orchard. Northern Spy, Jonathan, Arkansas Black, and even exotic apples like Winter Banana are available from mail-order nurseries. Focus on varieties that will bear in early summer, late summer, early fall, and later for good eating all season.

Whichever variety you prefer, remember that plant breeders also have developed productive varieties that are resistant to common diseases. Focus on those to save time and reduce the need for sprays. Some new varieties being introduced have bred-in disease resistance. They also retain the flavorful taste that made them popular. Plant breeders continue to develop even better apples, so let your taste buds guide you to new delights.

Favored Apples

For early eating, Lodi, Summer Rambo, and Grimes Golden are good. These are attacked less by insects and disease than varieties that ripen later. Prima ripens midseason with a dark red color on a yellow background. Macoun, also midseason, is a red-striped apple with crisp white flesh. Starkspur Golden yields especially flavorful fruit, bears more heavily than others, and is available as a semidwarf-size tree.

Redfree is bright red, resistant to apple scab and other problems, has a sweet, pleasant flavor for fresh use, and stores well in the refrigerator. It ripens in early August. Jonafree is an improved, bright red apple that resists diseases. Especially hardy, it ripens in mid-September. Grimes Gold is a rugged, hardy, disease-resistant variety that is tasty fresh and makes great applesauce. Yellow colored, it ripens in mid- to late September.

Empire has the sweetness of the Delicious type combined with the flavor of McIntosh. Highly productive, it resists problems and ripens mid-September. Liberty is another extra-disease-resistant McIntosh type with huge crops ready to harvest in late September. Granny Smith is a superb apple that resists cedar rust and diseases. It ripens in early November, has a tart flavor, and stays fresh in cold storage for several months.

FACT

If you like apples but live in warmer climates, take heart. Tropical Beauty was discovered in South Africa and has proven to be successful in warm areas, including Florida and Hawaii. It produces medium-size, carmine-red fruit with a mild flavor.

Different Taste Apples Worth Trying

Consider growing apples that will astound your family and friends. They offer taste appeal far beyond anything you'll find in supermarkets. Calville Blanc is the variety that is highest in vitamin C, a tender, sweet, and spicy apple excellent for sauces and desserts. Chenango Strawberry is great for eating or cooking. The fruit is long, conical, yellow with red stripes, and has the unusual ability to ripen over several weeks in September. The Duchess of Oldenberg is a tart, greenish to pale yellow apple with red stripes that ripens in August and is very hardy because it originated in Russia.

To be different, you can try growing Sheepnose, a Black Gilliflower that originated in the late 1700s. It has large, ribbed fruit that is deep black-red when ripe and a prize for baking or dessert. Sops of Wine is one of the oldest apples known. It originated in medieval England and is highly regarded for cooking and apple wine. There are dozens more, but Spitzenburg deserves note. It is Thomas Jefferson's favorite apple, one of the finest for eating and cooking. Fruit is bright orange, and it is a good keeper that ripens in late October.

Enjoy the Charm of Cherries

Sweet or sour, cherries have their own special charm. Modern breeding has produced many improved varieties. Cherry trees grow to medium height, between the size of standard peach and apple trees. They bloom earlier than most fruits. Their graceful shape, bountiful spring blossoms, and fruitful yields make them useful landscape additions.

Cherry Tips

Be sure that you select several varieties so that your trees achieve the proper cross-pollination to set fruit. Most fruit trees are not self-fruitful.

Sour cherry varieties pollinate themselves. They make better tarts and pies, but also are preferred by birds. Birds, it seems, like tart fruit rather than sweet fruit. Plastic netting solves that problem easily. Cherries prefer growing conditions suitable for peaches: full sun, well-drained sandy loam, and protection from prevailing winds.

Sweet cherry trees grow larger with upright growth and are tastier for eating fresh, but they have one disadvantage: They are not self-fruitful. You must grow two compatible varieties so they cross-pollinate to set fruit crops.

Tasty Cherry Samples

You don't have as many varieties among cherries as you do apples, but you can bet that what you grow will provide flavors better than standard supermarket types. Try Emperor Francis, which is among the best sweet cherries, with large fruit that resists cracking. Trees are vigorous, productive, and bear yellow-skinned cherries early. Napoleon is a high-quality yellow cherry, while Stella is a large, dark red type.

Among the best sour cherries for pie, jam, and tarts are Montmorency, Meteor, North Star, and Mesobi. All are relatively cold tolerant. Kristin is a proven winter-hardy variety from Norway to windswept Montana. Cherries are large, meaty, and firm, and with their winter hardiness, a sure winner for all gardeners in northern climates.

Dwarf North Star is another hardy cherry with an extra advantage. Trees mature at 6 to 8 feet tall, so picking is easy. It is a cross between a hardy Siberian cherry and the well-known English Morello, with very large, clear, bright red cherries.

Peaches Are Peachy

Peaches have gained wide popularity since the early Spanish explorers brought them here. Today, vastly improved, disease-resistant trees make them tasty favorites. You can even grow hardy peach varieties in northern areas because superb varieties have been perfected in Michigan and Canada.

Although peach trees can survive cold, their flowering buds are more tender than those of other fruit trees. Proper site selection is vital. Peaches love sun. Choose a spot with well-drained soil that gets full sun. Avoid frost pockets or areas punished by strong prevailing winds. The best site is a protected, sheltered, sunny area warmed by day and shielded from extremes of wind or frosty night air.

If you live in colder, northern areas, be certain to select the varieties that are noted and recommended for their winter hardiness. Your local garden centers may have some special varieties that have proven best for your area.

Every year, more new and improved peach varieties are being introduced. Here are some old, reliable varieties. You can begin with a selection of these and add others that are introduced in the years ahead.

Candor, Collins, Brighton, Harbinger, and Garnet Beauty are very early-maturing, delicious types. Prairie Dawn, Reliance, Redhaven, and Raritan Rose bear later. For midseason, you can pick Trigem, Eden, Glohaven, or Vanity. You can also think about the mouth-watering goodness of nectarines. These grow in the same type of soils, climates, and conditions as peaches.

Pick Perfect Pears

Pears are not as widely grown in home landscapes as they deserve to be. They are less troubled by most common diseases and insects than other fruits are. Once established, they require less pruning and care to produce abundant harvests.

Pears offer markedly different flavors and a range of texture, size, and shape as well. When you select varieties, remember that some are self-pollinating; others are not. Usually you need two varieties so they cross-pollinate to ensure adequate fruit set.

You'll also discover that many of the tastiest pears aren't in supermarkets because they are too tender to be handled and shipped well. That gives you a delicious opportunity to demonstrate your pear-growing prowess to family, friends, and neighbors. Think about the pleasure you can give when you present these exceptional treats.

Moonglow bears early. Trees are vigorous and upright, with large juicy fruits for eating fresh or for cooking. Magness bears late on spreading trees. Fruit is oval and of medium size, with a soft, very juicy, sweet taste. Seckel pears mature late on vigorous trees. They are very productive, yielding small, smooth fruit with white to slightly yellow flesh, which is aromatic and spicy. They also store well and longer than most pears. Bosc also ripens late. These large pears with dark yellow undercolor and fine russet vein have white, aromatic, tender flesh.

FACT

Pears, unlike most other fruits, should be picked "hard ripe" on the tree and allowed to reach their peak of flavor perfection off the tree. If pears begin to drop, you have missed the best time to pick them for the finest flavor.

Bartlett is a superior pear for fresh use. Trees bear large, golden yellow pears early and abundantly. Clapps Favorite looks similar but has pale lemon-yellow fruit with a bright pink cheek. Tyson is an early ripening sugar pear that is blight resistant. It is recommended for northern and central areas. Comice is a premium pear, the kind you see in fruit gift baskets—long, golden, blushed with red. Kieffer is a winter pear for all areas.

Plum Dandy Fruit

Plums are more easily grown in more parts of America than practically any other fruit tree. For one reason, you have a greater selection of species and varieties. Some can tolerate extreme cold, while others prefer warmer climates. Their small tree size lets you enjoy plums both as decorative landscape accents and for their abundant fruits.

Five Types of Plums

There are five basic plum groups, descended from European plum families. The Prune group provides plums that can be picked and dried with the pit intact. Green Gage plums are identified by round fruit with yellow, green, or reddish flesh, which is sweet and juicy. Yellow Egg plums are mainly commercial canning types. Imperatrice plums include most of the blue-colored ones that bear heavily, yielding medium-size, oval-shaped fruit with firm flesh. Lombard type plums are reddish, smaller, and somewhat lower in quality.

American and Japanese plums also are available now. The Japanese plums are especially attractive in blooming habit. However, generally speaking, the European plums have the best flavor and offer the widest selection of varieties.

Pick Plums to Taste

You can find many more plum varieties than most gardeners realize exist. As plums have gained popularity, nurseries have begun looking for new types to grow and introduce for American gardens. Here are some of the delights available for starters.

In colder areas, Mount Royal is good for dessert or jam and survives even icy Canadian winters. For warmer areas, Abundance is a heavy yielder of large, cherry red fruits.

Montfort is an old French blue plum with dark purple, juicy fruit. French Damson is vigorous, productive, and yields large plums, good for preserves, too. Green Gage is a favorite, with medium-size yellow-green fruit mottled with red, ideal for dessert. Leaton Gage bears quality plums on vigorous trees.

Fruit Tree Planting

Fruit trees do best when they receive full sun, have well-drained loamy soil, and are sheltered from strong prevailing winds. Since trees are permanent parts of your home landscape, dig deeply to prepare soil well for proper planting. If you have poor soil, add well-rotted manure, peat moss, or composted humus to improve growing conditions. Mix a bucket of compost or composted manure with each bucket of soil for a good fertile mix to give trees the best possible start.

Young trees can be swayed by winds and storms. It pays to give them some support for their first year or two as they set their own roothold in the ground. After 3 to 5 years, remove all stakes and guys on young trees.

Planting Essentials

Some trees are sold balled and burlapped, others in containers. Mail-order trees usually arrive bare-rooted, wrapped in moist moss. Plant them immediately. Make the hole at least twice as large as the root ball. Spread bare roots well. Pour a bucket of water into the hole. Place the root ball of container or burlap-wrapped trees carefully in the hole and fill halfway with soil mixture. Tamp it down and water well, with about half a bucket of water. Then, fill the hole with the remaining soil, tamp down to remove air pockets, and add another half bucket of water.

Leave a saucer-shaped depression around each tree to catch rain or irrigation water. Mulch around each tree with leaves, compost, peat moss, or grass clippings to smother weeds and help soil hold moisture better. Prune off any broken branches. Water weekly, with at least 1 inch of water, so your tree can send out new feeding roots and set a firm roothold in its new home.

Fruit Tree Spacing Guide and Bearing Age

Fruit Trees	Planting Distance	Mature Height	Bears Years After Planting
Apples (s/d)	12 × 12 feet	12 to 15 feet	2 years
Apples (S)	35 × 35 feet	20 to 25 feet	3 to 10 years
Apricots (d)	10 × 10 feet	8 to 10 feet	2 years
Apricots (S)	20 × 20 feet	15 feet	3 years
Cherry, Sour (d)	10 × 10 feet	8 feet	2 years
Cherry, Sour (S)	20 × 20 feet	20 feet	3 years
Cherry, Sweet (S)	25 × 25 feet	30 feet	3 to 4 years
Peach/Nectarine (d)	10 × 10 feet	8 to 10 feet	2 years
Peach/Nectarine (S)	20 × 20 feet	20 feet	3 years
Pears (s/d)	12 × 12 feet	12 to 15 feet	2 years
Pears (S)	20 × 20 feet	25 to 30 feet	3 to 4 years
Plums (d)	10 × 10 feet	8 to 10 feet	2 years
Plums (S)	20 × 20 feet	20 feet	3 years

S = Standard size, s/d = semidwarf size, d = dwarf-size.

Tree Care Considerations

If you have purchased a high-quality tree from a reputable local nursery or mail-order fruit specialists, pruning and fertilization will not be needed for the first full growing season. But do follow the directions that come with your plants. Some nurseries provide specific care details for their particular plants that should be followed. Trees need time to react and adjust to their new growing site. You should not add fertilizers, especially ones high in nitrogen, or do any pruning except for removal of declining or dying branches. After the first growing season, you can use a fertilization program.

Checklist for Fruit Tree Success

To achieve success growing fruit trees, follow this handy checklist.

- ☐ Choose trees that are right for the available space. For small yards, plant dwarf varieties that can be planted just 6 feet apart.
- ☐ Plant your trees as quickly as possible to avoid transplant shock.
- ☐ Mulch trees immediately after planting in spring to preserve soil moisture and stop weeds.
- ☐ Stake your trees immediately after planting.
- ☐ Check with local experts or your local extension agent to identify localized pests.
- ☐ When planting in the fall, wrap tree trunks with tree guards to prevent rodent damage and sunscald. Remove this barrier in mid-May each year.
- ☐ During the first few years, prune very lightly and remove only competing limbs.
- ☐ Fertilize your young trees with proper nutrients from the mail-order firms that have special starter fertilizer materials.

Never put fertilizers in the hole when you plant your tree. That can seriously burn or damage young tree roots. To improve soil condition, you can combine compost and well-rotted manure with the topsoil for filling the hole, but never any fertilizer.

Chapter 14

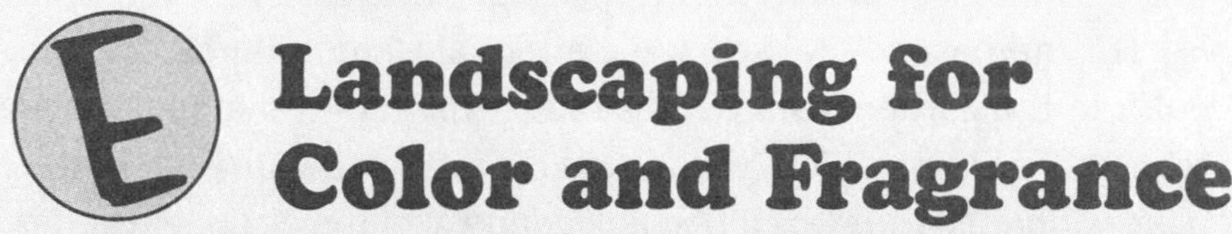

Landscaping for Color and Fragrance

As you plan your landscape vistas this year, think in many ways beyond the usual colors. Consider fragrance, ease of care, and especially color for dramatic effects. You'll surprise yourself as you expand your mind's horizons into new garden vistas for years to come.

Quick Tips on Color

There is a wide variety of colors out there—all you have to do is choose some. Easier said than done. Once you are faced with so many, it's hard to narrow it down. Take a trip to your local garden center and flip through magazines and mail-order catalogs. See what's out there and get a feel for your options. Then you can begin to make some decisions.

For the past several years, the National Garden Bureau has addressed color in the garden because it is one of the topics that generates many requests for information and advice. To help you with your color coordination, here are some key pointers courtesy of the National Garden Bureau.

Think Three Dimensional

When planning a garden, think of it as a three-dimensional painting. Focus on the colorful annuals and perennials for beds, borders, and containers as paints on an artist's palette. In artistic painting, some colors will dominate and be spread with broad brush strokes. Other colors will give depth and dimension with small dabs here and there. Try to envision an entire panorama of your garden as you want it to look when it is at its best. Then plan and plant to grow that panorama.

Brighten Shady Areas

To brighten shady areas use light-colored annuals such as white, light pink, or pale blues. Dark colors tend to get "lost" in shady areas. You can still use deep colors in a shady area, but be sure to use lighter colors around or behind them to provide contrast. That way they can stand out and be seen. For example, the contrast of burgundy impatiens surrounded by pale green coleus or coral impatiens will stand out nicely. Try to picture how colors of plants will blend or contrast with their surroundings.

Think of Theme Colors

Interior decorators often use three or four colors as a theme throughout a home. As an exterior decorator and landscaper, you can do the same. Repeated theme colors will unify different garden areas just as they unify the rooms of a house. For example, bordering all your garden plots with a row of yellow marigolds or creamy petunias can tie different garden areas together for a unified look.

Deep red geraniums or red salvia planted against a red brick or redwood fence will not stand out as well as white or pink geraniums. White geraniums will not stand out dramatically against a white fence or white siding.

Repeating the same colors but in different plant types can create the same effect. For example, if white and blue are your favored colors, try planting different types of flowers such as lavender, blue petunias, and blue salvia. For white use white geraniums, white impatiens, and white petunias to carry the theme but vary the look.

PLANT LIST—SUNNY WINDOW

Botanical Name	Common Name
1. *Juniperus sargentii*	Sargent's juniper
2. *Iris germanica*	German iris
3. *Pachysandra terminalis*	Japanese spurge, pachysandra
4. *Liriope sp.*	Liriope
5. *Paeonia*	Peony
6. *Hemerocallis*	Day lily
7. *Taxus cuspidata capitata*	Pyramid yew

▲ Plants for sunny window area.

Create a Focal Point

Each area of your garden should have a focal point. You can achieve that with decorative specimen trees or shrubs. If there isn't a natural focal point such as a pool of water or garden statuary, you can create one with color. Instead of long, uninterrupted rows of flowers, create a focal point by planting a mass of one color in the center of a bed; then surround it with flowers or plants that contrast in color, texture, or height.

If there is something unsightly in your view, such as a telephone pole or a fire hydrant, create a colorful focal point away from the object to draw attention in that direction and lessen the effect of a "problem" or ugly area.

Colors Can Affect Emotions

Advertising and marketing people have long known how to use colors to attract customers. Colors indeed can affect emotions. Bright colors such as red and yellow excite us and can make us feel warm. That is why they are often called "hot" or "warm" colors. Blue, lavender, green, pink, and peach are considered cooler and calmer. For the entrance to a home, you may want to create a feeling of warmth and excitement. For the entranceway you could choose stronger, more exciting colors such as yellow marigolds and scarlet dianthus. In the backyard garden or for patio containers, you may want to create a more relaxing and serene mood by choosing cooler or softer colors such as light rose shades with blue violas. Romantic flowers with fragrance also can set a mood.

Looking to the Future

Surveying garden authorities and landscape specialists, it appears that the future will bring brighter and stronger colors into popularity. That also seems to be what is more available as started bedding flower plants. Over the long term, the feeling seems to be that people will experiment more with color combinations as expressions of their own likes and personalities. The message to all: Be bold, be innovative, be assertive, and grow what you like. After all, it is your garden.

Avoid planting single flowers by themselves. Not only do they look lonely, but they seldom have sufficient visual impact to provide an appealing landscape scene. Groups are far better, especially when you wish to make visual statements with color.

Colorful Plantscaping

For many gardeners, adding color to their lives is often why they garden in the first place. Color can excite and stimulate. It also can soothe and refresh. Sitting in a garden and admiring a riot of color can inspire the artist in everyone. You, too, can use an imaginary artist's palette to combine tints and hues in exciting and dramatic floral illustrations.

Think in Colorful Ways

As you sit looking at your present garden or thumb through some garden catalogs on a frigid winter day, think more colorfully. Warm yellows, oranges, and reds excite and give a sense of exuberance. Think about a soft bark path lined with lemon marigolds, deep red snapdragons, and scarlet petunias to lead your eye to explore farther afield.

Cool blues, greens, purples, and pinks tend to calm and reassure people. These colors blend peacefully into the landscape. The heart of a quiet garden might be a Victorian urn from which sapphire lobelia and gentle white baby's breath cascade next to a simple bench for meditation.

White Is Basically a Blender

Landscape designers point out that white is the most versatile color of all. It actually blends other colors and lightens the garden. Whites tie garden areas together as they soften strong colors and lead the gaze from one area to another. Think about how pale colors such as pastel pinks and light yellows can subtly brighten dark corners of the garden or shady retreats. Dark colors will also add emphasis to darker areas when set off with white or silver blooms. Consider the following color combinations and then see if you can come up with some of your own.

- Pure deep blue with soft yellow or scarlet
- Clear pale blue with rose pink, pale yellow, or creamy white
- Deep maroon or plum with creamy white or pale yellow
- Flame pink with cool gray-blue
- Pure orange with brown and bronze

Use Monochrome Wisely

Monochromatic gardens are centered around one specific color. Once you decide on a color, look for foliage and flowers that are shades and tints of that color. For instance, you could have a garden with pale lemon, gold, and orange colors; sky, indigo, violet, and purple colors; or scarlet, pale pink, and cardinal colors. You could even have an all-white garden that is emphasized with shades of silver, cream, and pale yellow to set off the whites.

FACT

Expert landscape designers consider color blending to be an art form. However, you needn't be an artist to create a beautiful garden. With some practice and attention to what you wish to see as your favorite colors and combinations, you can achieve marvelous results.

Also Think Polychromatic

A polychromatic garden includes all colors, creating excitement and exuberance. In such a garden, you can use colors to set off some of your landscape or site features, such as the house, a fence, or a planter. For example, an old-fashioned weathered gray board fence is a spectacular backdrop for peach and salmon foxgloves and blue or purple delphiniums. Another example would be a white windowpane trellis or white picket fence draped with creamy peach sweet peas and bright blue morning glories.

Plan for all-season display. After the bright new greens of emerging leaves can come the bright yellows of daffodils; the pinks, reds, and yellows of tulips; the multicolors of pansies; and the pinks to reds of peonies. During summer, it is time for the brighter displays of yellows, oranges, and reds of sunflowers, lilies, and zinnias. Then, as summer fades, it's time to enjoy the fall displays of crimson and gold mums set amid blazing purple asters, perhaps with burning bushes as background.

Keep Winter Color in Mind

Don't neglect color potential in winter. Flowering shrubs that provide bright red or orange berries add appeal and feed birds, too. Crabapples, winterberry, and a variety of shrubs with distinctive and colorful bark patterns can brighten a drab winter scene. You can enjoy the muted greens and grays of evergreens against sparkling white snow, and the striking bark colors of red, gold, and velvety gray, punctuated with bright berries, on some shrubs brighten the scene.

Look up the more dramatic shrubs in nursery catalogs and envision how they can add to your winter garden pleasure. In Chapter 4, you'll find more winter color ideas for plants that provide blooms in spring and berries for fall and winter.

Vines Are Very Fine

The National Garden Bureau also points out the importance of vines. Here you will find their suggestions, hints, and tips for growing beautiful and useful vines.

There's something irresistibly romantic about a split-rail fence softened with intense clove-scented sweetpeas. Or, better yet for rose lovers, cascades of hundreds of bright red Blaze roses. Flowering vines of all sorts add an extravagant air to outdoor living areas. So do climbing roses, especially the old-time fragrant types.

Whether a living curtain of morning glories softly shading a west kitchen window or a white picket fence embroidered with a tumble of bright, sunny black-eyed Susan vines, flowering vines can add privacy, disguise harsh landscape elements, and give an aura of beauty.

Using Annual Vines

Many annual vines grow fast enough to cover a trellis in only a few weeks. By midseason, you can have an entire trellis attractively covered with foliage to block the winds, offer some shade, and add privacy.

Your options for using annual vines extend as long as your imagination. You can plant them in the ground in front of a windowpane arbor or up a tree wrapped with a flexible trellis. Use them in a planter box with a redwood fan, a pot with a topiary frame, or in a hanging basket or window box. One especially attractive option if you have limited room is to construct a trellis in a planter box on a deck or balcony. Annual vines covering the trellis will add beauty without sacrificing room.

Training Vines

Most annual vines attach themselves to a supporting structure with twining stems or tendrils. This allows them to attach easily to wire fences or thin strips of wood. Be aware that most vines will not cling to a brick or wooden wall. However, some ivies will do that, but will provide only their green foliage, without blooms to enjoy.

FACT

One of the easiest ways to train vines onto trellises is with vinyl-covered fencing. This is heavier than chicken wire, has holes about 1 inch by 2 inches, and lasts several seasons because of the vinyl coating. The vines and tendrils twine readily around the thin wires. This fencing is fairly inexpensive, and since the vinyl coating is green, it literally disappears from view when it's in place.

Vine Varieties

Now for the vines! You can enjoy sky-high beauty with some of these favorites that are easy to grow and will reward you with profuse blooms.

Sweetpeas (*Lathyrus odorata*) are old-fashioned favorites. They come in all sizes, from 2 feet and bushy to 8-foot climbers. Their pea blossoms range from scarlet to soft pink to white to purple plus combinations of bicolors. Their beauty can be dramatic, but their best trait is their intoxicating perfume. Sweetpeas bloom best in full sun and need rich soil that retains moisture. You can plant them directly outside after frost or start in pots indoors about 6 weeks before the last frost.

Morning glories (*Ipomoea purpurea*), with their familiar clear blue, pink, scarlet, or magenta trumpets, are among the fastest-growing annual vines. Buds unfurl gracefully each morning and fade by afternoon or early evening. Then they are replaced by new buds for the next morning's show. Morning glories are a logical choice for containers with trellises and will grow in almost any soil in full sun or partial shade. Plant them directly in the garden after frost is passed. Morning glory seed has a hard seed coat so be sure to soak seeds overnight before sowing in garden soil. Be patient. They tend to be slow starters, but once they begin, they seem to grow 1 or more feet every day.

When planning for annual vines, keep in mind that combinations can be especially appealing. For example, you can combine old-fashioned sweetpeas with morning glories to cover the upper and lower parts of a trellis.

Moonflower, or moon vine (*Ipomoea alba*), has bright white flowers that resemble morning glory blossoms. However, unlike morning glories, which peak in the morning, its blossoms open as dusk approaches and remain open through the night. As flowers open, their exotic perfume wafts through the evening air with a romantic fragrance. They require the same growing conditions as morning glories.

For a dense screen with unique flowers, consider the Balloon vine, or Love-in-a-Puff (*Cardiospermum halicacabum*), or Cup-and-Saucer vine

(*Cobaea scandens*). Both these vines will cover a trellis quickly to provide shade or a solid screen. Balloon vines can grow to 10 feet. They have tiny white, orchidlike flowers followed by appealing greenish balloon fruits. Plant Balloon vines in full sun in average garden soil after the danger of frost has passed. Cup-and-Saucer vines have unique reddish-purple cup-shaped flowers that seem to be nestled in light green saucers. Start seeds indoors about 6 weeks before the last frost or seed directly into the garden after danger of frost has passed. These prolific vines can stretch to 20 feet in one season.

FACT

Hyacinth Bean (*Dolichos lablab*) has distinctive blue-green leaves to complement its striking dark purple pealike flowers, which produce attractive purple bean pods. Hyacinth beans can grow to 15 feet or more in a summer in average garden soil with plenty of water. Sow seeds directly in the garden after danger of frost has passed.

Nasturtium (*Tropaeolum majus*) is another old-fashioned flower that deserves a place alongside other annual vines. Although it grows only to about 6 feet, it is a beautiful companion to other vines that grow higher. Its bright yellow, orange, red, and white flowers appear like jewels amid dusty green leaves. The blossoms have an extraordinarily sweet scent that will fill a room and are useful as cut flowers. Curiously, nasturtiums grow and bloom best in poor soil. Rich soil will produce abundant foliage but fewer flowers. You should plant nasturtiums directly in the garden after soil has warmed somewhat in spring.

Black-eyed Susan vine (*Thunbergia alata*) is a rather delicate vine that grows only about 6 feet long. It can be trained to a trellis but its best use is in a hanging basket or window box where its thin stems can dangle. Its blue-green foliage is decorated with typical bright orange, gold, or yellow flowers with dark brown eyes. The aging flowers will turn varying shades of cream to yellow. That gives you variations of color at any given time. Start seeds indoors 6 weeks before the last frost and transplant to well-drained soil in full sun.

New Roses Are Top Picks

Roses are gaining in popularity due to the several new varieties available. These new roses have a wonderful fragrance, grow well, and are nearly care-free. Ask ten of the top rosarians in the country for their favorite "no fear rose" and you can expect to get many responses. Some like landscape shrub roses; others like climbing roses; and yet others prefer the old-fashioned favorite, the hybrid tea rose. If you think you don't have the time, expertise, or even confidence to devote to roses, think again. Top rose growers were polled recently with this key question: What one rose would you recommend to nongardeners to plant in their gardens?

FACT

The purpose of the survey was to focus on roses that were the least amount of work—little spraying, pruning, or protecting in winter. Basically, the idea was to identify a rose someone could just plant, walk away from, and have success and beauty for very little work.

For those who are intimidated by the idea of growing roses, here are the roses to simply plant, water, and watch bloom, courtesy of some of America's top rosarians.

Donna Fuss of the Elizabeth Park Rose Garden in Connecticut nominated **Carefree Delight.** "It is the most disease resistant rose I've ever seen. In our garden it is extremely winter-hardy. Like its name, it is carefree. It is always in bloom. If there are any problems, it could be that it gets too big. But just a little pruning can curb its growth," she notes.

Dave Thompson from the world-famous Longwood Gardens in Pennsylvania also chose **Carefree Delight,** a small 3-foot-high and wide shrub. "It is a prolific bloomer and will be covered with fully-opened pink blooms, accented by tight red buds that look like little Christmas lights. Very carefree, as the name says, and perfectly hardy," Dave said.

Bob Downing of the International Test Rose Garden in Portland, Oregon, had trouble deciding on just one rose. He chose the **Landscape Rose, Carefree Wonder,** and the hybrid tea rose **Secret.** He likes Carefree Wonder because it starts blooming in the spring with semidouble blooms that combine a bold pink on the face of the petals with a creamy white on the reverse. This shrub rose is unusually vigorous and compact with a neat, orderly habit that never grows out of bounds. It's hardy from zone 4 and up.

Stephen Scaniello, a former rosarian at the Brooklyn Botanic Garden, chose **Knock Out,** another shrub rose and All-American Rose Selection award winner for the year 2000. This rose blooms continuously from summer until fall. "Never is there a day in the summer months from June through October that Knock Out does not have blooms," Scaniello promises.

Several leading rosarians had a secret, called **Secret.** It was the hands-down winner of the "no fear" contest. Bob Downing, Barbara Whitcraft of Hershey Gardens, and Diane Brueckman of the Missouri Botanical Garden voted for Secret. This rose's great pink blooms; fragrant scent; and rich, glossy foliage made it a favorite. Secret was named the All-American Rose Selection winner in 1994, with its classic bud and flower forms. This rose is a blend of creamy yellow shades suffused with pinks that vary from flower to flower during the season and depending on the weather. Diane Brueckman said, "This rose is hardy, grows for years and has a great fragrance. For a modern rose it's wonderful."

Favorite Colorful Climbers

For gardening higher than ever, climbing roses have won praise too in the easy-care survey.

Judy McKeon of the Morris Arboretum chose the climbing rose **New Dawn,** with beautiful, soft pink abundant blooms and a fruity, strong fragrance. This vigorous, hardy climber grows to heights of 20 feet.

Ray Reddell, another noted rosarian, picked **Polka** and explained why. "I have no fear that everyone can grow it well because it's so fuss free, no special needs other than reasonable planting and early training. Blossoms are drenched in perfume. This rose is irresistible."

For all who have ever hesitated about growing roses because they are worried about culture problems, the new breed of rose has opened up more landscape opportunities.

Grow a Patriotic Garden

You can celebrate America and grow a dramatic patriotic garden this year as a living American flag in your own yard. It's easy to plant a flag and then watch Old Glory wave its glorious red, white, and blue blooms with every breeze that blows. To grow a living flag garden, just pick a sunny spot, plot the stars and stripes where they should be on the ground, and select the right colored flowers for their appropriate places.

Pick Whichever Flag You Wish

Start with a thirteen-star Old Glory or today's fifty-star flag, as you prefer, and make it as large and impressive as you like. Once you have your site selected, apply a general all-purpose fertilizer to the soil before you spade or till the ground. Use 2 to 3 pounds of fertilizer per 100 square feet.

Plan to leave a wide margin around the edge of your living flag. That makes it easier to weed, remove old blooms, and water your garden during the growing season.

Find some pictures of American flags. Next, draw your plan for either straight rows or waving ones. Place stakes in the ground to mark rows. Stretch string or cord between the stakes. For a Colonial Old Glory, place thirteen wood stakes in a circle. That's where the white flowers for the thirteen stars representing the original thirteen states should be planted.

Next, plant your red and white flower seeds in the proper rows, just as the directions on the seed package tell you to. Cover them lightly with soil. Then, plant the seeds of the flowers to be your field of blue and cover them lightly. Next, plant the white flower seeds where you made the ring of stakes for a Colonial flag or the fifty stars for today's flag.

Tend Your Flag Well

Water your flag garden every day until seeds sprout, but leave the cord or string in place. That way you will know where your flowers will sprout and can remove any weeds that sprout between the rows. After your plants begin growing well, continue to remove any weeds. A mulch is helpful to smother weeds and preserve soil moisture. Use peat moss, compost, wood chips, or similar mulch materials.

For faster results, you can buy started red, white, and blue flower plants at garden centers or nurseries. This is easier and gives faster results, but is more costly if you plant a really large flag garden.

You can select a variety of different flowers for your patriotic gardens. Petunias are excellent because the new hybrids have such prolific blooms and withstand harsh weather better than older petunia varieties. Also, new types have larger blooms and more vivid colors.

Of course, you may prefer other flowers. Five kinds of popular, easy-to-grow annual flowers, regularly grown as separate colors and available from garden centers, produce all three flag colors. In addition to petunias, you can select asters, cornflowers, larkspur, and verbena as good alternates. Or, you can mix and match different flowers as you wish to achieve the red, white, and blue colors.

Red, White, and Blue Borders

You also can enjoy a glorious red, white, and blue flowerbed or border. To plant borders, spade or till soil 6 to 8 inches deep after you spread a balanced garden fertilizer on it. Apply 2 to 3 pounds per 100 square feet, such as in a flowerbed 5 feet wide by 20 feet long. After tilling, rake the soil evenly. Then mark the rows for your red, white, and blue flowers.

Plant seeds at the depth directed on the seed packets. Water well after planting and until seedlings are well sprouted. Then, add 1 inch of water per week. Keep the area weeded so seedlings get their needed nutrients and moisture and do not have to compete with weeds.

You also can enjoy patriotic colors in a wooden tub, box, or planter on a porch, patio, or balcony. As they burst into blooming beauty, you'll have good reason to say, "Hurray for the Red, White, and Blue!"

Fragrant Flower Favorites

Every year gardeners talk to each other and garden center owners. They write letters to mail-order seed firms. One of the ongoing topics is the desire for more fragrant flowers. For years, indeed decades, plant breeders had focused on creating larger, showier blooms with dazzling colors. They also wanted to build in disease resistance and did in many cases. Unfortunately, in the process, some of the fragrance of the original parent lines was lost. Happily, the plant breeders listened to the letters and calls from homegardeners. Fragrant flowers are making a remarkable comeback. You can find many listed in mail-order catalogs and as started plants in stores. To help you add fragrance to your gardens, here are some handy suggestions.

Fragrant Perennial Flowers

Here are some of the best perennials that provide fragrance. You can find more details about their cultivation in garden catalogs.

- **Bouncing Bet** (*Saponaria officinalis*) has clusters of pink, red, or white 3-inch flowers in summer and autumn
- **Creeping phlox** (*Phlox subulata*) such as Bruce's White is shade tolerant and has spring blooms.
- **Daffodil varieties** (*Narcissus*) in the poeticus, triandrus, jonquilla, and tazetta groups are highly fragrant, especially Buffawn, Canarybird, Kathy Rood, Trevithian, and Tripartite.
- **Daylilies** (*Hemerocallis*) can be fragrant including these key ones: Audacity Bound, Barbara Mitchell, Forty Carats, Fragrant Light, Kathy

Rood, Top Honors, and Vanilla Fluff.

- **Garden phlox** (*Phlox paniculata*) is an old-time favorite, especially Blue Paradise and pink Eden's Crush and Old Cellarhole, providing great all-summer blooms.
- **Giant lily** (*Cardiocrinum giganteum*) offers towering 5- to 12-foot-high spikes of fragrant white trumpet-shaped flowers in summer.
- **Hyacinths** (*Hyacinthus*) are among the most fragrant flowers for spring color and sweetness, especially Blue Jacket, pink Anna Marie, and white Carnegie.
- **Iris** (*Iris*) can be highly fragrant. For bearded irises, grow Fort Apache, Mary Frances, Scented Bubbles, and Thriller.
- **Lilies** (*Lilium*), including hybrid trumpet and oriental lilies, are strongly fragrant, especially the long-time favorite Casa Blanca.
- **Lily-of-the-Valley** (*Convallaria majalis*) is a low-spreading ground cover with white or pink spring flowers that prefers part shade.
- **Sweet violet** (*Viola odorata*) can have small purple, rose, or white flowers in late winter and early spring but also can overspread and crowd out other plants.

Fragrant Shrubs

Because shrubs are much larger than most perennials, they make great choices for maximizing fragrance in your landscape. Once planted, most are generally low maintenance and provide winter forms and early spring greenery.

- **Carolina allspice** or **sweet shrub** (*Calycanthus floridus*) has dark red 2-inch flowers in summer and grows well in sun or part shade.
- **Gardenia** (*Gardenia jasminoides*) is a long-blooming evergreen shrub that provides white flowers in summer with an extraordinary creamy fragrance.
- **Lilacs** (*Syringa*) are one of America's favorite fragrant shrubs. Among the hundreds of varieties of this popular 8- to 10-foot-high shrub, the most highly fragrant and disease-resistant choices are Excel, Vauban, and Miss Kim.
- **Mock orange** (*Philadelphus coronarius*) is one of the most fragrant of

all shrubs. Most varieties of this old favorite have strongly scented showy white flowers in early summer.

- **Koreanspice viburnum** (*Viburnum carlesii*) has powerfully fragrant small white flower clusters in spring and thrives in sun or partial shade.

Don't Forget the Roses!

Hand someone a rose and their first reaction is to bury their nose into its center to enjoy the splendid scent. Too often, breeders had sacrificed fragrance for the perfect bloom shape. Happily "Scent-uality" is back in roses. After more than 15 years of demanding research, crossing thousands of roses, and working with one of the finest fragrance companies in France, Conard-Pyle and the House of Meilland have introduced what American gardeners say they want: fragrant and hardy roses.

They thoughtfully selected an appropriate name for the new roses, Romantica. These high-tech garden roses combine the unbeatable characteristics of modern hybrid roses with the enduring qualities of old shrub roses. The result is what Conard-Pyle believes is the ideal rose for American gardeners, complete with sweet fragrances.

FACT

Romantica rose scent labeling information is gathered scientifically in the growing fields of France. Each rose is measured for the type and amount of essential oils that make up the fragrance of the flower.

Romantica roses offer a great medley of beautiful colors on easy-care plants with distinct fragrances ranging from strong to subtle. They have the traditional tea rose scent as well as uncommon rose scents such as grapefruit, lemon, cloves, anise, and even fresh dough.

The bushes are neat and compact and bloom all season, with some varieties boasting more than 130 petals on a single flower. In addition to their beauty in the landscape, they were bred to have the long sturdy stems of hybrid teas, so they are perfect for cutting and bringing indoors for arrangements, filling the house with sweet fragrance. The more they are cut, the more they prosper.

Enjoy Butterfly Gardening

When landscaping for color, you mustn't forget the color that butterflies will add to your gardens! Butterflies provide added excitement and color to your gardens, and children love them. Grow plants that attract these colorful winged friends and you'll be surprised at how they will entertain you every year. On a warm sunny day, these visitors provide color and motion that double the pleasure of gardening. It takes very little effort to make the yard attractive to butterflies!

Butterflies will visit and possibly stay to lay eggs wherever there is a variety of plants for food and shelter, some moisture, and an absence of pesticides. There are typically more species in warm climates than in cooler ones, but there are butterflies almost everywhere in the country. Their appearance in your backyard and their return to dine on flower blooms depends on whether their favorite plants are growing there. Some plants are needed to support their larvae, and others to support adult butterflies. One problem is that larvae can really eat a lot of the host plants, so you need to think through your butterfly attracting game plan.

FACT

The typical garden is not likely to have plants that host the larvae of most butterflies because they are usually unattractive, weedy, and wild plants. Adult female butterflies choose these particular plants; for example, Monarch moms must have milkweed to lay their eggs on. This assures that newly hatched caterpillars have their appropriate food immediately at hand.

Learn about Larvae

You do have some colorful choices of butterfly larvae–feeding plants. To attract butterflies to lay eggs, here are favorite larval host plants: aster, clover, hollyhock, lupine, mallow, marigold, passionflower, snapdragon, and violet. Baby caterpillars will virtually annihilate the host plant's foliage during their feeding frenzy. As they grow, butterfly larvae shed their skins four to six times before pupating. Then, they become immobile in a hard chrysalis suspended from a leaf or stem of the larval host plant, or hidden in leaf litter on the ground, until emerging as an adult butterfly. That stage is fun for youngsters to watch, of course.

Butterfly Gardens

Most gardeners prefer to have butterflies lay eggs elsewhere and then have adult butterflies come to visit flowers. Here's a list of all-time butterfly flower favorites. Many mail-order firms now offer collections of flowers for "Butterfly Gardens," and packaged sets are available at garden centers, too. Most butterflies seem to appreciate flowers with a flat contour so they can land and feed comfortably. Consider these butterfly-attracting flowers for your garden: aster, black-eyed Susan, butterfly bush, butterfly weed, coreopsis, lantana, liatris, and purple coneflower.

More Butterfly Know-How

Fortunately, adult butterflies have more cosmopolitan palates. The flower nectar they need for energy is available in lots of different flowering plants. They will visit in search of flowers that are most easily accessed by their long, coiled tongues, which enable them to reach deeply into the center of flowers for the sweet nectar. Botanists say that butterflies are particularly attracted to hot-colored, fragrant flowers.

If you really want to attract butterflies, then your challenge is to provide diversity of plants throughout your property to support both larvae and adults. Variety is one key. Wildflower meadows are one logical solution. You may let some of your property grow wild for that purpose. Also, let fresh water accumulate to support communal "mudpuddling," so butterflies get soil salts and minerals as well as moisture.

The more fragrant the plant, botanists explain, the better. You should also have plants at various heights because, like birds, certain butterfly species prefer to feed at certain heights. Different types have their preferences.

Chapter 15 Water Garden Wonders

This chapter isn't intended to be a complete how-to guide about water gardens and ponds. It will give you basic information and open the doors of knowledge to sources for the details you need for planning, purchasing, and maintaining various types of ponds, water courses, and water gardens.

What Type of Pond Is Best for You?

Water gardens and ponds offer a place of beauty and serenity. Perhaps this is the reason why water gardens are a trend that keeps gaining popularity. If this tranquil feature interests you, you'll soon find that there are several types of ponds to choose from.

The first thing to consider as you think about a water garden is what type of pond you really want. Do you want to grow beautiful water lilies? Do you prefer a natural fishpond that also includes other wild critters? Or, perhaps you want to create a replica of an Oriental koi pond? Where should you have your pond? How big should it be? Do you want to swim in it, too?

Where to Put the Pond

Veteran pond gardeners recommend that you locate your pond where you can see and enjoy it throughout the year. That includes where it provides a good view of your garden, so that when you sit there, you can see the beauty of flowers, shrubs, and trees around you. If you have a deck overlooking your yard, then it makes sense to plan your pond where you can see it from the deck.

Please keep in mind the safety of people and pets, and local ordinances that must be followed for pond construction. Local laws may limit what you can do, and may require safety fencing, too. Of course, safety and insurance considerations also are important.

Consider all seasons. Wild critters and creatures often visit at different times of year. They can be great fun to watch. Ducks and geese may explore it. Great blue herons may wade around it. Muskrats may find it a fine homesite.

Be aware that a pond or water garden is a major attraction. Guests often head right to the pond to see what's new there. Children love to walk around it, checking for frogs, turtles, and fish. Reverend

Marsh Hudson-Knapp built a water garden in the front of his church in Fair Haven, Vermont. He reports that he has met many people who stopped, sat next to the pond, and were deep in thought at times. You, too, may meet a lot of people this way and make new gardening friends.

Pond Considerations

As you dream of your water garden, it helps to make a checklist in your mind.

- Do you want goldfish or koi?
- Do you want only plants in the pond?
- Do you want a waterfall?
- Do you want to include ornamental rushes, grasses, flowering plants?
- Do you want a larger fishpond for bass?
- Do you want to raise baitfish like shiners?
- Do you want a pond big enough for swimming?

Avoid making the pond too small. It is far easier to plan ahead and dig the size you'll eventually want as you begin your pond, because expanding one is much more difficult. A small pond limits the number of fish and plants you can add. Most gardeners who have begun water gardens realize that a larger water garden allows adding reeds, rushes, and bog plants around the edges. They also can add a variety of flowering lilies to the pond, and many enjoy adding fish as a new type of pet.

Consider Adding Koi

Koi are unusual fish that are beginning to frequent Oriental water ponds and gardens. However, you won't necessarily be able to have a water "garden" if you decide to raise koi. Koi limit the amount of plant life you can grow because they eat some plants.

These fish will grow larger, so be sure you have created a big enough pond. Also, be sure to check with your local state fish and game authorities before bringing the koi home. Some states put restrictions on the type of nonnative fish that may be added to ponds and waterways.

FACT

Ornamental varieties of the common carp are called koi and are divided into two groups: the slender Asian forms and the broader European forms. Koi of various forms and coloration were bred in the late 1800s and are still popular today.

A koi pond should be no less than 1,000 gallons in volume; the bigger, the better. It also needs to have an area of the pond at least 3 feet deep, preferably 4 to 5 feet deep. A water garden typically has both koi or goldfish and a variety of aquatic plants. If you live in a moderate climate, plan for a 2-foot depth. In colder climates, pond experts suggest that you plan for a pond depth that provides at least 14 to 18 inches of water below the freeze zone.

Pick the Best Pond Site

After deciding what you want to grow and have in your pond, the next step is picking the best pond site. Most pond owners say they enjoy ponds that are close to the home. Choose an area where you can see the pond year-round, because ponds are great attractors of wildlife, including birds and butterflies. You might even want to consider a stream or waterfall in the long-range plan. It is worthwhile to discuss your water garden ideas with neighbors to keep peace.

A pond doesn't need to be round or oval. If you want a formal look to your pond stick with a square, circle, or rectangle design. The geometric shapes with balanced, mirror-image plantings are fine, but many gardeners prefer informal ponds without strict geometric shape. Today you have a choice of many styles and shapes.

Avoid placing your pond near trees. Otherwise you'll be busy cleaning leaves and other debris from the pond. Position your pond where it will receive at least 4 to 6 hours of direct sun if you want to grow water lilies. Shade is fine for fish-only ponds.

This warning may seem strange, but it is important. Create your pond where runoff from rain will not flow into it, because rainwater may carry fertilizer and pesticide residues into the pond. Fertilizer will cause algae problems, and chemical pesticides may kill or harm fish, frogs, and sensitive plants, especially if you have used herbicides on your lawn.

Pond Construction

If you've decided you just have to have a pond for your landscape, then you should be ready to get down to business. First, consider water circulation. In most cases, it isn't necessary to have water circulation, especially in larger natural ponds, but the use of a pump will allow you to keep more fish, and it will keep your plants healthier. Naturally, you'll need a pump to run a filter, fountain, or waterfall. The sound of running water adds greatly to the enjoyment of the pond.

Sizing a Pond Is Simple

The best way to size your pond is by using a rope or water hose to lay out the shape on the ground. As you measure, keep in mind that a finished pond will be about 30 percent smaller than you visualize it. So think bigger. A large pond is not only more inviting, it is also easier to keep and more stable.

Next, you will need to measure the maximum width and length. Use these measurements and add the depth twice. Then add 1 or 2 more feet for overlap. This figure will be the liner size. Naturally, having the pond supplier measure will be more accurate and probably a wise move. He can also estimate the amount of water you'll need to fill your pond. Generally, to determine the maximum amount of gallons in a pond, multiply the average length by the average width by the average depth by

7.48 (gallons in a cubic foot of water). This will tell you the maximum amount of water that will be in that size pond.

Take time to calculate the amount of water that will be in your pond. If it is substantial, make a written record of it and take it to your local fire department and insurance company. Sometimes fire departments may wish to put a "dry hydrant" at the pond for water in case of fire. A large water supply, especially in rural areas, may reduce your insurance premiums.

Dig Deep and Well

Digging a pond is hard work. Most likely you should have it dug by someone with experience and a backhoe. Frankly, most pond owners, including those who dug ponds themselves, believe it is far wiser, easier, and safer to have a pond dug and installed by experts. However, you should still be knowledgeable about what makes a good pond.

Basically you or they must dig the pond to the desired shape and dig a shelf around the perimeter of the pond about 1 foot deep and 1 or more feet wide. Then, filters should be positioned in their proper location, along with any skimmer devices that are to be used. Pond specialists noted that if a skimmer will be used, it is best to dig a ditch to the external pump and from the pump to the external filter or waterfall.

A pond for goldfish or water lilies needs to be only about 2 feet deep for horticultural zones 5 or warmer. Those that will contain koi should be at least 3 feet or deeper. Ponds built in colder areas may need more depth to keep the pond from freezing solid. You'll need to allow for at least 14 to 18 inches of unfrozen water below the freeze zone for the fish.

Use Pond Underlayment Material

The next step is to line the pond excavation with pond underlayment material. This should be cut with scissors or a utility knife. Tape small

STEP 1

Double the maximum measured length and width.

STEP 2

Inside measured area, dig your pool including shallow shelves in the walls. After taking out the rocks, add sand to your pool.

STEP 3

Place the plastic liner in the pool and use large stones to hold it in place.

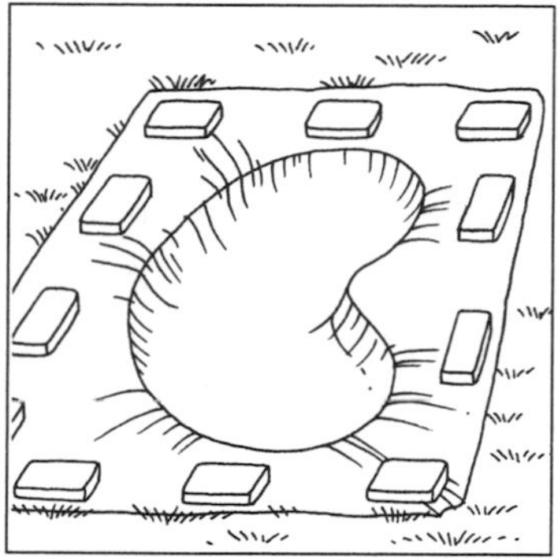

STEP 4

Fill in the hole with water. Do it so that the liner has time to slowly mold to the shape of the pool.

STEP 5

Make small folds in the side of the liner to fit the shape of the walls. You may need to put sand in the dug out shelves for support.

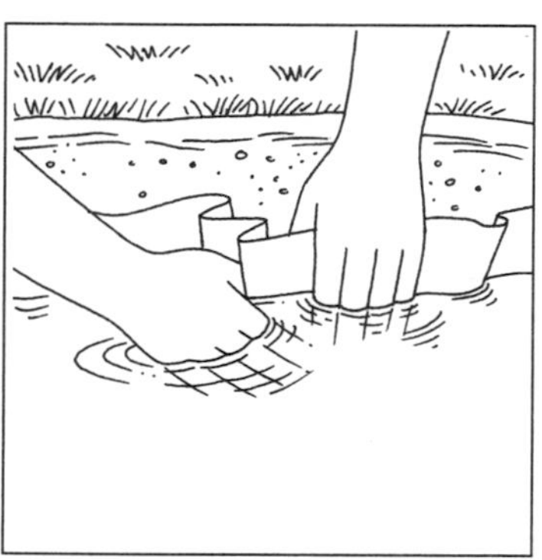

STEP 6

After this is completed, the large stones can be removed. The liner edge should be trimmed so that it overlaps about 6 inches.

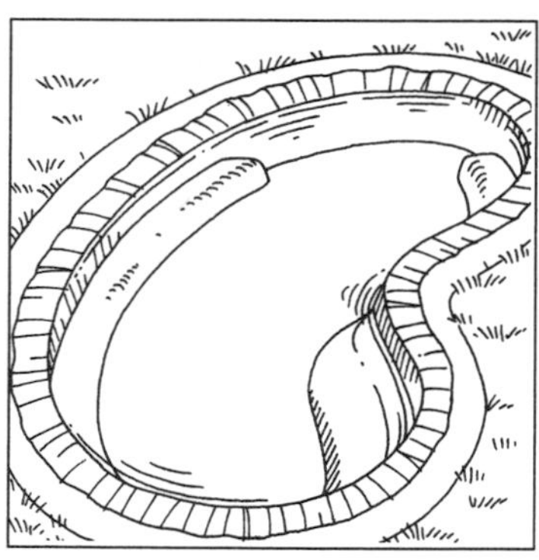

STEP 7

Use your choice of stones or bricks to decorate the outer edge of your pool. They should overhang the side of the pool a bit.

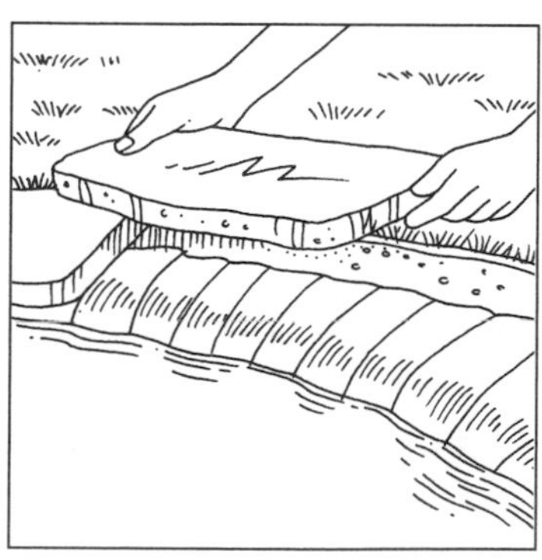

STEP 8

Make sure that the liner is entirely covered.

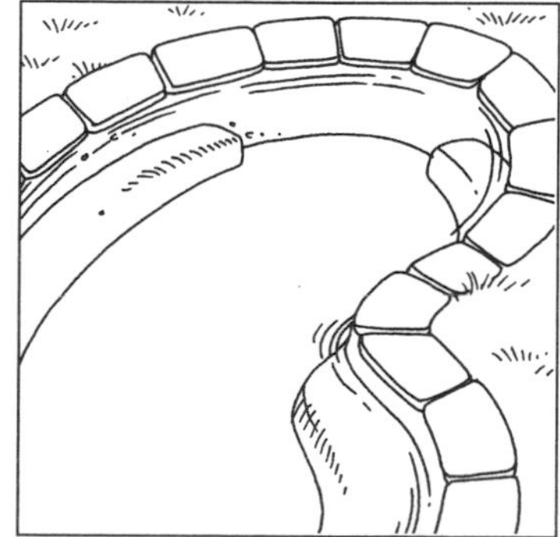

pieces together to keep them in place. Then unfold the pond liner and position it evenly in the pond. It is important to minimize folds and wrinkles.

If you are planning for waterfalls or need filters or skimmers, you should talk with professional water garden firms in your area.

Edging Your Pond

For most ponds, merely using a "necklace" of stone around the pond doesn't create a natural look. It is best to use several layers of stone to give a better appearance. That also lets water fluctuate without exposing the liner. Some people have used a layer of gravel around the edge. Then you can naturalize this area by planting shallow water plants. This will create a more appealing edge, with plants partly in and partly out of the water. Yellow flag iris and blue flag also work well. You can plant bare root plants directly into the gravel or place the plant with some soil still attached into the gravel. This will help the plant to establish more quickly.

Pond Care Tips

Here are some pond care tips, thanks to the folks at Lilypons.

In the spring:

- Clean the pond and top if off with water, if needed.
- When your fish are coming out of dormancy, feed them a food low in protein, such as Three Seasons Fish Food.

In the summer:

- Remove any debris from the pond surface and top off the pond with water, if needed.
- Remove any dead leaves from water plants.
- Fertilize water plants.
- Check submerged pump regularly for blockages.
- Test water for ammonia and nitrite levels.
- Feed fish once a day what they can eat in 3 to 5 minutes, using a high-protein formula.

- Keep an eye on the fish for any signs of illness.
- Remove any debris from the surface and again top off the pond with water, if needed.

In the fall:

- Remove any dead leaves from water plants and fertilize them.
- Feed fish once a day what they can eat in 3 to 5 minutes.
- Clean out as many fallen leaves as possible to prevent them from decomposing in the pond.

In the winter:

- Turn off any pumps or filters and remove.
- Thoroughly clean your biological filter, if applicable; drain and leave drainage valve open.
- Cut hardy water plants back and drop to the deepest part of the pond.
- Remove all tropical and annual plants.
- Keep an area free of ice over the winter to allow gases to escape and oxygen to enter.
- Eliminate feedings while the water temperature is below 50°F.

Favorite Pond Plants

Most pond gardeners grow some water lilies. There are many varieties and types: annual and perennial, small, large, and amazingly dramatic. You can see them in living color and get details about hundreds at The Water Garden, *www.watergarden.com,* and Lilypons, *www.lilypons.com,* Web sites. That's an Internet trip worth taking, plus you'll discover many more details about water gardens and lilies.

Lilies aren't the only potential water garden plants. For example, there are lilylike aquatics. These plants grow like water lilies. Some of these are perennial and will overwinter. Others are annuals and must be treated as such.

Pond Margin Plants

Marginal plants require their own individual containers of about 1 to 3 gallons. These marginal plants, which are grown in 2-inch net pots, should be planted without removing the net pot to protect the roots. Plant as you would the lilies in a loam garden soil. These plants should be fertilized about every 6 to 8 weeks. Marginal plants need to be lowered to a depth of only 2 to 3 inches. They are usually found at the water's edge.

Additional Plants to Consider

Also focus on floating plants, which require no planting. Simply place them in the water and they will grow. Many floating plants desire annual temperatures and cannot tolerate a frost.

Add water lilies and other plants with surface leaves to provide shade to approximately 66 percent of the surface area if in full sun. If in less than full sun, then less coverage is acceptable.

According to pond specialists at The Water Garden, the most important plant is Anacharis. This underwater plant helps to deter algae by consuming the nutrients the algae need. For ponds under 25 square feet, use one bunch for every square foot of pond surface area. For ponds 25 to 100 square feet, use one bunch for every 2 square feet of surface area. For ponds 100 to 300 square feet, use one bunch for every 3 square feet of surface area. Use one bunch for every 4 square feet for ponds over 400 square feet in size. Plant protectors will be needed for the Anacharis if you keep koi in the pond.

Try a Tub Water Garden

It is easy to create a tub water garden for a deck or patio. Just about any container that holds water can be used. Think of it as a different type of aquarium. If you use a 20- to 50-gallon container, you can even add a few goldfish. You'll need to use a water filtration system to maintain clear and clean water. Different types are available from various suppliers. Depending on size, you can grow some of the most beautiful water lily plants in a tub container.

Choose a container a few inches deep if you want only plants. For fish and plants, select a container at least 12 inches deep. Large tubs or barrel bottoms work well. Decide where you want the tub garden and position it. Water is very heavy, so moving a tub garden can be a problem. If you decide to grow water lilies, you'll need to place the tub garden where it will receive 4 to 6 hours of direct sunlight.

Check with reliable plant suppliers—The Water Garden, Lilypons, or others—to find other suitable aquatic plants for tub gardens. You'll be surprised at the variety of choices you have. Some floating aquatic plants look nice. Shallow-water plants can be set on bricks placed on the bottom. Water lilies, of course, should be in their own pots on the bottom of the tub.

You can pick small or large water lilies, depending on the size of your tub, but smaller lilies work best. A few bunches of Anacharis in the tub will keep the water clear. Once planted, aside from a bit of fertilizing, tub water gardens can be a delight and nearly care-free. Come winter in northern areas you'll need to dismantle the garden and store it, or move it indoors.

FACT

As water gardening continues to grow so rapidly in popularity, no doubt there will be many more suppliers of materials and plants. Those mentioned here have proved their reputations and back up their products with their own guarantees.

Consider Bog Gardens, Too

Do you have a wet area or soggy spot in your land? Perhaps you also get lots of rain runoff that soaks an area and prevents usual garden plants from growing well. Take advantage of the situation. Think about a bog garden. They can be fun.

One gardener calculated that the rain runoff from a roof was about 14,000 gallons of water a year. With a little bit of work, what had been a problem soggy area became a neat marsh garden. Now, butterflies play in the moist soil and cliff swallows use the mud to build nests and repay that gardener by eating thousands of insect pests while they raise their babies. Frogs arrived to welcome spring with their "spring peeper" chorus.

Simple Solution Works

To tap that surplus water, divert it with a gutter pipe to a flexible plastic hose to the soggy area. Water will drain away from your house to the marsh area. A mixture of compost and peat moss helps build a growing area for a variety of plants. Better yet, you can grow plants that are sure winners to attract butterflies and hummingbirds, because some prefer marshy growing conditions.

For example, consider spicebush, great blue lobelia, sweet pepperbush, joe pye weed, cardinal flower, buttonbush, white turtlehead, and swamp milkweed. Once the area takes root, you'll be surprised at the diversity of songbirds that arrive. Following are some key points to convert a seemingly useless part of your landscape to a beauty spot, using wastewater from your roof. Naturally, it is best to check local government rules about diverting water for such a project.

Pick Best Marsh or Bog Spot

Pick a site based on access to abundant rainwater, one that is flat enough to accommodate a marsh, and that has clay or peat moss soil to retain water. Happily, gravity guides the rainwater to the marsh for you.

As you select the site, think about the kinds of plants you want to grow. If you want bright, sun-loving plants, choose a sunny location on the south side of your home. If your only area is shady, then switch gears and pick shade-loving plants for it.

You also want to consider soil type. You really need either clay-type soil or to work in sphagnum peat moss so the soil holds water. Very sandy soil just won't work. Soil with a good deal of absorbent clay works much better.

Dig in for Marshy Fun

Outline the perimeter of the proposed site and strip the sod from the outlined area. Remove subsoil and rock to about 14 inches deep to allow for an overflow spillway at the lower end of the marsh, to get rid of excess water.

Of course, always check with local town or city regulations before making such major land changes, since there may be restrictions that prohibit or restrict what you can do.

Then, tap into your water supply. Connect a length of flexible plastic pipe to a downspout from your roof. Bury it beneath the ground and lead it into the marsh. Make sure the diameter of the pipe is great enough to avoid water backup during big rains.

Next, fill it with appropriate clay loam and peat or organic compost so you produce the desired marshy ground habitat that will hold water for bog plants. Finally, pick the bog plants you prefer. Many mail-order catalogs list them, and you'll be surprised how many types there are.

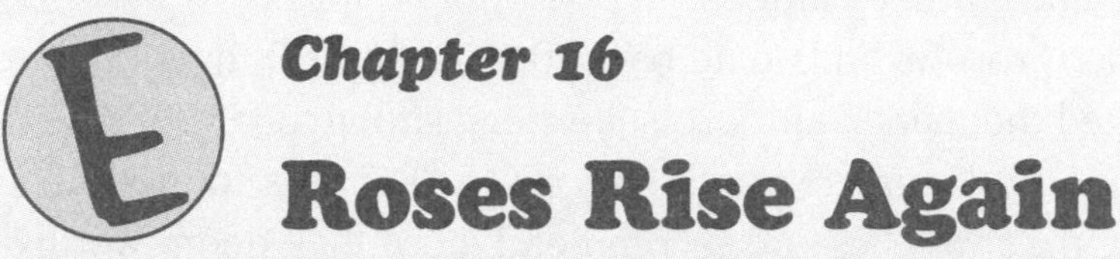

Chapter 16
Roses Rise Again

Roses are one of the world's best known and best loved flowers. Today you have more opportunities to put them to use around your home. It is nice to know that roses need very little for success. They are happiest with sufficient sun, air, water, food, and a little bit of love.

Deeply Rooted Rose History

In 3000 B.C., in what is now Iraq, the Sumerians created the first written record of the rose. Sappho made reference to the rose in her 600 B.C. "Ode to the Rose," calling it the Queen of Flowers, a reference that is still popular today. The rose was brought to North America by the Colonists. Rose tradition is deep indeed.

Modern rose hybrids date back to 1867. By 1920, hybrid tea roses dominated the market and are still selling strong today. As rose popularity continued, All-America Rose Selections (AARS) was formed in 1938 to test new rose varieties and recommend those they deem worthy to the public. All-America Rose Selections is a nonprofit association of rose growers and breeders dedicated to the introduction and promotion of exceptional roses. The AARS program has encouraged the rose industry to improve the vitality, strength, and beauty of roses for American home gardens. Today the AARS program is one of the most successful and highly regarded of its kind. The AARS seal of approval has graced outstanding new rose varieties that have withstood the test of time and Mother Nature.

FACT

For additional information about AARS, photos of the AARS winners, or to find a test or public garden near you, visit *www.rose.org* or contact All-America Rose Selections, 221 N. LaSalle Street, Suite 3500, Chicago, Illinois 60601.

A rose is a rose is a rose according to Gertrude Stein. If you sniff hard enough, you'll discover that there are hundreds of varieties of roses in the United States today. With such a rainbow of choices, there's a perfect rose for every space in your garden.

Defining Roses

Rose varieties vary in shape, size, growth habit, and leaf and flower color, texture, and form. Few other flowers bloom so readily the first year of planting, and roses reward you well by coming back year after year. Look around your home grounds for places where roses can provide their beauty. Whatever garden design you favor for roses, be sure to choose a sunny, well-ventilated area and plant roses 2 to 3 feet apart. Massed plantings of roses create a breathtaking effect.

Each rose variety has its own different look, from formal to free-flowing. Your choices of roses include hybrid tea, floribunda, grandiflora, miniature, shrub, and landscape roses.

Climber—Climbing roses help dress up any garden and are at their best when allowed to grow on a fence or trellis. They produce numerous flowers and can cover any type of supporting structure.

Floribunda—Floribunda roses are bushy shrubs and produce flower clusters of three to fifteen, which translates to floral abundance. These roses make any landscape design stand out with the most colorful of rose types.

Grandiflora—A grandiflora is a cross between a floribunda and a hybrid tea. This rose grows up to 6 feet tall and produces classic hybrid tea flower clusters.

LEFT: Floribunda "Bahia"

RIGHT: Grandiflora "Sundowner"

LEFT: Hybrid tea "Peace"

Hybrid—One of the most popular rose types, hybrid teas are the standard, classic rose with one flower per stem. Many varieties offer a beautiful fragrance. Some are beautiful but lack aroma.

Miniature—The smallest of the roses, miniature roses are often grown in containers. They mature within a range of 6 inches to 2 feet tall.

Shrub and Landscape Roses—Shrub and landscape roses offer you a wide variety of shapes, sizes, and growth habits. Shrubs are upright, and landscape roses have a low-growing spreading habit.

Tree Roses—These unique roses are made up of a hardy root stock grafted to a long stem that is in turn grafted to a rose bush at the top of the stem. They normally require special care in the winter.

Winning Roses

Two outstanding and delightful roses were named All-America Selections in 2002. Love & Peace is a classic hybrid tea, the most beloved of all types of roses, treasured for its long stems bearing striking individual blooms. Starry Night is a landscape shrub rose, the wellspring of inspiration to landscape gardeners.

"Love & Peace and Starry Night create a picture perfect combination nestled within a garden and promise to be real show stoppers," says AARS President Charlie Huecker. "They also offer excellent disease resistant qualities and easy maintenance."

Love & Peace

Love & Peace features a fruity scent and striking good looks. The high-centered, spiral-formed blooms of Love & Peace open into large golden yellow flowers edged with pink. Each flower has a minimum petal count of forty, surrounded by dark green glossy foliage. This classic upright, disease-resistant, hybrid tea grows to 4 to 5 feet by 3 feet. Love & Peace is perfect for framing a formal rose garden or creating a striking feature within a landscape. It also provides fragrant cut flowers.

Starry Night

Starry Night took top honors with its large clusters of pure white flowers. A landscape shrub, its medium green glossy foliage enhances the five-petal flower, which is 2½ to 3 inches in diameter. In cooler climates, Starry Night grows to 3 feet by 3 feet, and in mild to warm climates it can grow to 6 feet by 6 feet. As a landscape shrub, it is perfect for large plantings, borders, and ground cover. Its pure white sparkling flowers, which resemble dogwood flowers, are often referred to as a constellation of blooms.

Other Top-Rated Roses

Glowing Peace, a golden yellow and cantaloupe orange blended grandiflora, works well as a property divider, front hedge, or as a screen. This rose can also be planted in beds at the back-of-the-border position. This round, bushy grandiflora exhibits large round buds, which open to reveal full 3-inch blooms featuring twenty-six to forty-two petals, and will grow to 4 feet by 3 feet.

If you want to try something different, think small. Miniatures such as Sun Sprinkles can brighten up an evergreen foundation planting, small garden, deck, or patio. Sun Sprinkles exhibits pointed oval buds that spiral open to reveal 2-inch, petite, bright yellow double blooms with twenty-five to thirty petals and a moderate spicy fragrance with overtones of musk. It will grow to 18 to 24 inches.

FACT

The best time to smell roses is midmorning when the sun has just reached the garden. The fragrance will be most intense when the bloom is one-quarter to two-thirds open.

Guidelines for Growing Roses

Gardeners around the world know that roses return more to you for your time and effort than most other flowers, if you plant and treat them well. To grow roses successfully in any climate, you need only three things: lots of sun, water, and fertilizer.

Timing is important when planting roses. While spring is considered the ideal time to plant, other times of the year can work, especially in certain Sunbelt areas. For specific details on best planting times, contact your local County Extension agent or local garden center experts.

To produce fabulous flowers for dramatic garden displays and cut flowers, roses need adequate nutrition. Apply time-released rose food early in the season and a repeat application again in midsummer. During a drought or when roses look unhappy, add a fast-release rose food when you water and you will ensure brighter flowers and better bushes. Roses are thirsty plants. Be sure when you water to soak the soil. A rose that dries out is vulnerable to disease and other troubles.

Planting roses requires neither great gardening skills nor experience. Use your common sense in your choice of location and follow the steps outlined here to get your roses off to a healthy start.

Climbing roses aren't limited to walls or buildings. They may be trained to a post to create a pylon effect, and some of the less vigorous varieties may be pruned to form a pillar or large shrub effect. You can also enjoy them over arbors or on wire trellises to hide unsightly views, including compost piles.

Selecting a Planting Site

When selecting your planting site, remember these simple things:

- Roses need 5 to 6 hours of direct sun each day.
- Morning sun is best, but light afternoon shade is tolerated and even beneficial in hot climates.
- Good air movement helps dew and rain dry quickly, which helps

discourage disease. However, too much wind can damage foliage in the summer and canes in the winter. In windy areas, it is a good idea to protect roses with a building, wall, fence, or hedge.

- Roses don't like wet feet. Avoid wet or soggy areas. Wet roots, especially in the winter, can be fatal to roses. Check drainage at a potential site by digging a hole 18 inches deep and filling it with water. It should empty within several hours. If necessary, improve drainage with tile drains or consider raised beds.
- For less than perfect loamy soil, add organic matter like compost, dehydrated cow manure, or peat moss.

Don't plant near large trees or shrubs. They compete for light, water, and nutrients. Avoid eaves or gutters because rose bushes may be damaged by falling water, snow, or ice.

Tips for Planting Bare Root Roses

Some nurseries provide roses in a dormant, bare root stage. Here's how to get them planted properly.

1. Dig a hole 18 inches wide and 18 inches deep. Mix a quart of compost or peat moss with the soil and put the mixture in the bottom of the hole, forming a mound.
2. Position the rose on the soil mound. In warmer climates, position the rose so that the bud union is at or just above ground level. In colder climates, position the bud union 1 to 2 inches below ground level and mulch over. Carefully arrange the roots of the plant around the soil mound.
3. Work the soil mixture around the roots and firm it down to eliminate any air pockets. Add soil until the hole is three-quarters full.
4. Fill the hole with water and let it soak in, then refill. Trim canes back to 8 inches, making cuts at a 45-degree angle ¼ inch above outward-facing buds.
5. Create a 6-inch soil mound over the plant to protect canes from drying out. When buds sprout in about 2 weeks, remove the mound.

Tips for Planting a Container Rose

If you have purchased a container rose, which should already have plenty of leaves and perhaps some blooms, follow these basic planting steps.

1. Dig the planting hole for your rose bush the same depth as the container and about 18 inches wide.
2. Loosen the soil around the root ball to expose the roots. If the ball is rootbound, score it by making vertical cuts with a sharp knife. Open the scores about 1 inch to allow roots to form.
3. Center the rose bush in the hole and fill in with soil that's been amended with peat moss or compost. (Mix the soil with peat or compost so it feels crumbly.)
4. Work the soil mixture around the roots and firm it down to eliminate any air pockets.
5. Water thoroughly and mulch around the planted rose to stop weed competition and retain soil moisture.

Container Roses Provide Portable Beauty

If you are short on space but love roses, take heart. Don't miss out on rose delights because you don't have a big yard. Try a rose container garden! Many home gardeners have excellent success growing beautiful roses in containers on sunny balconies, decks, and terraces. Creative gardeners can even transform an exterior staircase or indoor window ledge into a bouquet of blooming roses.

Pick Attractive, Spacious Containers

Decay-resistant wooden tubs and boxes, porous terra-cotta or glazed pottery, and even plastic pots make good containers. Whatever container you choose, be certain it provides adequate drainage. Although roses are thirsty plants, they can't stand soggy roots. In fact, standing water around their roots can be fatal. There should be several holes in the bottom of the container and cleats or feet underneath to help keep the pot from sitting in water. For foolproof drainage and added mobility, consider attaching casters to the bottom of the pot. That also makes it easy to roll your blooming beauties here and there for party décor.

Use Soilless Planting Mix

Next, plant your roses in containers using a ready-made soilless mix or a growing medium composed of sandy loam and organic matter such as peat moss or leaf mold. Keep the soil evenly moist at all times and feed regularly with liquid or time-released fertilizer. Planting mixes are best because they prevent the introduction of disease organisms from garden soil.

Position Containers

Place containers where rose bushes will get at least 6 hours of direct morning or midday sunlight. Good air movement is important too so foliage is dry to discourage disease. In windy areas, place containers near a wall or building to protect roses from wind damage.

If the temperature is likely to drop below 20°F, move the containers to a frost-free location when winter begins. Remember also that strong winds in winter can harm roses, so move containers indoors and shield or mulch outdoor roses in your garden.

Your best bet is to purchase a blended planting mix that includes slow-release fertilizer in it so that your newly planted roses can be properly nourished as they set their roots in containers.

Shrub Roses Gaining Popularity

Roses that offer beauty plus toughness, easy care, and mobs of color are always popular. The term *shrub rose* is a catchall designation created by the American Rose Society that includes a wide variety of easily grown shrubby rose plants. The loosely defined category is comprised of roses ranging in size from low-growing 2- to 3-foot-tall "ground cover" roses like the Flower Carpet roses to mid-size English roses to climbing roses. Most are hardy and repeat-blooming, with flowers in single, semidouble, or double blooms in all rose colors. Depending on the cultivar, shrub roses may or may not be fragrant.

FACT

Shrub and other landscape roses are available at garden centers, nurseries, and by mail order. As heavy bloomers, shrub roses benefit from an appropriate diet of rose food and sufficient water. They grow best in 5 to 6 hours of full sun per day.

With thanks to veteran rose experts and the American Rose Society, here are some of the best performing and more popular shrub roses. They are easy-care and combine beauty with low maintenance and high levels of disease resistance. A big plus: They flower for months on end because they all are repeat-blooming types.

- **Carefree Wonder** is a shrub rose with semidouble pink flowers with a white reverse that grows 5 feet high by 4 feet wide, is disease-resistant, and is hardy to zone 4.
- **Flower Carpet Pink** is a ground-cover rose with semidouble fuchsia-pink flowers with subtle fragrance that grows 24 to 22 inches high by 4 feet wide. It is considered the most disease-resistant rose available, is excellent for mass plantings, and is hardy to zone 4.
- **Stanwell Perpetual** is a Scottish rose with double blush pink flowers with Damask fragrance on arching 3-foot bushes, is very disease-resistant, and is hardy to zone 3.
- ***Rosa rugosa,*** or **species roses** in many cultivars, typically have flowers with clovelike fragrance that are single, semidouble, or double, in white, pink, red, or yellow. They grow 3 to 6 feet high by 3 to 6 feet wide, are disease resistant, and have showy red hips each fall. They are hardy to zones 2 to 4, depending on variety.

Old-Fashioned Roses Gain Ground

Old-fashioned roses are making a popular comeback. Most old roses will give today's busy homeowner an appreciated rest from much of the heavy fertilizing, spraying, and nurturing demanded by fancier roses. Old rose specimens found in old cemeteries and abandoned homesites have survived even without care from human hands. Old garden roses are hardy even in poor conditions, but they will be at their loveliest if planted in a favorable situation with rich, well-drained soil.

Planting Tips

To prevent roses from drying out during planting, soak for about 1 hour before planting. Dig the hole large enough to accommodate the natural spread of the roots. Prune any roots damaged in shipping and spread the roots down around a pyramid of soil you place in the hole. Note the soil mark on the stem and plant the roses deep enough to reach or cover the soil mark.

Mulch, Water, and Feed Well

Mulch is helpful. Spread a 2- to 3-inch-thick layer of mulch around your roses. It will mean fewer weeds, less water stress, less heat stress, and healthier plants. Well-rotted compost is excellent. Check roses every few days, especially during droughts. Roses are thirsty plants and will look much better if they get a deep soaking every 7 to 10 days.

Most commercial rose foods and organic fertilizers are fine and give good results to feed roses. To keep roses healthy and vigorous, a feeding in spring and another in early fall should suffice. For peak performance, begin fertilizing your roses about 2 weeks before the last spring frost date for your area and continue at 4- to 6-week intervals until 6 weeks before the earliest fall frost date for your area to avoid forcing tender growth. Many gardeners prefer a basic spring and early fall fertilizer program.

Rose-Pruning Pointers

Old roses don't require the careful pruning that is needed by many modern varieties, but they still do need to be pruned. Ever-blooming varieties can be lightly trimmed several times a year because they flower on new growth. Roses that bloom only once are best pruned after they have bloomed. When pruning, remove dead canes or twigs, unbalanced growth, and a few inches overall. For climbing roses, remove only dead or unwanted canes.

A green-thumb rule is to clip back no more than one-third of the rose bush, encouraging full foliage and heavy bloom without destroying the vigor and attractive form of the plant.

Pick Most Fragrant Roses

Shakespeare said it best: "That which we call a rose by any other name would smell as sweet." Actually, not all roses are fragrant. Over the years, plant breeders created larger and more beautiful blooms among roses, but that sometimes was at the cost of fragrance. Old-fashioned roses are noted for their aroma. Others have been bred with top fragrance in mind. Here are some examples. You can find more at garden centers, and look for those featured for fragrance in mail-order nursery catalogs.

- **Just Joey** has petals that start out orange-apricot and fade to pink as they develop around the fragrant, high-centered bud. The overall effect is an orange bloom.
- **Mister Lincoln** is a high-centered and very fragrant dark red rose. It remains one of the finest red garden roses, with a strong growth habit and good disease resistance.
- **Fragrant Cloud** is a large-flowered coral red rose that will reach a deeper red hue in cooler climates. A low to medium bush, this rose loves sunshine and is very fragrant, with citrus-scented blooms.
- **Sutter's Gold** is aptly named for the colorful nuggets that sparked the 1849 California Gold Rush. This hybrid tea is a soft orange and yellow beauty, overlaid with pink, and very fragrant.
- **Crimson Glory** is perhaps the most scented of all roses. It combines

velvety crimson flowers with a full, lush rose fragrance.

- Two shrub roses, AARS 2000 winner **Knock Out** and its sister **Carefree Sunshine,** are rated as two of the best new fragrant roses introduced as part of the Meidiland Star landscape shrub roses.

Children Love Roses, Too

One of the fastest-growing segments of horticulture is gardening with children. More parents are actively trying to balance information with real-life experience. Introducing kids to gardening is a natural way to turn their attraction to dirt into a lesson about the importance of soil to everyday life and our ecosystem. Introducing kids to gardening with seeds is one way to open new discoveries and growing horizons of all types.

Don't underestimate children! Although many people consider the rose to be a plant for more mature gardeners, people of all ages are drawn to the rose's beauty, fragrance, and complexity. Kids love roses, too!

Gardening Teaches Responsibility

Planting their own roses and caring for them can help teach children responsibility and the importance of the environment. Gardening also helps kids build self-esteem, especially when observing the healthy growth of plants they have tended. Harvesting vegetables for dinner or creating a centerpiece for the table also helps instill in a child a sense of pride and accomplishment. Roses can also reach across the generations. As veteran gardeners have seen, an "I love you" bouquet of homegrown roses for Mom, Grandma, or a baby-sitter is a truly treasured gift.

Lessons of Life

It also is true that gardening enables youngsters to learn other important lessons for life. In the rose garden, kids learn how the elements affect all living things from people to plants. Roses require adequate sunlight, water, nourishment, and protection from extreme cold temperatures, just like people.

Kids learn how to nurture their rose garden by practicing proper site selection, watering, and pruning techniques as well as feeding their own rose plants. Most importantly, they see the blooming beauty that their efforts created, which they can share with others. That beautiful rose bloom they grow is like the pot of gold found at the end of the rainbow.

Chapter 17

Container Gardens for Landscaping

Containers provide you with a wide range of growing opportunities in pots, tubs, buckets, baskets, and window boxes. You can enjoy glorious flowers, the taste of herbs, the flavor of vegetables, and even try some special dwarf fruit trees in barrels. If you don't have much space, container gardening is for you!

Colorful, Flavorful Container Gardening

America is catching on to a trend that has been popular in Europe for several years: container gardening. Horticulturists estimate that Germany alone has 25,000 miles of container gardens. Window boxes and container gardens adorn many thousands of office buildings and homes in Switzerland, Austria, France, Great Britain, and elsewhere. Now it's your turn to enjoy a colorful, delicious new look on porches, patios, balconies, and even rooftops.

You have several options available for use as a container, so be creative! You can use anything that holds soil mix and provides proper water drainage. Garden centers and chain stores provide a wide range of shapes, sizes, and colors. Some are functional, others decorative. You also can shop flea markets and yard sales for old baskets, barrels, kettles, and buckets.

Keep raised beds in mind as you plan various types of containers, because container gardening can be as small as one pot or as large as good-sized raised beds. You may find that raised beds work well as large container gardens. They require less weeding, let you tend plants easily, and can be highly productive.

Container Basics

As you plan your own container gardening, keep these key points firmly in mind. Container plants need more water than those in backyard gardens because of their restricted growing habitat. Their roots cannot roam in search of moisture. They also are exposed to drying air on all sides from the sun and from the heat radiated from building walls. Check containers daily, especially smaller ones that can dry out faster. Poke a finger into the soil to check for moisture or dryness. Watering encourages deeper rooting for sturdier plants. However, proper drainage is especially important. Most plants hate wet roots. Two key facts to remember: too wet is bad and too dry is bad. Be certain your containers provide for drainage and escape of excess water.

Innovative new wick and trickle watering systems are available to

▲ Raised beds as "container"-type limited-space gardens.

provide moisture on a regular basis, even when you are away on vacation. Some fancier containers come equipped with their own bottom or wick watering systems. Those are a good investment for container gardening.

Soilless Soil

Another key to container growing success is "soilless" soil. Professional growers have used it with exceptional results for years. They call it the ideal plant-growing medium. Today, you'll find many different brand names of soil mixtures available in garden centers, supermarkets, and chain stores. They all have an advantage over typical backyard earth, which has soil bacteria, fungi, and insects in it.

Avoid evening watering because moisture left on foliage plants, especially in warm weather, invites plant diseases.

A Balanced Diet

Plants need a balanced diet, especially in containers where roots can't roam in search of food. Fortunately, many balanced fertilizer mixtures are available for container plant feeding. You have a choice of liquid fertilizer and prilled type or slow-release pellets that feed plants over a longer period. Always follow the directions for the type you use. Too much fertilizer can be as harmful as too little, especially in container habitats.

Made for Container Culture

Considering this container gardening trend, plant breeders have focused on producing ideal flower and vegetable varieties designed for containers. They have compact growth yet bloom beautifully and bear vegetables abundantly. Naturally, plants do require certain amounts of sunlight, moisture, and nutrients, but new varieties offer spectacular results.

Look through garden seed catalogs. You'll find many flowers and vegetables featured that are recommended for containers. You can even mix and match for tasty living and blooming beauty in the same containers. For example, surround a prolific producing tomato plant like Tiny Tim or Sweet 100 with dwarf marigolds for flavor and color.

Among vegetables, new hybrid cucumbers bear heavily from dwarf bushy plants. Bush-type hybrid squash yield well in container gardens. Rhubarb or Fordhook Giant Swiss chard provide tasty eating. Great Lakes, Buttercrunch, and Ruby lettuce offer salad fixings.

Consider Versatile Containers

One of the most versatile and easy ways to grow bushels of colorful annual flowers and a bounty of tasty veggies is in containers. The fast-growing popularity of "color bowls" is proof that container gardening is catching on.

Basically, if it holds soil, it is a container. Many people think primarily of plastic or glazed pots, terra-cotta, or half-barrels as likely containers for plants. Be imaginative. Shop flea markets for attractive containers that you can line with plastic bags to provide a proper growing habitat.

Containers Are Easy to Care For

Container gardens require less weeding than in-ground gardens, which makes them ideal for busy people who love gardening but have limited time. However, keep in mind that you must watch watering more closely. Containers in hot sun can dry out quickly. Even a light summer breeze can wick moisture from plants. Plan to water daily or even twice daily during long, hot, dry spells.

If no fertilizer was incorporated with the growing mix, be sure to fertilize plants so that they keep growing properly. Naturally, weed as necessary, but there should be few problems if you use proper planting mix, not garden soil.

Feed Your Container Plants Well

All plants need a balanced diet, just like you do. In containers, their roots can't roam in search of food, so it's up to you to provide their nutritional needs. Nitrogen, phosphorous, and potassium are the big three that all plants require. Nitrogen feeds vegetative growth. A soil mix deficient in nitrogen will produce stunted, pale green foliage. A nitrogen overdose produces fast-growing foliage with few flowers or vegetables. Too little phosphorous weakens roots, causing plants to lie flat rather than stand tall. Potassium deficiency produces strong-looking stalks that are actually weak, and vegetables that ripen before maturity.

Available Foods

Fortunately, you have many choices of well-balanced plant foods available today. Especially with the water-soluble types, it is easy to keep plants nourished and thriving. Many brands can be purchased at garden stores. Check which are recommended for container growing, since most brands come in several formulations. Some are best for flowers; others are best for vegetables.

Feed Just Right

You also can use slow- or time-release pelleted or prilled fertilizer with the soil mixture. Be sure the formulation provides sufficient food, since porous planting mixes are devoid of most nutrients. Some have limited amounts, but those nutrients tend to be used up early on by the developing plants, which then require additional feeding as they reach maturity, especially veggies.

Here's a general green-thumb rule. Begin weekly feedings of ½ tablespoon of 20-20-20 liquid fertilizer per 1 gallon of water when plants are about half mature. At blooming or bearing age, use a full tablespoon per 1 gallon of water weekly. This is just a guide. Your best bet is to follow the directions on the package of fertilizer you purchase.

Remember, too much is not only wasteful, but it can also harm the plants. It is better to feed your plants too little than too much. They'll tell you when they are still hungry. Yellowing or browning leaves may mean that more food is needed. In time you'll get the feel of feeding your various container plants, and they will reward you well for your tender loving care and attention.

FACT

Many flowers and smaller vegetables will grow well in containers that are 8 to 10 inches in diameter and 8 or more inches deep. Of course, taller and larger plants will need larger containers. Just be sure to find a container that will accommodate the mature plant size.

Be a Container Landscaper

Even container gardens benefit from your landscape design ideas. Consider color, texture, and flower form when designing a container garden. You choices of colors range over the rainbow. New and more beautiful hybrid flowers offer delightful bright colors or more subdued pastels. Pick and plant what you like best.

Your Container Garden Plan

What would you like to grow and where would containers look best and thrive? If an area receives full sun most of the day, you can choose from a wide selection of sun-loving flowers. If the area receives limited sun, choose plants that tolerate less light. Even if you have only shady areas, there are plants that prosper there. Another advantage with containers is that you can move them around to give the plants the growing conditions they need. Then, move them again to decorate an entertaining area.

You can mix and match different types of flowers and even flowers with veggies. But be aware of plant needs. A common mistake is choosing the wrong combination by mixing shade-loving plants with sun-loving plants in the same container. It's a green-thumb fact that shade plants will not perform as well in full sun, and full-sun plants will not perform their best in shade.

Take a look at some of the plants in this chapter and also in catalogs to pick your pleasures. Plan each individual container or grouping of containers to include plants of different heights, colors, and textures.

Flower Forms

When you plan your container flower displays, give some thought to flower forms or shapes.

- Use line forms like *Salvia splendens* or snapdragons, which are tall and spiky.
- Try mass forms such as daisies, petunias, or marigolds that have many small or large flowers.
- Exploit large flower forms such as large-flowered begonias, which are characterized by large, distinctive flowers. These can be especially dramatic.

Using Decorative Containers

First and foremost, your container should be large and deep enough to accommodate the plant as it reaches maturity. A container should also have a drainage hole at the bottom. Before adding soil, put 1 inch of gravel or pieces of broken pots over the hole to prevent the soil from washing out when watering. If your decorative container doesn't have a drainage hole, consider double potting. Simply place the original pot with its proper drainage system within the decorative pot. It's a good idea to put some gravel or pieces of broken pots at the bottom of the decorative pot. If a pool of water were to form in the bottom of the decorative pot, the gravel would keep the original pot from sitting in it.

To create a feeling of depth, plan groupings of three to five different-sized containers. You may want to have a couple of large pots that contain large plants that reach a couple of feet in height, and then surround the large with small pots containing small plants to give a three-dimensional look to your minigarden.

Container Garden Plantscaping

Too often, people use the containers in the same places every year. That can begin to look dull. Think about dramatic displays. Try five or more containers as a group to really get attention. For especially dramatic container plants, grow summer flower bulbs such as tuberose, oxalis, begonias, dahlias, and lilies.

When you begin with container plantings, you'll find places for them everywhere, even right in your outdoor garden. Actually, container gardening can be like painting. Let your imagination soar. You can create delightful compositions with your own choice combinations of color, form, and texture.

Brighten Up Dull Areas

Use your imagination to brighten dull areas around your property. Think about your side yards, walkways, decks, garage walls, or cement areas bounded by ugly chain-link fences. You can bring these areas to bright life with colorful flower container gardens. Morning glories in a wide range of new colors are available today, and various vines also lend themselves to dressing up dull areas, especially along fences. Flowers give you many ways to brighten your property.

Try Hot Tropical Plants

You can try some fun tropical plants for a different look with your container gardens. A few tubs or containers of giant leafy plants and vivid tropical colors can easily transform a scene from dull to "Wow!" Here are a few top container plants you might wish to try. They thrive in containers. All may be started from bulbs, and many may be purchased as bedding or container plants at garden centers.

Eucomis is a pineapple look-alike with a tuft atop a 15-inch spire of tiny greenish white flowers and a base of broad green leaves. The Eucomis bicolor is a tropical plant that blooms in July and August and retains an interesting look after flowering. It prefers full sun or light shade.

Cannas offer nonstop flowers from July till frost with distinctive tropical foliage of large brown or green leaves They bear gigantic red, orange, pink, or yellow flowers. To plant the canna root, lay it on its side, bury it 1-inch-deep in soil mix, and place in full sun.

Lilies will perform to their utmost in containers. Few flowers are as showy and impressive. Try three lily bulbs in a container 12 inches wide. Plant each about 4 inches below the soil surface. Both the early- to midsummer-blooming Asiatic lilies and later-blooming Oriental lilies do well in full sun or partial shade.

Caladiums thrive in the shade. Actually, the caladium's nickname could be "leaves-that-are-prettier-than-flowers." This appealing plant delivers attractive tropical color. Place it in partial or full shade and keep moist in hottest weather.

To enjoy success with these tropical plants in containers, follow these five simple steps:

1. Use commercial potting mix.
2. Give plants good drainage to keep their roots healthy. Be sure all containers have drainage holes in the bottom.
3. Choose containers deep enough for the plants, based on their planting instructions, so they have room to mature properly for best display.
4. Fill the pot one-quarter to one-third deep with soil and position plants at the proper depth based on planting instructions that come with the plants you buy. Fill in additional soil to 1 inch below the pot top to provide room for mulch, if needed, plus watering.
5. Group several pots together for greater visual effect and to minimize watering labor.

Bulb Container Gardens

The best time to plant a bulb container garden is in the fall. You can choose just about any type bulbs for whichever flowers you prefer. Consider blooming period, color, height, and fragrance. For example, early-flowering hyacinths offer a heady and fragrant choice for planting in containers combined with later-flowering daffodils and tulips as colorful follow-ups.

A Double Decker

One creative and easy planting technique especially suited to container gardens is the double-decker technique. Plant a layer of tall-growing bulbs such as pink tulips 8 inches deep in the container and make sure there are 3 inches of soil covering it. For the next layer, plant low-growing bulbs such as blue grape hyacinths. Cover this with 5 inches of soil and 1 inch of mulch. Then, water well. In spring, you'll see the results: The blue grape hyacinths will create a carpet lining the container, and the pink tulips will flower above, creating a striking display. Try out different combinations of flowers, but make sure they will bloom at the same time. If you are feeling especially creative, you can add a third layer. For example, you could add a layer of Tête-à-Tête narcissi between the grape hyacinths and tulips.

FACT

You can obtain dramatic containers that can be used to create a distinctive and appealing look. Look for some of the new fiberglass, resin, and synthetic containers now available. Many are lightweight, can overwinter outdoors without cracking, and are often copied from rare old estate containers in handsome designs of pseudostone, terra-cotta, and even cast iron.

Consider Cold Time Needs

Aside from good drainage, the most important requirement for spring-flowering bulbs is temperature. Bulbs have to have at least 15 weeks of cold temperatures, but they also cannot freeze. Bulbs in containers are vulnerable to extreme temperatures. It's best to move small containers to a sheltered place if your area suffers heavy freezes. Large containers are better for cold protection and can be wrapped or padded in burlap or blister wrap or even set into bales of hay. When spring comes, place the containers back out in the sun for glorious spring blooms.

Best Spring Bulbs

To grace your containers, whether fancy decorative types or others that you prefer, here are some of the best spring bulb flowers to consider:

- *Anemone blanda,* also known as Greek windflower
- Chionodoxa, glory of the snow
- Crocus, all species and Dutch crocus cultivars
- Hyacinth, all cultivars
- Miniature Iris, *I. danfordiae* and *I. reticulata* hybrids
- Narcissus, including taller cultivars and, especially, shorter-stemmed and miniature varieties

- Tulip, shorter-stemmed cultivars and species such as *T. greigii, T. kaufmanniana,* and *T. fosteriana,* and taller tulips including Darwin hybrids, Lily-flowering, double early, single early, and Triumph hybrids

Best Vegetables for Containers

There are a variety of excellent, tasty, and new hybrid vegetables that thrive and perform well in container gardens. If you want to enjoy some taste treats, grown by themselves or in combination with flowers, here's a list recommended by top veteran gardeners.

- **Beans:** All varieties
- **Beets:** Burpee's Golden and Little Ball
- **Cantaloupe:** Bush Musketeer, Bush Star Hybrid, Honeybush, and Minnesota Midget
- **Cucumber:** Bush Champion, Bush Whopper, and Spacemaster
- **Lettuce:** Green Ice, Loosehead, Little Gem, Cos, Butterhead, Minetto, and Crisphead
- **Pea:** Edible pods Sugar Ann and Sugar Daddy; standards Laxton Progress and Sparkle
- **Pepper:** New Ace Hybrid and Big Dipper
- **Radish:** All varieties
- **Summer Squash:** Cocozelle, Crookneck, Peter Pan Bush Scallop, Scallopini, Sunburst Bush Scallop, and all zucchini types
- **Winter Squash:** Autumn Queen, Early Butternut Hybrid, Table Ace Acorn, Table Queen Acorn, and Bush Vegetable Marrow
- **Tomato:** Baxter Bush, Pixie II, Indeterminate, all varieties (staked)
- **Watermelon:** Bush Jubilee, Sugar Baby, and Sugar Bush

Vegetables suitable for indoor production include those that can be "mowed" to grow again, like leaf lettuce, spinach, endive, and Swiss chard. You can savor root crops such as radishes, dwarf carrots, and bunching onions from container gardens. Beets and turnips are as valuable for their edible greens as their roots. Good fruiting vegetables for indoors also include squash, cherry tomatoes, bush cucumbers, and snap beans.

Try New Roses, Too

Americans are wild about roses. They're our national flower and one of the most perennially popular garden plants. Americans also have fallen in love with container gardening. Combining the two passions by planting roses in containers is another growing horizon for you. A new generation of easier-care landscape and shrub roses and new, high-tech garden containers offer even novice gardeners the opportunity to grow roses in containers.

The attractive properties of new high-tech composite and fiberglass containers make container gardening easier than ever. Today's containers offer striking imitations of classic materials such as terra-cotta, cast iron, and stone. Happily most of today's containers are affordable, lightweight, weatherproof, and retain moisture well. By mixing, matching, and moving container plantings, you can add a whole new dimension to the landscape and around the house.

Gardeners have begun using containers right in the outdoor landscape with dramatic effect. Today, containers are finding themselves featured beyond the bounds of deck and terrace and used as decorative elements in the landscape itself, an idea well worth trying.

Pick Best Roses for Containers

Technically, almost any rose can be grown in a container, but traditional roses often quickly grow too large for pots. Today you have a solution. Use "garden roses" that are bred to offer florist-type flowers on vigorous, fully leafed garden bushes. Examples include the new Dream Rose series in pink, yellow, red, and orange.

Smaller ground-cover and shrub roses are ideal for container gardening. They offer abundant colorful flowers, an extended bloom season, and easy-care habits. Any of the popular Flower Carpet ground-cover roses will be excellent choices due to their exceptionally long bloom season, natural disease resistance, and cascading canes. These include Flower Carpet Pink, Flower Carpet Appleblossom, and, just introduced this spring, Flower Carpet Coral. There's also Red Flower Carpet and Flower Carpet White. Don't be misled by the "ground cover" name. Flower Carpet roses grow up to 3 feet tall and nearly as wide to fill out a container nicely. Other top shrub rose choices for containers include Weeks Roses' delightfully fragrant *Rosa* Flower Girl and Mix 'n' Match, and Meideland's Rosa Bonica, Carefree Wonder, and Carefree Delight.

Keys to Container Rose Success

Roses in containers will need a bit more care than roses planted in the garden or landscape. Use good-sized containers. Roses have deep, thirsty roots. Containers should be 18 to 24 inches in diameter at a minimum. Larger containers insulate against excessive heat and cold that can damage roots. They also allow the roses to go longer before becoming root-bound, with the subsequent need to repot them. Water often and deeply. As with all containers, soil tends to dry out quickly, so frequent watering is vital. It also is important to water thoroughly.

Warning: It is possible to give a container a good dousing but still leave the root ball in the center dry. To avoid this, water well once; then do it again, letting excess water drain from the bottom. This helps ensure that water will get to the thirsty roots and not run down the inside of the container and out.

Feed roses well. Container-grown roses need more frequent feeding. The water that runs out of the holes in the bottom often takes essential nutrients with it. If you use a fast-release rose food, feed weekly. It is better to use a slow-release formula that saves you work and will keep a rose bush just as happy by feeding only a few times per season, depending on the formula. The right roses in the right containers can be grown alone or combined with annuals or perennials in limitless combinations of color and texture.

Chapter 18

Solving Problem Areas

Every gardener has faced problems, from soggy areas and droughts to poor soil that desperately needs improving to grow beautifully blooming flowers and shrubs and abundant veggies and fruits. This chapter gives you some of the time-tested solutions to basic garden problems.

Improving Landscapes to Solve and Prevent Problems

Thoughtful landscaping can help prevent more problems than you may expect and also help you solve other problems around your home grounds. For instance, if you are having problems with your water quality, landscaping can help. Proper landscaping reduces surface water runoff, which can keep phosphorus and other pollutants from lawn fertilizing and weed treatment out of waterways. A dense cover of plants and mulch holds soil in place. That helps keep sediment out of lakes, streams, and storm drains. Or if you are suffering from noise pollution, good landscaping will help to reduce city noises and even glare from headlights.

Think about Energy

An unprotected home loses much more heat on a cold windy day than on an equally cold still day. Well-located trees and shrubs can intercept the wind and cut heat loss, reducing fuel consumption by 10 to 30 percent. Prairie farmers knew that windbreaks could indeed stop chilling winds, so they added trees to their homesteads as one of the first steps in providing comfortable living.

FACT

The height and density of trees determine the amount of protection they may provide. Windbreaks of two to five rows of trees and shrubs generally provide good protection.

A study in Nebraska compared two identical houses for the amount of fuel required to maintain a constant inside temperature of 70°F. The house protected by a windbreak used 23 percent less fuel. In another study, an exposed, electrically heated house in South Dakota used 443 kilowatt-hours per month to maintain an inside temperature of 70°F. An identical house sheltered by a windbreak used only 270 kilowatt-hours. The difference in average energy requirements for the whole winter was 34 percent.

The amount of money you may be able to save with a windbreak will vary depending on the typical climate, home location, and construction material. The facts are there. In addition to reducing the force of the wind, windbreaks can also reduce the wind-chill impact on people outside the house.

Foundation Planting Also Helps

Lower-growing trees and shrubs next to buildings also reduce wind currents that would chill the outside surface. These foundation plantings create a "dead air" space, which slows the escape of heat from a building and also helps reduce air infiltration around a house foundation. Evergreen trees and shrubs, such as yews and junipers, are thicker and are more effective than deciduous plants. Create a tight barrier by planting them close together.

Summer Energy Savings

Another key landscape value is saving energy in the summer. Well-placed trees and shrubs can also help cut air-conditioning costs. Trees, shrubs, and even ground covers reduce solar radiation more than structural devices such as deck covers or window awnings. Deciduous plants that drop their leaves in winter let the sun reach buildings in the winter for warmth, yet they provide welcome, cooling shade during the summer.

Shade trees reduce air temperatures indoors in the summer because trees soak up the sun's heat while transpiring cooling moisture into the air. It is best to plant trees on the south and west sides of your house. Planting shrubs around an outdoor condenser or heat pump also saves energy.

FACT

Vines help cool homes. Deciduous vines on trellises can be used to cool walls that face south or west. Behind the trellis, a convection current carries warm air away from the wall, according to energy research scientists.

Disentangle Overgrown Landscapes

Without pruning, shrubs and trees can overgrow their area. Take a hard-nosed look at your landscaping. Are your junipers blocking the living room windows? Do some shade trees seem to have more dead than live branches? Are your shrubs wearing the paint off your house? Perhaps your landscape needs renovation. Before you reach for the pruning saw or shears, pause a minute. Start with a pencil and paper. That way you won't cut or chop away some of your landscape anchor plants.

Do a Landscape Sketch

Draw your house and landscape to scale. Then do a survey of your favorite plants. Next, tape a piece of tracing paper or a plastic sheet over the house plan and add in all of the existing plants. Identify problem areas: wet spots, slopes, shady areas, dog runs, unsightly walls or views.

Next, color on your sketch map those plants you wish to keep. Then add a list of plants you want to add that would be more appealing, add color, or dress up the property better. Make a consolidated landscape plan and list priorities to decide how much can be done at a time, within a reasonable budget. Renovation may take several years. Do it with a plan in mind, and you'll find that the results will grow into place as time and budget allow.

Remember some basics. Hazards exist when plants block or conceal windows or doors, house numbers, or utility accesses. In emergencies, fire and police need to be able to locate your home.

Trimming Trees and Shrubs

You can have large trees trimmed professionally to allow more light to filter through to the ground. Even then, tree roots may still compete for nutrients and require extra effort and shade-tolerant grasses, plus extra fertilizing to keep the area looking nice.

You should consider trimming back overgrown shrubs or removing them entirely if they are no longer desirable. Although the plant may be visually unattractive for a while, consider a severe trimming nearly to the ground to rejuvenate old and woody shrubs. Fall is a good time to do severe trimming, as shrubs go dormant in most northern areas. By spring, they'll begin growing again from their established roots. Then you can control them with periodic pruning.

Remember that any plants in the ground around the base of a tree compete with tree roots for water and nutrients. One way to make areas beneath trees more attractive is to use raised beds. You can also use portable containers to add color and changes to the scene.

Win the War on Weeds

Winning the war on weeds is important. If they gain a roothold, they rob other valuable plants of nutrients and water and detract from the appeal of your desired plants. You don't need to reach for weed-killing chemicals when weeds first appear. Weeds grow either from seed or reproduce from roots. As weed roots grow outward from the parent plant, some new plants may sprout up. Weeds that reproduce from their roots are usually more difficult to control.

Mulch First

Think mulch first. You can use new weed-controlling fabrics on beds and borders and around trees and shrubs, disguising them with a light layer of mulch. Another approach to weed control is an ongoing mulching program. Keep adding peat moss, wood chips, compost, or other mulch materials to smother weeds.

Even with fabrics and mulches, weeds have a way of gaining on you. Make a pledge to yourself. Pick and pull weeds each week early in the gardening season. That's what veteran gardeners do, and it makes sense. The weeds are easier to remove then; they haven't set roots too deeply or taken over part of your garden.

Chemical Weed Controls

There are two types of chemical weed controls: postemergent and preemergent. Basically, postemergent herbicide kills weeds that are actively growing. A preemergent prevents weed seeds from germinating. Within the postemergent category, there are selective and nonselective herbicides. Generally speaking, a selective herbicide kills the broadleaf weeds but doesn't harm the grass. A nonselective herbicide kills any plant it touches. Before you begin using herbicides, think carefully about what they do, and read the directions and safety precautions thoroughly.

Gardening safety rule number one: Read the labels and follow the safety precautions whenever you use pesticides. They are designed to do specific jobs such as kill weeds or insect pests. Always follow directions exactly and wash well after using them.

Roundup

Roundup has become a popular herbicide due to its effectiveness. Spray Roundup only on the foliage of the weed. It is then absorbed and sent through the root system, ultimately killing the plant. The manufacturer claims that Roundup does not have any residual effect, which means that you can safely plant in an area where Roundup has been used. No residual effect also means that this material has no effect on weed seeds, so there is absolutely no benefit to spraying the soil. Naturally, carefully read the package directions before using it.

Never spray on windy days, and be sure that herbicide spray doesn't drift to your desirable plants. To prevent spray drift and protect your plants, you can construct a cardboard shield and place it around only those plants you want to kill.

Beat the Drought

Sometimes droughts arrive. Veteran gardeners know the usual weather cycles in their areas, so ask them what they recommend for landscaping. Where droughts occur periodically, it pays to pick plants that can take that punishment.

Drought-Resistant Plants

Most of the new landscape roses can handle long dry periods. Knock Out, a pink All-American Rose Selection winner, and Carefree Sunshine, a bright yellow single-petaled rose, were both bred for tough conditions and are extremely drought resistant. Other shrubs that are particularly drought resistant, once they get established, include Euonymus Emerald Surprise, or Moonshadow, and Juniper Gold Lace and Emerald Sentine.

In addition, you can choose drought-tough perennials such as yuccas and any plant in the sedum family. Both are hardy and undemanding and nearly all have the ability to tolerate drought and poor soil. Yuccas are so drought resistant they will bloom without rain since their taproots go so deep.

Reduce Your Watering Needs

When droughts occur, sometimes water for lawns and gardens is restricted. Here are ideas to reduce your water needs from the American Nursery and Landscape Association as part of their Water Wise program.

- Plant plants in groups according to the amount of water they need so you won't end up over- or underwatering any parts of your lawn or garden.
- Establish watering priorities. Take care of new and young plantings first, and then more mature trees and shrubs that usually can tolerate dry periods better.
- Plan a watering schedule to minimize your water consumption. Try to water in the early morning to take advantage of the cooler temperatures and reduce evaporation.

- Water slowly and deeply to avoid water runoff. Spot-water areas that dry out more quickly.
- Continue mulching, pruning, composting, and fertilizing. Strong plants require less care than weaker ones.
- Shelter container plants by moving them to shady areas to reduce water loss due to evaporation.
- Consider installing a drip or trickle watering system, which can save up to 60 percent of the water used by sprinkler systems.
- On sloping land, place plants with low water needs at higher elevations and those that need more water at lower elevations. Water from the higher areas will trickle down to those plants that require more moisture.

New Science Helps Gardeners

New scientific discoveries are being introduced to help gardeners every year. Because droughts periodically plague gardeners, scientists have been focusing on that problem. "Drought is as common as thunderstorms and hot summer days," says Don Wilhite, director of the National Drought Mitigation Center in Omaha, Nebraska. "It's a normal part of all climates."

One of the newest introductions to the gardening world is water-retention crystals. Many mixes, like the soilless Pro-Mix, contain water-holding crystals. The water-absorbing crystals hold water and ration it to the plant as it needs it. Some gardeners even mix this formula right into the topsoil with their plants and shrubs to help retain moisture longer.

Focus on mulching. According to research at Texas A&M University, unmulched soil may lose twice as much water to evaporation as mulched soil. Mulched soil also allows water to penetrate more deeply, and it stops water-robbing weeds from growing.

FACT

When watering, keep in mind this important fact: It's best to water deeply every 3 or 4 days. This practice not only uses less water, but it also forces the roots to grow down deeply to seek out the water.

Winter Protection Rose Tips

If drought has taken a toll on your roses, here are things you can do to help them. Rose experts advise that you give them a good soaking before winter arrives and well before the ground freezes, using a soaker hose for 30 minutes to a few hours, depending on how dry the ground is. It pays to prune roses back, too. Around Thanksgiving is a good time to remove a few inches of the twiggy top growth of the plants. That will prevent snow and ice from accumulating and possibly breaking the plants during the winter.

Mulching also helps insulate roses from winter cold. The most serious damage to tender-type roses happens when the ground is frozen and the roots cannot take up moisture. The most common type of winter protection is to mound soil 6 to 10 inches up the canes of the rose. For added protection, place leaves, evergreen boughs, or similar material among the plants as insulation against winter winds or extreme cold. Then, in spring when forsythia starts to bloom, carefully remove the winter protection from around the canes.

These tips apply to conventional garden roses such as the hybrid teas, grandifloras, and floribundas. The new landscape shrub roses are especially hardy and relatively easy-care. That's why some of these newly introduced rose varieties have become so popular. They are hardy, need little pruning, and survive winters without extra care.

Clean up the ground around the roses of any fallen leaves or other plant debris that might be harboring parasites or disease organisms. If you have had disease problems, apply a fungicide spray to roses before winter and be sure to spray the ground under and around the roses as well to reduce black spot problems next spring.

In Need of Light

If you find that some plants don't perform as well as they should, perhaps they need more light. Consider moving these to another area of

PLANT LIST—SUNNY WINDOW

Botanical Name	Common Name
1. *Juniperus sargentii*	Sargent's juniper
2. *Iris germanica*	German iris
3. *Pachysandra terminalis*	Japanese spurge, pachysandra
4. *Liriope sp.*	Liriope
5. *Paeonia*	Peony
6. *Hemerocallis*	Day lily
7. *Taxus cuspidata capitata*	Pyramid yew

▲ Plants for sunny window area.

the garden and finding new, shade-tolerant plants to replace them. Begonias, impatiens, coleus, and other shade-tolerant plants can give a bright show of color where petunias and marigolds don't perform well.

Hostas remain one of a gardener's best assets for shady spots. Many new varieties are being introduced with attractive bicolor, mottled, and distinctive foliage. Another advantage is that once planted, hostas require virtually no care.

If you are unsure how a plant will perform in a problem area, try one or two plants of the types you would like, perhaps in a container, and test them for one season. Many gardeners try out new plants on a small scale to see how they really do in their gardens before going through a considerable amount of effort to create the effect they want.

PLANT LIST—SHADY WINDOW

Botanical Name	Common Name
1. *Kalmia latifolia*	Mountain laurel
2. *Convallaria majalis*	Lily of the valley
3. *Clematis*	Clematis
4. *Caladium bicolor*	Caladiums
5. *Hosta sp.*	Hosta lily
6. *Hypericum*	Hypericum
7. *Sedum acre*	Moss sedum

▲ Plants for shady window area.

Match Plant Needs to Your Garden Spots

To prevent problems, it helps to match plants to their needed growing conditions in various parts of your garden. You'll find some key plants here based on the type of habitat they prefer. Talk to your local garden expert or consult catalogs and magazines if you are unable to find your desired plants listed here.

Trees That Tolerate Standing Water in Spring

- Balsam Fir (*Abies balsamea*)
- Red Maple (*Acer rubrum*)
- Silver Maple (*Acer saccharinum*)
- Alder (*Alnus*)

- River Birch (*Betula nigra*)
- Green Ash (*Fraxinus pennsylvanica*)
- Winterberry (*Ilex verticillata*)

Plants That Tolerate Drought

- Japanese Barberry (*Berberis thunbergii*)
- New Jersey Tea (*Ceanothus americanus*)
- Hawthorns (*Crataegus*)
- Dwarf Bush Honeysuckle (*Diervilla lonicera*)
- Russian Olive (*Elaeagnus angustifolia*)
- Green Ash (*Fraxinus pennsylvanica*)
- Common Juniper (*Juniperus communis depressa*)
- Eastern Red Cedar (*Juniperus virginiana*)
- Red Pine (*Pinus resinosa*)
- Scotch Pine (*Pinus sylvestris*)
- Fragrant Sumac (*Rhus aromatica*)

Plants That Tolerate Shade

- Balsam Fir (*Abies balsamea*)
- Amur Maple (*Acer ginnala*)
- Sugar Maple (*Acer saccharum*)
- Juneberries (*Amelanchier*)
- Winged Euonymus (*Euonymus alatus*)
- Smooth Hydrangea and its cultivars (*Hydrangea arborescens*)
- Japanese Yew (*Taxus cuspidata*)
- Arborvitae and its cultivars (*Thuja occidentalis*)
- European Highbush Cranberry (*Viburnum opulus*)

Chapter 19

Memorable Biblical Gardens

The Bible is alive with colorful descriptions of plants. For landscaping purposes, this chapter will focus on the flowers (typically bulbous plants) native to the Mediterranean area. If biblical gardens entice you, you may want to explore further. Therefore, this chapter also offers some great sources of information.

Biblical Flowers Featured

This chapter focuses on biblical plants that meet several criteria. First of all, they must be authentically identified plants of the Bible that grew in the Holy Land during the time in which the Bible was written. Second, they must be available today as specimens, seeds, roots, or bulbs from reliable sources. Third, they must be reasonably easy to grow in gardens in North America. You'll probably be surprised that you already know many of these beautiful flowers. Much of the information you'll find in this chapter is based on *Flowers of the Bible* by Allan A. Swenson. These chosen flowers include:

- Crocus
- Cyclamen
- Hyacinth
- Iris
- Lily
- Narcissus
- Tulip

Perennial Beauty for Years

One of the best things about biblical flowers is that they are perennials that will reappear to add their glorious displays to your landscape for years to come. In fact, some will actually multiply with underground bulblets that mature to produce profusions of blooms in mass groups in the future. Because they have such value, these are some of the first plants that you should add to your gardens.

To take a virtual tour of the world's largest biblical garden, the 625-acre Biblical Landscape Reserve in the Holy Land, fly there on the Internet and walk the trails illustrated with beautiful plants at *www.neot-kedumim.org.il*.

Land Stewardship Important

There are many valuable lessons about gardening in the Bible. An important one is that all people must be stewards of the land. You, too, can help make every square yard of your garden ground more abundantly productive. And that also includes revitalizing and beautifying empty city lots, turning ugly spaces into garden spots, perhaps with help from family, friends, and neighbors.

Every conservation-minded gardener can do much to make this world a better place, a fruitful place, a more beautiful place. There actually are Bible admonitions to let the land rest. That is the first teaching of crop rotation.

Your Soil Is a Bank

As gardeners, think of your soil as a bank. Your plants can take out only in proportion to what you have put in. You certainly cannot take more money out of your bank account than what you have put in, and the same theory applies to the soil. For example, the plants you plant will take all that they need to survive from the soil; therefore, you should put back those elements, by making deposits of fertilizer, compost, and mulch to keep the soil balanced.

Facts about Biblical Flowers

The Holy Land, Asia Minor and the countries bordering the Mediterranean Sea, are the sources of the classic bulbous flowering plants so popular in America and Europe today. From these regions have come our crocuses and cyclamens, hyacinths and irises, lilies and tulips. These flowers developed there under the hot dry season that forced them into dormancy, and then experienced a brief moist period that forced them into bloom.

The Meaning of Bulb

The term bulb is a horticultural term that is usually interpreted rather broadly. It includes the true bulbs, which have food storage parts within the bulb. For example, cut a tulip or narcissus bulb in half and you will see the makings of a complete plant: leaves, stem, and flowers, with its food stored within. Today, the word bulb has also come to mean similar bulbous roots that are called corms, rhizomes, and tubers by botanists. These plants are ideally suited for survival and adaptation.

Flowers, Passages, and Latin Names

Biblical gardens have become increasingly popular lately. More are being planted at homes as well as at places of worship and religious schools. For historical reference, here are key biblical flowers that can be traced to actual scriptural references. You can look them up in various translations and versions of the Bible as you wish. All grow well as potted plants and also are available at florist shops.

- **Anemone** (*Anemone coronaria*): Matthew 6:28
- **Saffron Crocus** (*Crocus sativus*): Isaiah 35:1, Song of Solomon 4:14
- **Cyclamen** (*Cyclamen persicum*): Song of Solomon
- **Daffodil or Narcissus** (*Narcissus* or *N. tazetta*): Matthew 6:28, Isaiah 35:1
- **Hyacinth** (*Hyacinthus orientalis*): Song of Solomon 6:2–3
- **Iris, Yellow Flag** (*Iris pseudacorus*): Hosea 14:5
- **Lily, Madonna** (*Lilium candidum*): Song of Solomon 2:1–2
- **Tulip, Sharon** (*Tulipa*): Song of Solomon 2:12

There are many other flowers that could be identified as having been mentioned in the Scriptures, but in more generic terms.

FACT

Here's another newsworthy fact: More people have been growing pots of these biblical flowers to give to friends when visiting because of their special significance as flowers of the Holy Land and Scriptures.

Attractive Anemones

In early spring in the Holy Land, many thousands of crown anemones appear. They are dramatic in scarlet but also appear in purple, pink, blue, and white blooms. The fields, wastelands, and hills throughout the Mediterranean area are colorfully alive with this delightful flower. A passage from the Scriptures describes that beauty well.

And why take ye thought for raiment? Consider the lilies of the field, how they grow; they toil not, neither do they spin: And yet I say unto you, That even Solomon in all his glory was not arrayed like one of these.

—Matthew 6:28–29

Many scholars believe anemones are the flower meant in these passages, not the lily. The Madonna lily is not especially common in Israel. Most authorities now agree that the Madonna lily cannot be the "lilies of the field" of Matthew 6:28 and Luke 12:27. Since most authorities today regard the Palestine anemone, *Anemone coronaria,* as the famous "lily of the field," we are inclined to accept the majority viewpoint.

Your Choice of Anemones

If you prefer bright red anemones, select De Caen Hollandia, a special variety now widely available. Plant them in groups. Each tuber produces four to six single flowers at intervals of 1 to 2 weeks. For bright blue anemones, select De Caen Blue Poppy, which adds rare blue blooms to your summer garden.

You also have another option, the Japanese anemone, *A. japonica,* which is an autumn-blooming species. Adding these to your garden lets you enjoy both a spring and a fall display of anemones. Plants grow 12 to 15 inches tall. Space corms 2 to 3 inches apart. They grow nicely in horticultural zones 6 to 10. Plant these anemones in groups in borders or beds. They also make excellent displays with other flowers. You can use them to brighten vegetable gardens, too.

Growing Tips

Anemones grow well from tiny tubers, which should be soaked for 24 hours in warm water before you plant them in the ground after all danger of frost has well passed in the area in which you live. Anemones are useful as ground covers and prefer light shade.

Plant tubers about 2 inches deep and 2 to 4 inches apart in cool, moist, and well-drained soil. In northern states, plant anemones in the early spring or fall. In southern areas, plant in the fall and cover with mulch during the first winter. Although they thrive wild in rocky, poor soil, for best results in gardens they should have compost and fertilizer periodically. Cover with mulch to save moisture and thwart weeds.

Use anemones in rock gardens, under shrubs, and beneath trees. They are excellent for tucking into many spots to brighten landscapes every year.

Crocus Is Calling

The Saffron Crocus, *Crocus sativus,* is native to Asia Minor and Greece, and is also found in other Mediterranean countries. After the stigmas and styles (those distinctive reproductive parts of the flower) are gathered, they are dried in the sun, then pounded into small cakes. This expensive product is used primarily as a yellow dye and also for coloring and flavoring in curries and Oriental foods. Another pleasant passage reminds us of the beauty of the crocus.

> *The desert shall rejoice and blossom; like the crocus it shall blossom abundantly, and rejoice with joy and singing.*
>
> —Isaiah 35:1–2

Welcomers of Spring

Crocus, a genus comprised of closely related plants with a single name, are hardy perennial plants that produce a single tubular flower from a corm. They have grasslike leaves that grow in a rosette pattern. The common fall crocus, *C. sativus,* has bright lilac-blue flowers. Spring-flowering crocuses, including the early-flowering so-called Dutch crocus, are available in violet to purple hues and in various other colors.

The saffron crocus closely resembles our springtime crocus, but it actually blooms in its native habitat in late autumn. The saffron crocus is a tiny plant with a subterranean corm. It produces several narrow leaves and one or more large, bluish-lilac flowers. You may choose the purple-blue spring crocus for your garden or the purple fall crocus that also thrives across northern regions of America.

Crocus bulbs are easy to plant. No garden should be without these cheerful welcomers of spring. By planting the largest, earliest-flowering varieties, you often will be greeted by their colorful blooms even before all snow has melted. The fall types multiply rapidly without care or trouble.

Growing Tips for Crocuses

Plant autumn crocuses in the spring, in sun or light-shade areas. As a perennial, they become a permanent part of your plantscape beneath trees, under shrubs, in beds, and along pathways. Spring-flowering crocuses should be planted between mid-September and early November, before the ground freezes. Plant bulbs 3 to 4 inches deep in clusters or groups.

FACT

For best results, it pays to obtain larger corms, which cost a little more but produce bigger blooms and get your garden started better. That fact is true for all bulbs. Larger ones produce better, bigger blooms the first year and are worthwhile investments for your perennial bulb gardens.

The Captivating Cyclamen

Most likely, the cyclamen is another prime contender as a "lily of the fields," according to botanists. There are many scholars, botanical and biblical alike, who have been researching the history and heritage of Holy Land flowers for centuries. Often they focus on key scriptural passages in their attempts to determine the true identify of the actual flower. When earliest translations of the Bible were made, there was no botanical nomenclature. The term lilies was loosely translated to mean a variety of common flowers.

Cyclamen persicum is also called by a common name, alpine violet. It grows wild in stone walls, among rocks and crevices, and along roadways in the Holy Land today. This plant prefers an acidic soil and some shade from the afternoon sun. Cyclamens offer a long blooming period compared to most other flowers. Now that hardy varieties are more readily available, they are prime candidates for every biblical garden.

Cyclamen persicum closely resembles the cyclamen of the Holy Land. This hardy cyclamen needs a soil with lots of sand and composted leaf humus for zones 6 through 9. Space them 8 to 12 inches apart. Mulching is important in fall to insulate the ground from freeze-and-thaw cycles that can damage even hardy types.

Another type, *Cyclamen neapolitanum,* also is hardy and ideal for gardens and naturalizing. It is good for rock gardens or shaded areas under trees and shrubs, as is *Cyclamen cilicium,* another hardy cyclamen that performs well as a ground cover.

Hail the Hyacinth!

Hyacinths are one of the most welcome delights among biblical plants because of their marvelous fragrance. These distinctive flowers originated in Palestine and the Middle East, and ancient writings reveal that they were cultivated by some of the world's earliest gardeners.

> *I belong to my beloved and my beloved to me, who pastures his flock among the hyacinths.*
>
> —Song of Solomon 6:3

Their true significance and identity as a flower mentioned in the Scriptures has been debated for centuries. *Hyacinth* is the common name for a genus of plants of the lily family, *Liliaceae.* They have been cherished as garden and houseplants for centuries in temperate and tropical climates around the world. Hyacinths are bulbous plants with sword-shaped leaves. Flowers appear on long spikes and have three petallike sepals, three petals, and six stamens.

Hyacinth Advantages

In Palestine and other areas of the Middle East, the hyacinth flowers profusely in the wild, bearing deep blue, highly fragrant spikes. You can obtain good hyacinth bulbs in local garden centers or departments that will provide excellent flowers on sturdy stems. For the largest blooms, you should order mammoth bulbs 18 to 20 centimeters in size, which produce glorious displays. Like tulips and daffodils, hyacinths have been hybridized to exceptional quality and growth performance by plant breeders.

The Goodspeed translation of the Bible makes a point of focusing on the hyacinth in The Song of Solomon 2:1–2: "I am a saffron of the plain, a hyacinth of the valleys."

Hyacinths have another marvelous advantage. They produce magnificent blooms in special hyacinth-growing glasses. You can obtain kits of these giant bulbs that nestle in the tops of these glasses at some of the major chain stores like Wal-Mart and Home Depot. Local garden centers also often carry them. This makes a fun family blooming project from late October to December to give you the color and fragrance of a biblical garden indoors.

Dig Deep to Grow Hyacinths Well

Hyacinths will produce blooms in any type of reasonably fertile soil that is well drained. They, like most other bulbous plants, do not tolerate soggy root conditions. Because they are spring-blooming, hyacinths should be planted in the fall, between the middle of September and late October.

For hyacinths, you should dig more deeply than is required by other bulbous plants. They prefer 12 inches of well-drained soil under the bulb since roots grow about 10 to 12 inches deeper down in the soil. It pays to dig down deeply, plant well, and enjoy this most fragrant of biblical plants for decades to come.

Growing Tips for Hyacinths

Plant actual bulbs 6 inches deep and give them sufficient room by spacing them 5 to 8 inches apart in beds. Hyacinths can remain in that location for years. If you want really massed color, plant bulbs closer to one another but be prepared to compensate for close planting with extra fertilizer each year. In outdoor gardens, be sure to let foliage ripen after plants have bloomed. The leaves must manufacture food and store it in the bulbs to produce and nourish next year's plants. A light mulch helps prevent bulb heaving in cold winter areas.

Hyacinths thwart squirrels, chipmunks, and even deer. There are irritating chemicals contained in the bulbs, which even give some people an itchy rash. If you have sensitive skin, wash well after planting them.

Enjoy Irises

In the Holy Land you will see what appear to be yellow irises along waterways and moist areas. Many scholars believe it probably is the yellow water iris, commonly called the yellow flag iris today. Many species of iris grow on hills and mountainsides, in fields, and even in drier areas. One particular scriptural passage relates to this plant, which does indeed "cast forth its roots," giving botanical scholars a clue to the plant's true identity.

> *I will be as the dew unto Israel: he shall grow as the lily, and cast forth his roots as Lebanon.*
>
> —Hosea 14:5

The yellow flag displays its beauty along streams and waterways, often in masses of color. Because it flourishes along the edge of streams where you also find poplar and willow trees growing, botanists believe the yellow flag may be the plant indicated in the passage from Hosea.

The Eurasian yellow flag, *I. pseudacorus*, is actually one of the most common wild irises in the world, blooming in June and July in temperate climates. You can also find a wide variety of beautiful irises that are related to the biblical yellow flag irises. Many gardeners prefer these new hybrids for gardens, so you'll find directions for growing both types below.

Growing Tips for Wild Iris

Wild irises, like their domesticated and hybrid relatives, can be transplanted easily by moving entire clumps or dividing the rhizomes with a sharp knife. Iris rhizomes must be planted right at the surface, never beneath soil. If planted deeply, iris won't thrive. Cultivated hybrid Irises prefer well-drained soil, but they'll grow in sandy to clay, and they prefer full-sun locations. July to September is the best planting time. Space rhizomes 1 to 2 feet apart. Set with tops just beneath soil surface, spreading roots well. Water well and periodically until plants set their roots.

Growing Tips for Yellow Flag

For success with the yellow flag, which likes wet locations, plant in the muddy shores of streams or ditches, or keep soil moist. Divide rhizomes with a sharp knife and plant at the soil surface. Move entire clumps if available and set into wet-soil areas.

Visit your local garden center or check through mail-order catalogs to find the best-looking yellow iris as a representative biblical iris.

Nurture the Narcissus

The narcissus is thought by some to be the biblical lily. Many biblical and botanical scholars also believe that the narcissus fittingly represents the flowers noted in Scriptures, and some base their determination on their analysis of this passage.

The wilderness and the solitary place shall be glad for them; and the desert shall rejoice, and blossom as the rose.

—Isaiah 35:1

Despite the use of the word *rose,* scholars have noted where such plants live in the Holy Land and have mostly agreed that the narcissus is truly a flower meant in scriptural passages. Actually, narcissi were notable in ancient times and still grace the wild areas of the Holy Land today each spring.

Description of Narcissi

The plants have long, slender leaves growing upward from the bulbous root. The flowers usually have six petallike sepals, a corolla of six united petals, six stamens, and a solitary pistil. The cup-shaped crown, called the corona, rises from the inner surface of the corolla. Flowers are usually yellow, with combinations of shades.

FACT

Narcissi are also called daffodils by many and are one of the first harbingers of spring, blooming right after crocuses do. Their large flowers appear early and they thrive in moist soil, doing best in temperate climate areas.

Dutch hybridizers have made their talented contributions to this plant, too, creating hundreds if not thousands of variations. You can put them to dramatic accent use in your garden; naturalize them in meadows, under trees, or under shrubs; or use them to create giant flowering crosses in green lawns for spring display.

Growing Tips for Narcissi

Dig deeply for fall planting so roots can grow and establish the plant before cold weather arrives to freeze the ground. Plant narcissus bulbs at least 4 to 6 inches deep between September and mid-November. Water well as you plant and moisten again weekly so they begin their life in your garden properly.

Narcissi are beautiful in massed springtime displays. They also are appealing in beds and borders, under trees and shrubs. Many gardeners consider these flowers one of the most versatile and long-lasting perennials to use in home garden landscaping.

Narcissus bulbs contain alkaloids that are poisons and can cause severe vomiting and convulsions. Exercise caution as you plant them so children and pets are kept safe.

Tempted by the Tulip

The vibrant wild tulip of the Holy Land bears a single, bright red flower. Ancient records tell us that tulips were cultivated ages ago in Turkey. The name *tulip,* some linguists believe, comes from a Persian word meaning "turban." No doubt their roots are set deep in antiquity, and they still grow wild in modern Israel. Since they do, and are such lovely flowers, they deserve a prominent place in any biblical flower garden.

Tulip is the common name for a genus of spring-flowering, bulbous flowers of the lily family, *Liliaceae,* that are native to the Mediterranean area. Thousands of glorious and dramatic hybrid types have been created by plant breeders to grace our gardens.

Botanical wild tulips from the Dutch Gardens mail-order firm offer a low growing size. A collection of red and yellow colors provides a pleasing contrast and bloom mid- to late spring, with flowers only 4 to 6274inches tall with open blossoms. They naturalize well for years of perennial beauty.

Typically, tulips are erect plants with long, broad leaves and cup-shaped, solitary flowers at the tip of the stem. Red Emperor is one of America's best-loved tulips. It produces large, bright red blooms on stalks about 14 to 16 inches tall. Space 4 inches apart in zones 3 through 8 for early spring flowering. Red Riding Hood and Scheherazade are others that provide a dramatic red color mass.

Other Special Tulips

Greigii species and hybrids are other attractive types of tulips. They offer you large flowers as well as attractive foliage. Related to the wild Oriental Greigi tulip, these plants do well in good sun or semisun. Species tulips are particularly valuable because they multiply and require little care. They bloom very early and are attractive in rock gardens, along walls and walks, and in naturalized settings.

Praetans tulips seem remarkably close to the wild tulip of the Holy Land as well. Princeps have brilliant scarlet color for dramatic displays. Check different types of tulips out in colorful mail-order catalogs.

FACT

A favorite cultivated tulip that closely resembles the native Holy Land tulip is a praetans called Fusilier. It matures at 8 to 10 inches high in zones 3 through 8. A vivid, early spring–flowering tulip, it fits rock gardens and nooks and crannies, naturalizes well, and produces five to six flowers on each stem, which is unusual, and gives massed color when spaced 4 inches apart.

Growing Tips for Tulips

Plant tulip bulbs between early October and mid-December for strong spring growth. Ideal soil is a light, fertile, well-drained loam. Well-rotted compost made from manure, weeds, and other organic material is a good soil additive to improve growing conditions. Leave tulip foliage alone until it finally yellows. Foliage is the food-building part of these plants.

Informative Sources

This chapter is based on several reliable resources. First is *Cruden's Concordance,* written in 1737 by Alexander Cruden, which contains 200,000 references to words of the Scriptures found in both Old and New Testaments, providing the books, chapters, and verses in which the words were used. Another informative and illuminating book is *Plants of the Bible* by Harold N. and Alma L. Moldenke. This is the classic, highly respected book that provides probable botanical names and logical alternatives in its plant-identifying process. Finally, *Plants of the Bible and How to Grow Them* is a modern reference by Allan A. Swenson that traces the botanical identifications to the Scriptures and then provides how-to details for growing all the major plants traced to Scripture in North America.

Chapter 20

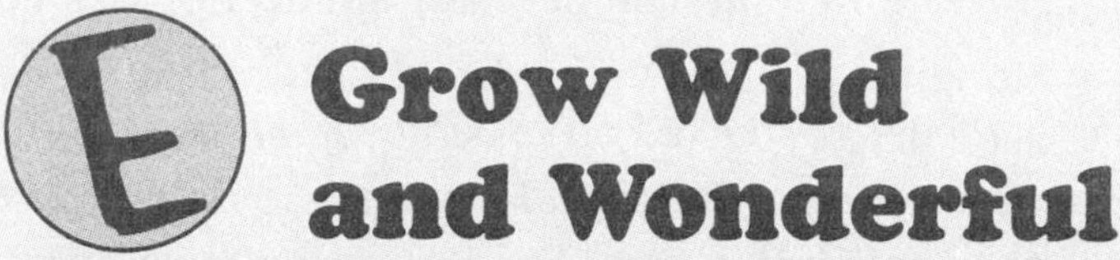

Grow Wild and Wonderful

Don't mow miles of lawn this year. Grow wild instead. You'll save gas, dollars, and time. Best of all, you'll see your unmowed lawn become a blooming meadow of wildflower beauty. If you are hesitant to do so, at least give it a shot on a small area of your site. You may discover how wonderful and naturally beautiful it can be.

Let Your Mind Run Wild

You'll be amazed at how many delightful, different flowers will grace a natural meadow. Many sprout from roots or dormant seeds. Others begin their life cycles when birds or wind carry seeds from one location to another. New wild beauty will sprout, grow, and delight you from spring to fall with virtually no work and little need for fertilizer or pest control chemicals.

One veteran gardener conducted an experiment. He simply left one area of his lawn alone to see what would happen. He didn't mow or cultivate, just let nature take its course. You can imagine his delight when he ended up with a gorgeous wildflower meadow.

No Mow Secrets

He shared his secrets. Frankly, he just didn't mow about a quarter acre of lawn. First came glorious golden dandelions. Next, in early spring, hundreds of tiny bluets appeared. Violets appeared next. The second year, the lawn area gave forth a purplish haze for several weeks during spring. Lupines appeared with 8- to 10-inch purple bloom spikes for dramatic displays.

Then hawkweed sprouted. What seemed to be dandelions at first glance were 10-inch-tall stalks with yellow blooms. They flourished. Next, daisies bloomed in June. Their fernlike foliage matured, supporting bright white ox-eye blossoms with golden yellow centers. Red and white clover reappeared, beckoning bees to a harvest of pollen. By July, scattered black-eyed Susans burst forth. Their radiant yellow petals surrounding dark centers brightened the unmowed, waving grass. Finally, asters sprouted, cascading white and even purple-hued blooms through the fall. Perhaps the richest reward was the time saved. He used it to enjoy this natural wildflower world, a colorful bouquet in his own backyard. It grows on to this day, glorious and untended, naturally.

Advantages of Wildflowers

Wildflowers have natural advantages over cultivated ones. They are naturally hardy, usually self-propagating, and almost as indestructible as weeds. Better yet, they provide the beautiful answer to the question of what to do with those areas plagued with inhospitable soil.

Growing Tips

Here are tips for growing wild.

- Select healthy material and give plants the same soil in which they grew in their native habitat.
- Always plant immediately after you bring plants home. If you can't plant, dig a trench in the ground and set their roots in it. Cover the plants with soil and keep them moist until you are ready to place them in their permanent location.
- Set plants at the same depth at which they grew naturally. It pays to gather extra soil with the plants you dig up so they will be comfortable in their new setting.
- Clear space around the new planting to avoid competition from weeds. A layer of mulch helps smother weeds until your wildings get well rooted.
- Water during the first few days and then weekly until they are established.
- Collect decaying humus from around the plant when you take it from its native ground. Then spread it around the plants to mulch and to let the natural soil organisms work their wonders as they did where the plants grew originally.

Before collecting wildflowers, always find out if the flowers are on any rare or restricted lists. These flowers should be left alone in their native habitat. This information is available from your state conservation officials or a local garden center expert. Also be sure to get permission from landowners before you dig up plants on their property.

Start simply in a small way, a few clumps of plants at a time. Always match their growing needs to conditions around your home. Plants, like people, have a fondness and a need for certain types of living conditions.

Mulch during the first winter with dead leaves to reduce the risk of frost heaves. In spring, clear away this mulch gradually and carefully as the weather warms.

Visit wildflower specialist nurseries. They often provide individual plants, seeds, and collections of mixed varieties that are native to certain areas. Those specialty firms also provide you with helpful tips, ideas, and advice invaluable to the success of your wildflowers. Wildseed Farms and the Vermont Wildflower Farm are both great sources for information.

It's Easy to Grow Wild

You can enjoy a beautiful wildflower garden by following these easy steps. You start with a natural advantage. Wildflowers are native. Therefore, they are both hardy and acclimated to your area. Begin simply. Try a few wild plants that catch your eye. Add to your collection gradually so that you get a feel for the adventure of growing wild.

Select healthy material, whether dug from the wild with permission of the landowner or purchased from a wildflower specialist. Set your wild plants in the ground the day you obtain them.

FACT

If your plants are collected from the wild, bring sufficient woodland litter and soil from their native location to provide conditions as close as possible to those in which the plants normally grow. Give each plant the same soil in which it grew wild.

Be sure to provide your wild plants with the same type of location and the same amount of sunlight or shade they are used to. Set them at the same soil depth at which they grew originally. Water the first few days or until you see that your new wild plants have settled in well. Protect them from dogs, cats, and children who might unwittingly trample them.

Mulch the first year with similar materials to those that fall naturally where the plants grew. Clear mulch gradually in the spring but leave some to decompose. That adds valuable humus to promote the growth of wildings.

Finally, spend time with your wild wonders. Observe their growth and tend to their needs. Most will require little care once they become well rooted. Grow wild this year. You'll find new natural beauty all around you, and growing wild is a fun side of gardening naturally.

Delightful Daisies

You'll enjoy more than a daisy a day when you grow ox-eye daisies. They'll reward you with backyard bouquets every day throughout much of the summer. Daisies are easy to grow, delightful to view, and surprisingly prolific.

Daisy Description

Originally from Europe, these well-established flowers are truly naturalized Americans. They grow well all across the United States. Fernlike leaves give the plants a graceful look. The sparkling white petals surround bright yellow-gold centers. Blooms stand 15 to 23 inches tall on sturdy stems. Flowers are 1 to 1½ inches across. They are ideal for cutting and are long lasting in water for indoor decorations.

FACT

Daisies long have been lauded in poems and songs. Children have traditionally used them to make daisy chains. Young lovers have pulled the petals saying, "he loves me, he loves me not." Daisies are deeply rooted in folklore.

Satisfy Their Needs

Daisies love sun. They are found in open fields, along roadsides, and in empty city lots. Since they thrive on a wide range of soils, daisies are easily grown in most garden areas.

The best planting time is spring or fall. From wild plants, select and divide large clumps. Keep roots wrapped in moist moss covered with plastic until you plant them. You also can grow ox-eye daisies from seed. Collect seeds in late summer from mature plants. Sow them in the fall, as nature would, or save until the spring

Black-Eyed Beauties

Black-eyed Susans will never give your garden a black eye, despite their name. You'll delight in their nodding blooms of bright golden petals around the dark brown "eyes," the centers of these wildflowers that give them their popular name. They are hardy native Americans that prefer well-drained, even fairly dry soils. Their ability to grow well even in poorer, sandy soils makes them a perfect match for daisies and clover in a natural meadow habitat.

Foliage and leaves are rough and bristly. Flowers burst into bloom on stems 2 to 3 feet tall. Blooms of golden yellow petals with purple-brown centers may be 1½ to 2½ inches across, and they add a colorful display in late summer to wild areas and cultivated flower borders alike.

Mature plants can be moved easily in the fall. Young plants can be set in early spring. Seeds are widely available from mail-order firms, or you can collect your own from wild plants. Sow seeds in summer. They will germinate and overwinter as young plants, to bloom the following year. Once established, these delights will display their beauty year after year.

Glorious Goldenrod

In Europe, especially in England, goldenrod is a prized plant for borders and flower gardens. Goldenrod doesn't cause hay fever. Its pollen is too heavy to be carried by wind. Ragweed is the real culprit, but since goldenrod blooms at the same time and is more visible, it gets the blame. Once you understand that, you can begin to appreciate goldenrod's value as a decorative garden plant.

FACT

Goldenrod grows tall, from 2 to 5 feet. Because it is a hardy native, it is easy to grow and maintain. Blooms are myriad golden yellow flowers borne as a crest on the tall stems. Leaves are typically lance-shaped, toothed, and somewhat woolly beneath.

Varieties of Goldenrod

There are many varieties of this distinctive yellow wildflower, from classic Canadian to lance-leafed, from seaside to more common fall goldenrod. All display their golden yellow finery in late summer through most of the fall. Many types survive early frosts to carry color well beyond the typical garden season.

Goldenrod Growing Tips

You can divide old clumps from the wild, matching their growing situation to the desired location at home. Most types prefer somewhat acid soil, so applications of oak leaf and sawdust are much advised. Seeds also sprout well. You may wish to collect mature flower heads and simply bury the dried heads, which contain hundreds of seeds, to establish new plants for the next spring and add a golden glow to fall.

Violets Love You

Violets are true blue, plus white, purple, yellow, and lovely shades in between. You have a wide choice among the wild violet family. Some like sun; others thrive in shade. Some tolerate poor soil while others prefer richer conditions. All grow nicely low, so they fit well into beds and borders, around trees and shrubs, and in rock gardens, too. With time, most will form dense clumps. Those that don't will proliferate to carpet an area with dozens to hundreds of tiny plants.

No matter where you live, there are wild native violets for rock gardens, beds, borders, or just growing wild in your uncut lawn areas. Transplant by dividing clumps in spring or fall. Most root readily and spread themselves by seeds through the years.

Try fragrant sweet white violets. They're adaptable to acid or alkaline conditions in dry or moist ground, light or heavy soil. Common violets are uncommonly easy to grow. They prefer loamy soil and sun and grow

3 to 7 inches tall with ½-inch rich purple flowers. Bird's foot violets, with odd-shaped leaves, thrive in the acid soil of open woods and sandy fields. These plants have light violet blooms ½ inch across.

Downy yellow violets are native to dry, rich woodland soil. The ¾-inch flowers bloom in early spring on 6- to 15-inch plants. Their downy leaves are attractive, too. A smooth yellow variety prefers moist woods and stream borders. Woods violets, thin-leafed, early blue, and a dozen other varieties are native to different regions.

Wild Iris Are Elegant

Iris blooms have been admired throughout recorded history. The fleur-de-lis pattern has been captured in tapestries, carvings, and ceremonial banners from ancient times through the present. Wild flag irises have a long, hardy tradition that you can add to your home gardens. The large blue flag iris shoots its lance-shaped leaves from wet meadows and pastures in early spring. Its neatly furled buds burst into violet blossom on 16- to 30-inch stems. Although this iris prefers marshes, wet pastures, and banks of streams, it will flourish in moist garden soils or boggy areas if provided regularly with ample moisture.

Try Blue or Yellow Iris

Blue flags will reward you more profusely each year with violet-blue, purplish, and slate blue blooms. Southern varieties tend to be short but just as decorative for gardens and wild areas.

Yellow flag or sword flag iris produces 3- to 4-foot stems, flanked by 12- to 18-inch leaves. This, too, is a marsh plant, favoring borders of swamps, ditches, and streams. It must be well watered to thrive. The crested dwarf iris with light blue to violet blooms prefers a slightly drier habitat. The slender blue iris has violet-blue blooms veined with deeper blue.

Iris Growing Tips

All wild irises, like their domesticated relatives, can easily be transplanted by moving entire clumps. Or, you can divide the rhizomes with a sharp knife. Then replant the rhizomes at the soil surface, just tucked in enough to stay in place. If they are too deeply planted, they won't thrive.

Fall Is Aster Time

Wild asters give us sparkle and color in the fall after most other flowers have passed their prime and gone to seed. They are prolific, hardy, and grow well even in poorer soils, so they deserve a place wherever you wish to grow wild. Low-growing types cling to the ground and are ideal for rock gardens, slopes, low beds, and borders. Taller types 2 to 5 feet tall and bearing profuse blooms can be used as a backdrop for lower plants. Some asters are common in sunny meadows, along roadsides, and at the seashore. Other types prefer shade and thrive in wooded settings.

Look over your home grounds. Then find and transplant the appealing varieties that match your own habitat. Many asters are now available from wildflower seed firms and mail-order catalogs. New England asters provide shaggy flowers of dark purple with golden center blooms in late fall. Other, dense-flowered asters have tiny white blooms on plants 1 to 6 inches high. White wood asters, with 1-inch blooms on 2-foot-tall plants, prefer dry, open woods and thickets. Calico aster, michaelmas aster, willow aster, sharp-leafed, and others all have their own appeal.

The best method of propagation is by dividing mature clumps in late summer. The second best is by collecting their seeds and scattering them in the fall in areas that match their native locale.

Super Sunny Sunflowers

Marvelous sunflowers turn their beautiful blooming heads to follow the sun in its daily journey east to west across the sky. These radiant flowers are hardy natives nationwide. Sunflowers are highly regarded for food, for humans as well as birds. The giant cultivated varieties have huge seed-filled heads. Early Spanish explorers introduced these valued, prolific plants to Europe centuries ago. Sunflowers are now well rooted there and a major cultivated crop around the world.

QUESTION?

What exactly is a wildflower?

Simply put, wildflowers are flowering plants that grow in their natural state with little interference from man. They are not bred or cross-bred the way hybrids and cultivated annuals and perennials are. Basically, wildflowers may be considered "natural" because they grow without someone planning where they should be planted.

You'll enjoy the sparkling displays that wild sunflowers provide for weeks during the summer. Their golden yellow blooms are common in fields and meadows in sunny areas only, of course. They thrive even in poor, sandy, gravelly soils, but are most productive in sandy loam. The common sunflower is an annual with yellow petals radiating from a darker yellow center. The stems are 3 to 10 feet tall, while blooms are 3 to 6 inches across.

The best propagation is from seed for both common and giant varieties. You can easily gather seeds in your travels during the fall, drying them for spring plants. Most wildflower nurseries offer these glorious plants. Sunflowers will grow in all states but do best outside the Deep South.

The Call of the Wild

One of the many appealing qualities of wildflowers is that they are low maintenance. Once established, wildflowers usually require less attention than "cultivated" types of plants. Their less formal nature is also very appealing. As named, they are more "wild" than "tamed." Deciding which wildflowers to grow depends on where you live and where in your garden you want to grow them.

Learn Wildflower Names

It pays to learn their real names, because wildflowers can be purchased as seeds or plants, as a single species, or in mixes. The common names of plants can vary from one area to another. For example, one name for *Centaurea cyanus* is "cornflower." However, "Bachelor's Button" is yet another common name. To avoid confusion, get to know the botanical names of those flowers you want to plant. By law, the packaging of wildflowers must list genus and species, so finding what you want shouldn't be too difficult. Check catalogs for scientific names of wildflowers.

New Wildflower Growing Help

As the wildflower-growing trend has expanded, many helpful aids have been introduced. No longer do you need to find wild plants and ask permission to dig a specimen, or gather seed and worry through the first year's growth, as early wildflower gardeners did. There are a number of easy-to-plant-and-grow wildflower products available to help you succeed. With all these helpful aids, it's time to think about going a little wild in the garden.

Popular with those wanting to grow wild gardens are seed packets that offer a variety of wildflower types ranging in sizes, colors, and textures. These packets are often available for particular regions, such as the Midwest, New England, and the South. Started plant mixtures are also available.

Canned Wildflowers

You can find cans of wildflower seeds in retail and mail-order outlets. The cans are often designated for specific regions and contain a variety of wildflowers that is native to that particular region. Sometimes, the cans are designated for growing conditions (shade or sun) instead. They also contain inorganic carrier materials such as vermiculite that aid in spreading seed evenly, especially in large areas.

Preseeded Wildflower Mats

You can also buy wildflower seed mixes in mat form. The mat form makes it easy and convenient for you to produce a wildflower garden. The mats are available in a range of sizes and already contain the wildflower seeds. All you have to do is lay the mat down, water it, and wait for the flower to spring up! Mats are often made of a wood fiber material and are biodegradable. Of course, not all mats are the same: some provide nutrients, others don't. Be sure to read the directions on the package.

Wildflower Sods Available

If you'd rather purchase started plants to get a jump on blooming beauty, then you have the option of buying wildflower sods. The sod contains already-established plants and requires you only to lay it down on prepared soil and water. Pretty easy. An added advantage is that the sod can be cut into any shape you desire.

FACT

For more information about wildflower seed suppliers, contact the National Garden Bureau, Suite 310, 1311 Butterfield Road, Downers Grove, IL 60515, and ask for a list of the bureau members who offer wildflower seeds and products.

Grow Your Own State Flower

Native American wildflowers are delightful additions to any home garden. Being native, they are hardy and adaptable. Best of all, they are beautiful. Some states have selected native wildflowers as their official state flowers. You'll find them here. Other states have selected flowers that may be cultivated plants but that truly represent the state well.

Every state has its official flower, selected for its unique beauty as a true representative of that state. Sometimes two states share the same flower. By growing these flowers, you can cultivate the plant of the state where you were born or salute the state where you have been transplanted.

Here's a list of all of America's state flowers. Dig in and grow those that please you most.

State	Flower
Alabama	Camellia
Alaska	Forget-me-not
Arizona	Saguaro cactus
Arkansas	Apple blossom
California	Golden poppy
Colorado	Columbine
Connecticut	Mountain laurel
Delaware	Peach blossom
District of Columbia	American Beauty rose
Florida	Orange blossom
Georgia	Cherokee rose
Hawaii	Hibiscus
Idaho	Syringa
Illinois	Violet
Indiana	Peony
Iowa	Wild rose
Kansas	Wild sunflower
Kentucky	Goldenrod
Louisiana	Magnolia
Maine	Pine cone and tassel
Maryland	Black-eyed Susan
Massachusetts	Mayflower
Michigan	Apple blossom
Minnesota	Lady's slipper
Mississippi	Magnolia
Missouri	Hawthorn

State	Flower
Montana	Bitterroot
Nebraska	Goldenrod
Nevada	Sagebrush
New Hampshire	Purple lilac
New Jersey	Violet
New Mexico	Yucca flower
New York	Rose
North Carolina	Dogwood
North Dakota	Wild rose
Ohio	Scarlet carnation
Oklahoma	Mistletoe
Oregon	Oregon grape
Pennsylvania	Mountain laurel
Rhode Island	Violet
South Carolina	Yellow jasmine
South Dakota	American pasque flower
Tennessee	Iris
Texas	Bluebonnet
Utah	Sego lily
Vermont	Red Clover
Virginia	Dogwood
Washington	Rhododendron
West Virginia	Rhododendron
Wisconsin	Violet
Wyoming	Indian paintbrush

Growing wild and wonderful is easy, colorful, and can be really dramatic. Wildflowers can thrive in poorer soils than cultivated plants require. A final point is that wildflowers can grow and prosper in parts of your landscape that have been a problem to decorate with fancier plants. Try growing wild and you'll probably be amazed at the beauty wildflowers can provide as natural parts of your landscape.

Appendix A

Glossary

Accents: Usually part of a landscape planting, plants that provide special interest with their specific forms, textures, colors, or other attributes.

Acid soil: Soil with a pH value less than 7 on the pH scale of 1 (acid) to 14 (alkaline).

Alkaline soil: Soil having a pH greater than 7 on a soil test.

Annual: A plant that completes its life cycle from seed to mature plant and that produces seed itself in one growing season. Annuals are noted for their intense flowering but must be replanted each year because plants are not cold-hardy.

Bacteria: Microscopic, one-celled organisms that lack chlorophyll, multiply by fission, and live on nonliving organic matter, thereby helping break it down into humus.

Balance: The relationship between elements in the landscape. Formal balance usually means that one side of the landscape mirrors the other. Informal balance is when plant sizes and numbers are only relatively similar on both sides.

Base map or plan: A drawing that incorporates all information collected about the landscape and provides basic elements to be used in the landscape designing process.

Biennial: A plant that requires two growing seasons to complete its life cycle and then dies. Typically, vegetative growth takes place the first year and flowering and fruiting the second year.

Border planting: A plant or grouping that divides spaces or elements in a landscape or between adjacent property borders.

Bract: A leaf that grows below a flower or cluster of flowers that is often colorful and might be mistaken for a petal.

Bud: Naked or scale-covered embryonic tissue that will eventually develop into a vegetative shoot, stem, or flower.

Bulb: An underground stem that stores energy in modified leaves, as with daffodils and tulips. Botanists distinguish between bulbs, corms, rhizomes, and tubers, all of which have underground storage organs that store plant needs to grow each year. Strictly speaking, a bulb has enlarged scales where most of those nutrients are stored and a small basal plate where the next season's roots and shoots are. A corm has small scales and its nutrients are stored in the enlarged basal plate. Rhizomes and tubers are two types of enlarged stems that also store nutrients.

~

Chemical fertilizer: This is man-made fertilizer, made without carbon or derived from nonliving material.

Cold hardy: Refers to plants capable of withstanding cold weather conditions. Cold-hardiness is relative and is usually expressed in mail-order catalogs by indicating the horticultural zones in which plants can grow.

Compost: The end product of decomposition of organic matter such as plant residue, weeds, manure, lawn clippings, and other natural materials.

Corm: An underground stem that stores energy in modified stem tissue, such as a crocus corm.

Corner plantings: Any planting group that occupies a corner location, typically the corner of a property, and is used to blend border plantings together.

Crown: A plant's crown is where its roots and stems meet.

Cultivar: Synonymous with *variety* except that it refers only to cultivated plants. A cultivar or variety is a plant that has been selected or bred to have a specific trait or traits different from other members of its species and that has been given a unique name.

~

Decomposition: Breakdown of organic materials into their constituent parts due to the action of bacteria and microorganisms such as in compost.

Direct seeding: Planting seeds outdoors where you want them to grow in your garden.

Dividing: Making more plants from one by dividing it into two or more pieces.

Draft designs: Preliminary designs consisting of key plants as well as concept lines and spaces. Draft designs become a completed landscape plan as specific plants are selected for each location and put into the plan.

Drip irrigation: A system of adding water to garden soil in a slow, gentle stream from sources such as a perforated hose or one with a bubbler or slow-release action. This watering method prevents soil from being disturbed and reduces water runoff.

~

Easements: An interest in land owned by another person that entitles its holder to a specific limited use, most often access to cross other land.

Entry garden: A landscape area near the entry to a building that calls attention to the entry area and to certain plants there that are used to catch the eye.

Environmentally sound: A landscape that does

not harm the environment, soil, water, and air. An environmentally sound landscape is less dependent on pesticides, fertilizers, and water to maintain its appearance and often utilizes native plants and wildflowers.

Foliar fertilizing: Applying plant nutrients mixed in water directly to leaves rather than soil so that leaves absorb nutrients to feed the plant.

Forcing: Making plants or bulbs bloom at a time that is not natural for them to do so.

Foundation plantings: Plantings located in beds surrounding the base of a structure such as a home that usually provide transitions to lawns or other gardens.

Freestanding plantings: This refers to plantings that are apart from a structure or other plantings and are sometimes called island plantings. These often contain groups of plants or special specimen trees or shrubs.

Genus: Closely related plants grouped together under a single name, known as the genus. Species are plants within a genus that can be separated from each other by recognizable individual characteristics. Each different plant is assigned a specific epithet. The genus and specific epithet form the species name.

Germination: Sprouting of a seed.

Grafts: The process of splicing parts of two or more plants together to make one plant.

Habitat: The region in which a plant is found growing wild.

Humus: Organic matter that has decomposed to the point that it is no longer distinguishable from the soil itself. It is produced from recycling organic matter in compost piles and is a vital ingredient for improving soil.

Hybrid: Many new varieties are created when plant breeders combine the characteristics of two different plants into a new one by taking pollen from one plant to pollinate the other. Plants that grow from those cross-pollinated seeds are called hybrids.

Insecticide: Also called pesticide, insecticide is a substance that kills insects by poisoning, suffocating, or paralyzing them. There are stomach poisons, contact poisons, and fumigants. Many different types of insecticides are sold in garden stores under brand names and in combination pest-control spray mixtures. Organic gardeners avoid chemical pesticides but may use natural ones such as pyrethrum, made from plant flowers.

Key plants: This refers to landscape plants placed in a highly visible location, often for screening or softening building corners, steps, fences, and unsightly areas.

Landscape architect: A licensed professional who plans and designs landscapes. In some states this designation can be used only by certified professionals. Landscape architects are usually trained in engineering and architecture and typically work on projects larger than residential properties.

Landscape designer: A professional who plans and develops landscapes, usually at a residential or small commercial level. Landscape designers are usually skilled in the use of plant materials and other horticultural aspects of landscape design. They also may be called landscape horticulturists, who have a stronger focus on plants and their uses.

Legume: A plant characterized botanically by fruit called a legume or a pod. This includes alfalfa, clover, peas, and beans, which are associated with nitrogen-fixing bacteria that take nitrogen from the air and fix it on plant root nodules. This provides nitrogen to the soil when the plant is plowed under or rototilled to make a garden.

Loam: Soil that contains silt, sand, and clay, which are the major components of balanced soil. Ideal proportions of loam are 30 to 50 percent sand, 30 to 50 percent silt, and the remainder as clay. In those proportions, the soil holds water well but is loose enough for the roots and air to penetrate soil easily.

Mass plantings: Plantings where many plants of the same species are used to fill an area. Mass plantings are used to achieve dramatic, colorful effects and as connections between other planting groups or as ground covers.

NPK: This is the basic formula for fertilizer and is found on all bags and packages. *N* = nitrogen, *P* = phosphorus, and *K* = potassium. *N*, *P*, and *K* are the major nutrients most garden plants require for healthy, productive growth in varying proportions, depending on the plant and what stage of its development it has reached.

Peat moss: Partially decomposed vegetative material from sphagnum moss that is useful as mulch or as a soil additive to increase moisture-holding ability and also add porosity to soil.

Perennial: A woody or herbaceous plant that lives from year to year. The plant's life cycle doesn't end with flowering or fruiting. Valuable for gardeners because they grow and bloom every year without the need for planting more seeds or seedlings.

Petal: One of the showy, usually colorful portions of a flower.

Petiole: The stalk of a leaf.

pH: A term that represents the hydrogen ion concentration by which scientists measure soil acidity. The pH acidity scale measures from 1, which is acid, to 14, which is alkaline, with 7 as a neutral point.

Phosphorus: An essential macronutrient for plant growing. Its major function is promoting root formation in plants.

Pistil: The female reproductive structure of a plant, found in the flower.

Pollen: Tiny grains that carry male reproductive cells, which are borne on anthers of the bloom.

Potassium: Potassium, or potash, is another essential macronutrient of plants. It is important for plant maturity, flower development, and hardiness.

Rhizome: A horizontal underground stem that gives rise to roots and shoots.

Rototilling: Garden soil preparation done with a rototiller, which turns the soil to create a fine seedbed and area for planting.

Scale: The relative size of one part of a landscape to another. Scale may be the proportion or ratio of size to other components in the landscape.

Seed: A fertilized, ripened ovule (egg) that can grow into a new plant.

Sepal: One part of a whorl of green leafy structures that is located on the flower stem just below the petals.

Soil: Basically a natural layer of mineral and organic materials that covers the surface of the earth at various depths and supports plant life. Soil is created by the action of climate, water, time, and the interactions of living organisms and microorganisms on the parent material.

Species: A group of individuals forming a subdivision of a genus with similar characteristics but differing from the genus too slightly to form another genus.

Specimen plants: These can be part of a larger planting but usually stand alone in the landscape to provide specific seasonal interests or color through distinctive shape, flowers, fruit, or leaves.

Stamen: The male reproductive organ of the pollen-bearing flower, the top part of which is the anther.

Stigma: The terminal part of the reproductive organ of the female flowering plant, which receives pollen.

Sucker: A bud that forms and grows into a branch in the crotch between another branch and the main stem and can crowd out the original branch if left to grow. Also, new plants, especially from berries, that emerge from underground roots.

Sustainable landscape: A landscape designed, installed, and maintained that is maintainable, environmentally sound, cost effective, and visually pleasing.

~

Taproot: The first root that many plants put down when they germinate, which grows straight down into the soil and is like a stem that all the other roots grow from. Some trees have much deeper taproots than others.

Terminal bud: The bud that is borne at the tip of a stem.

Texture: The coarseness or fineness of the plant. Texture is created by leaves, branches, and bark.

Tuber: A swollen, underground stem modified to store large quantities of food for the plant.

~

Unity: This refers to how well the entire landscape design comes together to form one landscape look so that all aspects of the landscape complement one another rather than compete for attention.

~

Variegated: Leaves that have different colors are called variegated, such as coleus and hostas. Variegation is most often white or yellow, but it can also be bluish or reddish, depending on the plant, and can change due to light or soil conditions.

Variety: Refers to a group of individuals forming a subdivision of a species with similar characteristics but differing from the species too slightly to form another species.

Appendix B

Great Gardening and Landscaping Web Sites

Today there's a growing wealth of gardening know-how to harvest when you know where to dig it up. Here are some great garden information Web sites. Dig up as much information on whatever special topics you want. Some sites also offer opportunities for you to ask questions and get answers in return. More companies are offering that service every year to attract and retain valued customers. Check out the sites and you will be surprised and pleased at the bounty of worthwhile information available to you.

All-America Roses:	*www.roses.org*
All-America Selections:	*www.all-americaselections.org*
Antique Flowers:	*www.selectseeds.com*
Bartlett Tree Company:	*www.bartlett.com*
Bluestone Perennials:	*www.bluestoneperennials.com*
Breck's:	*www.brecks.com*
Burpee Seeds:	*www.burpee.com*
Carnivorous Plants:	*www.peterpauls.com*
Charley's Greenhouse Supply:	*www.charleysgreenhouse.com*
Clyde Robin Wildflower Seeds:	*www.clyderobin.com*
Cook's Garden:	*www.cooksgarden.com*
Drip Rite Irrigation:	*www.dripirr.com*
Dutch Gardens–Bulbs:	*www.dutchgardens.com*
Ferry Morse Seed Company:	*www.ferry-morse.com*
Fine Gardening Magazine:	*www.gardenguides.com*
Garden Net:	*www.gardennet.com*
Garden Web:	*www.gardenweb.com*

Gardener's Supply Company:	*www.gardeners.com*
Garden's Alive:	*www.gardensalive.com*
Gardenscape Tools:	*www.gardenscapetools.com*
Gurney's Seeds:	*www.gurneys.com*
Henry Field's:	*www.henryfields.com*
High Country Gardens:	*www.highcountrygardens.com*
Johnny's Selected Seeds:	*www.johnnyseeds.com*
Lilypons Water Gardens:	*www.lilypons.com*
Mailorder Gardening Association:	*www.mailordergardening.com*
Mellinger's Gardens:	*www.mellingers.com*
Miller Nurseries:	*www.millernurseries.com*
Monticello:	*www.monticello.org*
National Garden Bureau:	*www.ngb.org*
National Gardening Association:	*www.garden.org*
Neot Kedumim Bible Gardens:	*www.neot-kedumim.org.il*
Netherland Bulb Association:	*www.bulb.com*
Organic Gardening:	*www.organicgardening.com*
Park Seeds:	*www.parkseed.com*
Raintree Nursery:	*www.raintreenursery.com*
Seeds of Distinction:	*www.seedsofdistinction.com*
Spring Hill Nurseries:	*www.springhillnursery.com*
Stark Bros. Nurseries:	*www.starkbros.com*
Thompson & Morgan Seeds:	*www.thompson-morgan.com*
USDA Gardening:	*www.usda.gov*
Van Bourgondien:	*www.dutchbulbs.com*
The Water Gardens:	*www.watergarden.com*
Wayside Gardens:	*www.waysidegardens.com*
Wildseed Farms, Ltd.:	*www.wildseedfarms.com*

Index

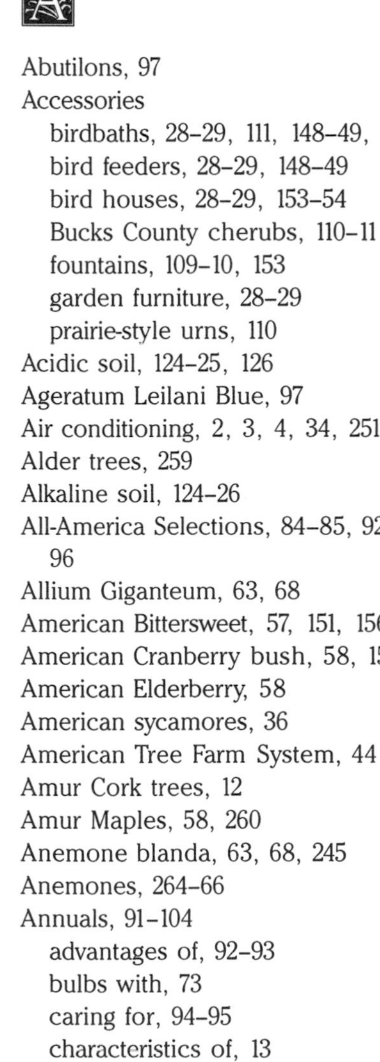

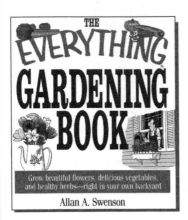

Everything® **Civil War Book**
Everything® **World War II Book**

HOBBIES

Everything® **Bridge Book**
Everything® **Candlemaking Book**
Everything® **Casino Gambling Book**
Everything® **Chess Basics Book**
Everything® **Collectibles Book**
Everything® **Crossword and Puzzle Book**
Everything® **Digital Photography Book**
Everything® **Drums Book (with CD), $19.95, ($31.95 CAN)**
Everything® **Family Tree Book**
Everything® **Games Book**
Everything® **Guitar Book**
Everything® **Knitting Book**
Everything® **Magic Book**
Everything® **Motorcycle Book**
Everything® **Online Genealogy Book**
Everything® **Playing Piano and Keyboards Book**
Everything® **Rock & Blues Guitar Book (with CD), $19.95, ($31.95 CAN)**
Everything® **Scrapbooking Book**

HOME IMPROVEMENT

Everything® **Feng Shui Book**
Everything® **Gardening Book**
Everything® **Home Decorating Book**
Everything® **Landscaping Book**
Everything® **Lawn Care Book**
Everything® **Organize Your Home Book**

KIDS' STORY BOOKS

Everything® **Bedtime Story Book**
Everything® **Bible Stories Book**
Everything® **Fairy Tales Book**
Everything® **Mother Goose Book**

NEW AGE

Everything® **Astrology Book**
Everything® **Divining the Future Book**
Everything® **Dreams Book**
Everything® **Ghost Book**
Everything® **Meditation Book**
Everything® **Numerology Book**
Everything® **Palmistry Book**
Everything® **Spells and Charms Book**
Everything® **Tarot Book**
Everything® **Wicca and Witchcraft Book**

PARENTING

Everything® **Baby Names Book**
Everything® **Baby Shower Book**
Everything® **Baby's First Food Book**
Everything® **Baby's First Year Book**
Everything® **Breastfeeding Book**
Everything® **Get Ready for Baby Book**
Everything® **Homeschooling Book**
Everything® **Potty Training Book, $9.95, ($15.95 CAN)**
Everything® **Pregnancy Book**
Everything® **Pregnancy Organizer, $15.00, ($22.95 CAN)**
Everything® **Toddler Book**
Everything® **Tween Book**

PERSONAL FINANCE

Everything® **Budgeting Book**
Everything® **Get Out of Debt Book**
Everything® **Get Rich Book**
Everything® **Investing Book**
Everything® **Homebuying Book, 2nd Ed.**
Everything® **Homeselling Book**
Everything® **Money Book**
Everything® **Mutual Funds Book**
Everything® **Online Investing Book**
Everything® **Personal Finance Book**

PETS

Everything® **Cat Book**
Everything® **Dog Book**
Everything® **Dog Training and Tricks**
Everything® **Horse Book**
Everything® **Puppy Book**
Everything® **Tropical Fish Book**

REFERENCE

Everything® **Astronomy Book**
Everything® **Car Care Book**
Everything® **Christmas Book, $15.00, ($21.95 CAN)**
Everything® **Classical Mythology Book**
Everything® **Divorce Book**
Everything® **Etiquette Book**
Everything® **Great Thinkers Book**
Everything® **Learning French Book**
Everything® **Learning German Book**
Everything® **Learning Italian Book**
Everything® **Learning Latin Book**
Everything® **Learning Spanish Book**
Everything® **Mafia Book**
Everything® **Philosophy Book**
Everything® **Shakespeare Book**
Everything® **Tall Tales, Legends, & Other Outrageous Lies Book**
Everything® **Toasts Book**
Everything® **Trivia Book**
Everything® **Weather Book**
Everything® **Wills & Estate Planning Book**

RELIGION

Everything® **Angels Book**
Everything® **Buddhism Book**
Everything® **Catholicism Book**
Everything® **Judaism Book**
Everything® **Saints Book**
Everything® **World's Religions Book**
Everything® **Understanding Islam Book**

SCHOOL & CAREERS

Everything® **After College Book**
Everything® **College Survival Book**
Everything® **Cover Letter Book**
Everything® **Get-a-Job Book**
Everything® **Hot Careers Book**
Everything® **Job Interview Book**
Everything® **Online Job Search Book**
Everything® **Resume Book, 2nd Ed.**
Everything® **Study Book**

All Everything® books are priced at $12.95 or $14.95, unless otherwise stated. Prices subject to change without notice.
Canadian prices range from $11.95–$22.95 and are subject to change without notice.